PROBLEMS OF INTERNATIONAL FINANCE

This volume studies several aspects of the current problems concerning international finance.

Robert Z. Aliber considers the role of international finance in allowing adjustment to economic shocks to be spread over time so as to reduce costs of adjustment. He discusses the problems which have arisen because of the growth of a large volume of international debt without any institution able to provide quality regulation or to perform the lender-of-last-resort function of national central banks.

Geoffrey W. Maynard considers the increasing role of banks in international finance, especially in recycling the OPEC surpluses since 1973, and examines the problems arising from flexible exchange rates and high and fluctuating interest rates.

David T. Llewellyn analyzes the motives of the various parties to international loans – the ultimate lenders, the ultimate borrowers, and the institutions which provide financial intermediation – and examines the relations between these groups.

K. Alec Chrystal considers the non-speculative motives for holding foreign money, and discusses the development of international monies.

Nicholas C. Hope and **David W. McMurray** look at the place of international lending in financing the non-oil developing countries.

Bahram Nowzad stresses the problems of debt burden for these countries.

Kate Phylaktis and **Geoffrey E. Wood** examine the theory of the operation of exchange controls on capital movements under different exchange-rate regimes.

Finally **Emmanuel Pikoulakis** considers the theory of monetary and fiscal policies in an open economy with a flexible exchange rate.

The general consensus is that current problems in international finance, while serious, are not out of control, and that there is reason to hope that the world financial system can find ways of surviving its current difficulties.

John Black is Professor of Economic Theory at the University of Exeter and a former Chairman of the International Economics Study Group. He was formerly Fellow and Tutor in Economics at Merton College, Oxford. He is the author of *Essential Mathematics for Economists* (with James F. Bradley) and *The Economics of Modern Britain*, and editor (with Brian Hindley) of *Current Issues in Commercial Policy and Diplomacy*, (with John H. Dunning) of *International Capital Movements* and (with L. Alan Winters) of *Policy and Performance in International Trade*. He has been an editor of *The Review of Economic Studies* and *The Economic Journal*.

Graeme S. Dorrance has recently retired from teaching at the London School of Economics and the University of Maryland.

––––––––––

Also from St. Martin's Press

CURRENT ISSUES IN COMMERCIAL POLICY AND DIPLOMACY
Edited by John Black and Brian Hindley

POLICY AND PERFORMANCE IN INTERNATIONAL TRADE
Edited by John Black and L. Alan Winters

PROBLEMS OF INTERNATIONAL FINANCE

Papers of the Seventh Annual Conference of the
International Economics Study Group

Edited by
John Black
and
Graeme S. Dorrance

St. Martin's Press   New York

ISBN 0–312–64767–0

Library of Congress Cataloging in Publication Data

International Economics Study Group. Conference (7th :
     1982 : University of Sussex)
     Problems of international finance.

     Includes index.
     1. International finance – Congresses.   I. Black,
John, 1931–   .   II. Dorrance, Graeme S.   III. Title.
HG205 1982   332′.042   83–24747
ISBN 0–312–64767–0

Contents

List of Tables

List of Figures

Notes on the Contributors

Robert Z. Aliber	Professor of International Economics and Finance, University of Chicago
K. Alec Chrystal	University of Essex
Graeme S. Dorrance	London School of Economics
Nicholas C. Hope	World Bank
David T. Llewellyn	Professor of Money and Banking, Loughborough University
Geoffrey W. Maynard	Chase Manhattan Bank, Visiting Professor, University of Reading
David W. McMurray	World Bank
Bahram Nowzad	International Monetary Fund
Kate Phylaktis	Lecturer in International Finance, The City University
Emmanuel Pikoulakis	University of Hull
Geoffrey E. Wood	Reader in Banking and International Finance, The City University

Introduction

The International Economics Study Group is one of several study groups in economics in the United Kingdom funded mainly by grants from the Social Science Research Council. It organises one-day meetings and an annual conference. These provide a forum in which professional economists from British universities, polytechnics, government departments, banks and business meet to discuss research papers by members and foreign visitors.

Since 1976 annual conferences have been held at the University of Sussex Conference Centre, Isle of Thorns, Sussex.

The 1982 conference, convened by Graeme Dorrance, was held from 17 to 19 September 1982. The International Economics Study Group would like to thank the Social Science Research Council, Barclays Bank, Lloyds Bank and Shell International for grants which made it possible, as well as all who took part, especially Graham Bird, Anthony Bottrill, Helen Hughes, James Riedel and Martin Wolf, who acted as discussants on the papers.

The topic of the 1982 conference was a consideration of problems of, and approaches to, current international financial relations, and of the prospects for international borrowing and lending. The meetings were held when the problems relating to the Mexican 'debt crisis' were the subject of widespread comment and it was being suggested that the international financial system was facing a serious breakdown. This collection of essays comprises the papers presented against this background.

The general tenor of the discussions was relaxed. It was recognised that the international financial system faced a number of short-term difficulties, but it had faced such obstacles on a number of occasions in recent years, and there was no reason to believe that the current difficulties could not be overcome if proper policies were followed in the future. In general, proper policies had been followed in the past, and the International Monetary Fund and others, such as the Bank for International Settlements, appeared prepared to be innovative. It was largely accepted that the institutional arrangements that would develop by 1990 would be as different from those prevailing, as the 1980s arrangements are from those in existence in the early 1970s. Yet the possibilities of a serious financial crisis, or of a breakdown of the international financial system, were regarded as being remote; and even to say this, it was felt, might overstate any inherent weaknesses in the international financial system. In large part, this rather optimistic consensus resulted from the long-term horizons accepted by these authors who refused to be stampeded by short-term rumours.

I THE BACKGROUND

Three general, but overlapping, themes dominated the discussions. First, with the background of the Mexican and similar 'crises', the stability of the international financial system was questioned. Here, the long-run views taken by all the authors, and practically all the participants in the conference, contributed to the relaxed atmosphere. Second, there was considerable interest in the lines that should be followed in analysing the institutional and statistical information that is becoming available on the operation of international financial institutions. Finally, there are some more theoretical questions that warrant further examination.

Most discussions of international financial transactions are based on considerations of national current account or capital account surpluses or deficits unless they are examinations of the types of instrument traded in the markets. Today, most national capital markets are linked through the international markets and it is not countries, but individual economic agents, that borrow and lend. For any economy, the ex post international capital account balance will be the net of the capital surpluses and deficits of its domestic agents. Domestic borrowers and lenders compare the alternative opportunities in their domestic markets to those available to them in international markets, and individually decide to have recourse either to domestic or to international markets. Even though many individual agents do not have effective direct access to international markets, if some important marginal borrowers or lenders have access to these markets, the domestic markets will reflect the conditions on international markets. Further, as financial intermediaries were very innovative in the 1970s, the effective access to international markets has broadened. Money-market and similar funds have made deposit-type assets available to a wide range of domestic lenders, but have made loans on the international markets as counterparts to these liabilities, paying interest to domestic lenders based on the returns on international assets. Similarly, merchant banks and similar organisations with access to international markets have developed networks of branches making loans to domestic borrowers who would have difficulty in achieving direct access to international markets.

The fact that transactions on international capital markets are completed by independent agents rather than by countries makes it quite normal that residents of individual countries should be concurrently lending and borrowing on international capital markets. For certain types of transaction, the economies of scale and the limitations of international institutions to large transactions can make international deposit and similar rates higher than comparable rates on domestic markets. The absence of a reserve ratio 'tax' on international transactions can also contribute to this disparity; at the same time, international lending rates are lower than comparable domestic rates. Hence, concurrent borrowing and lending by residents on international markets may be encouraged. This concurrency is likely to be particularly important in countries where the domestic financial system is developing rather than sophisticated; yet, on many occasions US residents have had concurrent recourse to international markets. It also frequently reflects the more efficient transformation activities of institutions, including foreign branches of domestic institutions, engaged in the international capital markets. Thus, for example, many OPEC official agencies and private lenders had a strong desire for deposit-type assets, while the borrowers, particularly those facing extended economic adjustment problems, wished to borrow on medium- to long-term bases. Much of the recycling of petro-dollars reflected a transformation of short-term sources of funds into longer-term loans. Even individual agents may be concurrent borrowers and lenders. Thus some national Treasuries that have been active borrowers at medium- to long-term have also been active accumulators of international reserves (that is, deposit lenders) during the 1970s and early 1980s.

While international capital transactions are flows of funds they are also the product of shifts in the portfolio structure of individual economic agents, including the financial institutions engaged in the international markets. Some of these movements may be fairly stable over the long-term, as investors build up their wealth and only slowly change its composition. Other movements are the product of short-term changes in portfolios that continue until portfolio structures are adjusted and then cease or continue only at markedly diminished rates. The adjustment in US bank portfolios between 1974 and 1976 that reflected the pent-up demand arising from US capital outflow restrictions from 1963 to 1974 is one example of such a sudden surge. Similarly, the adjustment of UK institutional portfolios following the abolition of exchange controls in 1979 is another example.

The growing popularity of international investments with primarily domestic financial institutions during the 1970s represented a shift in portfolio
structures that extended over an unusually long period and contributed to
the high annual flows from the early 1970s to the early 1980s. It is as yet
(1983) unclear whether the surprises of 1982 will lead many of these
institutions to readjust their portfolios towards a lower proportion of
foreign assets.

The international debt burden problem has been a specific aspect of
international financial relations that has attracted considerable attention in
recent years. The increased attention to this problem can be partly explained by the change in the structure of international financial flows. In
the 1940s and early 1950s, aid and loans on concessional terms accounted
for the major part of international resource transfers. As the international
financial system was liberalised in the 1950s, residents of the important
net savings countries, primarily large companies, looked to opportunities
for investment in the expanding net borrowing countries, such as the
European reconstructing countries and some of the less developed countries
(LDCs). This direct investment involved no fixed repayment and profit
transfers were dependent on profit earnings – these transfers did not
involve fixed debt burdens. With the growing importance of institutional
investors in all middle and high income countries, and the growth of
available savings in a relatively few non-industrialised countries (such as
some members of OPEC) international financial flows tended to become
institutionalised. Lenders looked for deposit-type or negotiable security
assets and borrowers wished to accept debt with predetermined maturities.
In some cases, the borrowing countries preferred financial obligations that
enabled them to finance domestic investments where the operations would
be subject to domestic sovereignty rather than controlled by foreign trans-
national companies. However, one of the costs of this institutionalisation
was the growth of predetermined debt-servicing charges in the place of
foreign capital servicing that was related to domestic earnings.

Institutionalisation has also tended to accelerate the rate of debt
repayments. In many cases, direct investments are never redeemed. As long
as a foreign-owned enterprise earns profits, the investors are satisfied to
accept the stream of profits. In fact they usually forgo the transfer of
some of the profits earned, reinvesting a considerable part so as to augment
their income streams. On the other hand, financial institutions, which
accept liabilities that are legally repayable at definite times, can only make
loans that are also repayable on predetermined terms. With many of the
savers desiring liquidity as well as income, the financial institutions, satisfying this demand by accepting short-term liabilities, are restrained in their

freedom to make longer-term loans. It was generally accepted that financial institutions had engaged in considerable maturity transformation so that their assets tended to be of longer average maturity than their liabilities, but that there were limits to this transformation.

II THE CONTRIBUTIONS

Many of these theses are reflected in Aliber's chapter which indicates how the international financial system has allowed adjustment to the stocks in goods and service markets to be spread over fairly lengthy periods, thereby lessening the adjustment costs. In fact, LDC borrowings have been larger than would have been required to adjust smoothly to the change in petroleum prices. The countries with high returns on capital have been able to draw resources from the countries with excess savings. Aliber acknowledges that certain countries may have borrowed more than could be justified on purely market criteria. He also recognises that most domestic financial systems have a lender-of-last-resort to guarantee the essential liquidity of the system. Such a safety net is not yet available on the international scene and in this chapter he argues that it is difficult to foresee how such a guarantee mechanism might evolve.

While the discussion of this argument tended to accept its general conclusions, certain reservations were expressed. The high level of debt, particularly the LDC debts, was accepted as a matter of concern. The fact that, in some cases, this was the product of inappropriate fiscal/monetary policy mixes indicated that lenders should be more prepared to examine the domestic policies of borrowing countries when making country risk assessments. In particular, it was maintained that they should be concerned to ensure that foreign loans provide the marginal finance for productive investment rather than supporting high levels of consumption or financing investments with low social returns. It was suggested, however, that undue attention had been directed to the distortions arising from inappropriate borrowing – some of the individual cases are horrendous. On the whole most financing has, in fact, been directed to the support of investment projects. Foreign borrowing that financed consumption was undertaken primarily to facilitate the adjustment processes that were made necessary by the shocks to which individual countries had been subjected in the 1970s.

Some of the effects of the institutionalisation of international capital transfers are outlined by Maynard who concentrates on the role of banks in the international financial intermediation process and draws attention to a major change in the structure of international capital flows during the 1970s. In the 1950s and 1960s these markets tended to be ones where residents of the industrial countries were not only the major lenders but also the major borrowers, and most of the borrowers were private enterprises. After the 1973–4 increase in oil prices, OPEC countries (particularly a few with large current account surpluses – Iraq, Kuwait, Libya and Saudi Arabia) became important lenders in the international markets and developing countries entered the markets as important borrowers. Maynard points out that these lenders wished to acquire liquid assets, while the borrowers wished to be free of the immediate burden of short-term debt. The banks – in the widest definition of this term, including some underwriting houses – moved into the breach to accommodate these discrepant desires. As a result, total international lending rose from slightly over 10 billion dollars per year at the end of the 1960s to over 100 billion per year at the end of the subsequent decade, and the developing countries' share of this total rose from slightly over 1 billion dollars per year to approximately 50 billion per year.

This rapid growth occurred when exchange rates were becoming more volatile and more uncertain and interest rate volatility was also increasing. Maynard draws attention to the growth of variable-rate debt instruments as a means of reducing the costs of interest-rate volatility for lenders, and, to a certain extent, for borrowers. The increasing levels of debt also have raised concern regarding the debt burden and the stability of the international financial system. Here Maynard is more optimistic than many commentators. He sees the recent relatively high growth rates in most of the borrowing countries, and the rising level of domestic investment in most of them, as signs that 'international capital markets did a better job at redistributing world savings to areas where the real return on capital remained relatively higher than they have been given credit for so far'.

Attention should finally be drawn to Maynard's views on the need for a 'lender-of-last-resort' or an international safety net held by the IMF or some international central banking group. This idea has certain appeal as it fits in with generally accepted domestic banking theory. One of the surprising aspects of the 'international financial crises' of late 1982 and early 1983 was the ease with which they were met. They provided more income for financial journalists than real worry for lending institutions. If the inter-governmental community were to move further in the direction of underwriting the lending institutions' operations it could well encourage greater irresponsibility by these institutions and raise serious questions of moral hazard.[1]

Llewellyn deals mainly with the relation between domestic and international financial transactions. He indicates some of the criteria, particularly portfolio criteria, that must be observed in any further studies of international capital market questions, and argues quite strongly for the need to integrate international capital market studies with domestic flow of funds and balance sheet analyses. He also finds some evidence to support these views but, in general, this must be taken as a guide to further work rather than as a group of startling conclusions.

In the discussion, it was recognised that Llewellyn's presentation was a preliminary framework intended to provide a basis for further development. The suggestion was made that he concentrated too much on overall surplus and deficit agents and that many international capital transactions arose from the specific need of individual agents to use certain types of credit (for example, trade credit) and to have certain types of asset (for example, liquid deposits or income-earning direct investments). These specific requirements could explain many of the concurrent borrowing and lending transactions. It was also suggested that the model should be developed to incorporate interest-rate effects into what was essentially a price-free structure.

Chrystal's contribution is a specific example of the type of analysis proposed by Llewellyn (although it is clear that Chrystal reached his conclusions following lines of thought quite different from those pursued by Llewellyn). Chrystal examines some of the influences on those parts of portfolios that are held as foreign currency trading balances – he specifically abstracts from all speculative demands for international balances. He recognises that the international currency markets are highly institutionalised. Most traders in goods and services either buy foreign exchange from, or sell it to, domestic banks and, as a consequence, trading balances are held predominantly by banks – most dealers in goods and services either sell export proceeds only or cover import requirements only. Very few individual agents (chiefly large multinational companies) both buy and sell exchange. He also recognises that direct dealings between particular currencies (for example, trading drachmas for cruzeiros) involve high transaction costs. Consequently, the trading balances of banks will reflect their portfolio targets, as they are both buyers and sellers of exchange. By combining the demands and supplies of many agents, they can minimise balances below the levels that would be required if all agents were holding individual transaction balances. There are markedly different transactions costs in different markets (for example it may be easier to sell drachmas against dollars and to buy cruzeiros with dollars than to attempt to buy cruzeiros directly against drachmas). It is reasonable therefore for banks' holdings of transactions balances to be concentrated in such intermediary currencies as the dollar, DM, or yen, irrespective of the currency in which individual transactions are invoiced (that may, in fact, not be the currency of settlement between individual traders). Chrystal examines some of the conditions that will influence the size and composition of these primarily institutional trading balances.

Some objections were raised to the development of a model that excluded speculative and foreign interest rate considerations. Speculative and trading balances are frequently consolidated and held in interest-bearing form (overnight Euro-dollar balances have recently carried interest higher than the transaction costs of moving into and out of them). It was also suggested that any model of liquid foreign balances should incorporate the relation between changes in these balances and domestic monetary policy. Admittedly, Chrystal included a domestic interest rate in his model, but it would be desirable to relate the size of foreign exchange balances to domestic monetary aggregates.

Hope and McMurray each dealt specifically with the debt burden and debt management problems. Their chapter draws attention to the fact that, in many respects, there is no 'developing country' financing problem. Rather, each country's problems are, in a sense, unique. However, they indicate that there are certain similarities in the problems faced by countries that have relied primarily on borrowing on international financial markets. These are different from those of countries that have been able to rely on aid to meet their balance-of-payments deficits. There is an intermediate group that has relied on a mixture of aid and market borrowing. A major part of the paper is devoted to a review of the criteria that a developing country should adopt in its international debt strategy. Hope and McMurray start with the fact that, when considering future borrowing, the authorities should know the amount of their country's outstanding debts. This seemingly simple point has yet to be acknowledged by many countries, despite the efforts of the World Bank, the IMF, and the OECD to compile such data, not only for their own use, but for policy determination by individual countries. The chapter emphasises the relation between appropriate domestic financial policies and long-term access to capital markets on reasonable terms.

Along with several other contributors, Hope and McMurray draw attention to the growth during the 1970s of bank financing as a source of international capital. On an optimistic note, this paper suggests that the growth of institutional lending has provided a degree of sophistication in international financing that has produced benefits for those countries which rely on international borrowing. They express a view, similar to the one that 'it is not true that developing countries as a whole borrowed excessively, that they squandered the proceeds, and that they now face a generalised debt problem. There is no generalised debt crisis.'[2]

Nowzad directs attention to the debt problems of the developing countries. He shows that many developing countries have, in fact, faced external debt difficulties that have had serious consequences for their growth prospects, and in the view of some commentators are putting strains on the international financial system. He points out that these problems arise not only from unwise borrowing policies followed by countries, but also from unwise lending policies adopted by financial institutions. Part of the difficulties reflect the changes in the terms of international borrowing. Over the 1970s, average maturities have tended to shorten (if anything, the terms for private lending have lengthened, but there has been a marked substitution of private for longer-term official loans) and interest rates (reflecting inflationary expectations) have tended to rise. However, an examination of individual cases suggests that, aside from the Eastern European countries, those countries that have experienced serious debt problems have tended to be ones with relatively slow growth rates and relatively high inflation rates compared with those of the developing countries that have not experienced serious international debt problems. That is, there is evidence that international financing problems were, in a number of cases, the product of domestic policies. On a slightly different line, Nowzad finds little, if any, evidence to support the view that, allowing for recent changes in policy, the international financial system is under serious strain.

In discussion at the conference, attention was drawn to the number of cases where inappropriate exchange rate policies were the most damaging of domestic financial policies. It was also indicated that the assessment of the debt burden problem may be even more complex than Nowzad suggests − no single ratio, or even several, can be used in measuring the problem. For example, the most commonly used debt service ratio includes amortisation together with interest payments. In many instances there may be a strong case for refinancing amortisation payments. Further, if interest payments include an element of inflation compensation, they also include, in effect, an element of advance redemption or reduction in the real value of the debts.[3] Hence, there may be a case for borrowing to meet part of the interest payment so that the stream of amortisation is stable in constant-price terms. In brief, an assessment of the debt burden problem is complex.

The increasing freedom from direct controls and of competitiveness have contributed markedly to the growth of international capital markets. Phylaktis and Wood draw attention to the fact that exchange controls still exist in many countries and that any analysis of capital movements should take account of these controls. They suggest that in most cases, it is possible to derive a 'tax equivalent' effect of exchange controls. These tax-equivalent effects will influence portfolio adjustments and the exchange rate. At least in the long-run, interest parities and purchasing power parities, adjusted for the effects of exchange controls, may be expected to prevail. In fact, after the monetary effects of changes in capital transactions lead to new portfolio structures, interest rate parities will probably be maintained. As emphasised at the conference, the adjustment process resulting from any imposition of exchange controls is likely to be extended over time and may not be completed if there are expectations that a subsequent change in exchange controls is possible.

Finally, Pikoulakis examines some of the adjustment reactions within a system of fluctuating exchange rates where allowance is made for current account trade in goods and services, and capital account adjustment of portfolios, but where different types of asset are imperfect substitutes for each other. He suggests that this imperfect substitutability may contribute to stability in the international monetary system — a theoretical conclusion that is consistent with the more optimistic views of several of the more pragmatic papers included in this collection.

NOTES

1. On this point, see Dorrance (1981).
2. World Bank, *World Debt Tables, 1982–1983 Edition*, p. vii.
3. See Nowzad and Williams (1981).

REFERENCES

Graeme S. Dorrance (1981) 'Would Loan Guarantees Undermine International Capital Markets?', *The Banker* (December).

Bahram Nowzad and R. C. Williams *et al.* (1981) *External Indebtedness of Developing Countries*, International Monetary Fund Occasional Paper 3.

World Bank, *World Debt Tables, 1982–3 Edition*.

1 Capital Flows, External Debt and the International Adjustment Process

ROBERT Z. ALIBER

INTRODUCTION

Under the Bretton Woods System, one of the major concerns was that the supply of international reserves would be increasingly inadequate. At the macro- or international level, the shortage would prove deflationary and lead to both declines in the world price level and restrictions on international trade and payments; at the country level, the shortage might lead to excessively abrupt adjustments in exchange rates and exchange controls. In the 1960s, especially toward the end of the decade, many analysts believed that because international reserves were inadequate the speed of adjustment to payments imbalances would be too rapid and so excessively costly. The view was that if international reserves had been larger or had increased more rapidly countries with payment deficits would be able to adjust at a less rapid pace, and so their costs of adjustment would have been smaller. Moreover, more of the burden of adjustment would have fallen on the surplus countries. The argument is that the costs of adjustment to payments imbalances vary with the speed of adjustment to the new balance of payments equilibrium. For each distribution of imbalances there is an optimal speed of adjustment. That adjustments must be made to restore payments equilibrium is generally recognised, except in those cases when the disturbance is temporary, and the return to the pre-disturbance equilibrium 'automatic'. Hence the argument is that for each disturbance, there is an optimal adjustment path, and any deviation from this

1

path creates excess costs. These excess costs of adjustments are measured in terms of the costs of excess demand or excess supply (under-employment of resources or inflation) or in terms of the decline in economic efficiency and welfare from the resource re-allocation, the continual or sporadic shifting of productive resources between markets in the surplus countries and markets in the deficit countries. The concern about a reserve shortage led to attention about how to optimise the choice between financing payment imbalances, and adjusting to payments imbalances. Acceptance of the arguments about the reserve shortage eventually led to the establishment of Special Drawing Rights.

One of the ironies of international finance was that soon after acceptance of the need for a more rapid increase in international reserves on a planned basis, the stock of reserves surged, a result of the massive US payments deficit. Between 1965 and 1972, the stock of reserves doubled. A second irony became evident with the move to floating exchange rates in 1973 — a move which had been recommended as a solution to the reserve shortage. Concern with reserves was supposed to be redundant in a world of floating exchange rates, for the price of foreign exchange was supposed to adjust continuously to any incipient payments imbalance. Yet the stock of foreign exchange held as international reserves increased from $146 billion in 1972 to $350 billion in 1981 — and only partly because of OPEC payments surpluses. Finally IMF quotas were increased in 1977 and again in 1979, and at $60 billion, are twice as large as in 1975, SDR allocations have increased, and new windows have been opened at the IMF. However, Fund quotas have fallen significantly relative to world reserves. Moreover, if monetary gold is valued at $400 or $500, the market price in recent years, international reserves are five or six times as large as a decade ago.

Now there is concern that international reserves — or at least IMF quotas — are too small, a view prompted by the debt service problems of Argentina, Brazil, Mexico, and a number of other developing countries. At the aggregate or macro-level, the argument that there is a shortage of reserves is not intuitively plausible; international reserves seem much too large in nominal terms and have increased very rapidly in real, or price-level adjusted terms in the last decade. At the macro-level, the world price level continues to increase at a double-digit rate. Yet at the country or micro-level, the reserve shortage is said to be severe, especially in relation to the external debt of the developing countries. Hence there is a significant distinction between the role of reserves in facilitating the adjustment to payments imbalances and in facilitating the re-financing of existing external debts.

The secular increase in the demand for reserves is related to the optimising choice between financing payments imbalances and adjusting to payments imbalances present under pegged exchange rates and also evident under a floating exchange rate regime. Only under the most limiting and heroic of assumptions about the nature of disturbances would non-intervention be optimal. The major difference between the exchange rate regimes is that with floating exchange rates, the monetary authorities have continuous options about whether to adjust or finance; financing involves discretionary exchange market intervention. With a pegged rate regime, in contrast, the authorities are obliged to finance payments imbalances; the commitment to peg means that the authorities cannot use the exchange rate as an adjustment variable, except when they adjust the parity. Financing imbalances automatically leads to adjustment through changes in the money supplies, unless these changes are neutralised.

The choice to finance or adjust is usually examined in terms of flows of international reserves undertaken by the monetary authorities. The flows of finance may be market-induced and responsive to changes in interest rate differentials in relation to expected changes in exchange rates. In a world of private capital mobility, official financing of payments imbalances must be related to the private financing of payments flows.

The domestic economic counterpart to the concern with reserve adequacy in the international economy is whether the supply of money or credit grows at an appropriate rate. A subsidiary question is whether there is an adequate institutional arrangement for a lender-of-last-resort. If these aggregate conditions are satisfied, then private capital flows finance the deficits of particular sectors. Virtually all countries supplement private flows with public credit flows, although in most instances these public flows are intended to stimulate particular activities rather than compensate for inadequacies of private credit flows.

The test of the adequacy of international reserves is that in response to various shocks, both structural and monetary, the supply of finance permits various countries (and their trading partners) to adjust with the minimal disruption to their long-run target-growth trajectories. Thus adjustments to shocks that may cause a deviation from the growth trajectories which will be reversed in the future when the shock abates may be minimised. Monetary shocks are likely to cause primarily a deviation from the growth trajectory, while structural shocks are likely to cause shifts in the trajectories, although even a monetary disturbance, by altering the levels of international indebtedness, may cause a shift in the unplanned growth of reserves.

This chapter is about the adequacy of mechanisms for financing payments imbalances in response to structural and monetary shocks. Attention is given to the adequacy of private or non-governmental mechanisms, and then to the role of official flows of finance to supplement or supplant the private flows. The next section of this chapter reviews the applicable theory primarily to determine some conceptual benchmarks for the adequacy of private flows. The subsequent section relates the pattern of capital flows to the adjustment process in the last decade, with special attention to a number of issues, including the payments surpluses of the oil-exporting countries, and to the payments deficits of the developing countries. The last section comments on the adequacy of international reserves.

II   THE THEORY OF RESERVE ADEQUACY

One approach toward determining whether international reserves are too large or too small involves an extension of the quantity theory of money to the international context — if the world price level is increasing, then reserves are increasing too rapidly. However the causation may be from the price level to the level of reserves rather than from the level of reserves to the price level. An alternative approach is to list the phenomena likely to be observed if reserves are growing too rapidly or too slowly, especially changes in trade controls. A third involves comparing the growth of reserves are growing too rapidly or too slowly, especially changes in trade controls. A third involves comparing the growth of reserves with the growth of trade and payments. None of these approaches appears widely acceptable. A fourth relates the cost of holding reserves to the costs of changes in income associated with adjustments to reduce imbalances (Heller). A fifth relates reserve growth to world welfare. Few of these approaches are readily operational.

The relationship among interest rates in the countries with payments surpluses and those with payments deficits provides an insight into the effectiveness of the adjustment process. Consider two groups which are prevented from transacting in securities by barriers; the prevailing interest rate between borrowers and lenders in one group will almost certainly be higher than that in the other group. Within each group, following Fisher, the interest rate equals the group's time preference. Reducing the barriers to trade in securities between the two groups means that the interest rates in the two groups will move toward equality; community welfare will be enhanced as a result of trade in securities. If trade in securities continued until interest rates in the two groups were not significantly different aggregate welfare would be maximised.

Consider the Kemp–MacDougall approach to allocation of the stock of physical capital among countries at a particular moment – the test of optimal allocation is whether there is any other allocation of which this capital stock which would lead to a higher aggregate level of income in the capital exporting and the capital importing country. The optimal allocation occurs when the interest rates in the capital importing countries have declined so that they are not significantly higher than the interest rates in the capital exporting countries. While the traditional argument ignored the distinction between nominal and real exchange rates, the argument involves the approximate equality of real interest rates. The Kemp–MacDougall argument is a geographic extension of Fisher's argument; borrowers and lenders are not randomly distributed among countries. One country has relatively more borrowers; the other has relatively more lenders.

Whenever there are disturbances – a change in time preference in Fisher's model or in the marginal product of labour in the Kemp-MacDougall model, the interest rate changes. The implicit assumption is that there is an immediate stock adjustment, since in both cases stocks of assets are being priced. The change in the market clearing price almost certainly has some impacts on future flows of finance.

These two arguments, one in time and one is space, involve the distribution of a given stock of physical capital. Changes in the location of the stock of wealth are represented by changes in the allocation of titles to ownership among individuals in the several countries.

The Kemp-MacDougall argument does not explicitly recognise that the transfer of physical capital among countries is a response to the flows of financial capital. Trading in financial assets occurs in the debt and equity markets, while trading in physical wealth occurs in the goods market. Trading in financial assets 'drives' the goods market. Both Fisher and Kemp–MacDougall assume a frictionless transfer of financial capital. The larger the frictions to the transfers of capital among countries the greater the deviation from the optimal allocation.

These types of model might be used to provide a basis for models of the balance-of-payments adjustment process. In the pre-disturbance equilibrium interest rates are not significantly different among countries. Financial capital flows occur between countries just as they do between individuals – some countries (the savers) have current account surpluses and others (the borrowers) have current account deficits. Current account surpluses and deficits are not inconsistent with payments balance – when there are no flows of money or reserves among countries. Disturbances affect the current account and hence the flow of reserves.

The Kemp-MacDougall approach might be extended to deal with

monetary and structural disturbances. In the post-disturbance equilibrium the interest rate equalities should hold. The adjustment to the shocks might involve either a stock adjustment or a flow adjustment; the concern is the process by which a new equilibrium is established, and with whether that process is optimal, in the sense that the costs of adjustment are minimal.

As long as the interest rates and yields in the several countries are not significantly different, it might be inferred that there is no evident inefficiency in the operation of the capital market. What must be answered is whether efficiency in the capital or financial market implies that the balance-of-payments adjustment costs are minimal — and the dual namely, whether minimal adjustment costs imply that the capital market is efficient. If the capital market equivalence relationship is violated, either by the disturbance or by the adjustment toward equilibrium, the implication is that some other distribution of the capital stock would have resulted in a higher level of aggregate welfare.

Within a domestic economy, shocks may also cause countries to deviate from their optimal growth trajectories. The argument that there is an optimal level of the money stock is that the real costs of adjustment are minimal if investors believe that the anticipated rate of increase in the price level is zero. In response to a shock, the authorities may increase (or reduce) the money supply as a way to maintain the price level targets.

At the international level, disturbances may occur and adjustments may have to be made; these adjustments, however, should be no different in an international context than in a domestic context. Adjustment costs are minimised if the rates of return are not significantly different in the surplus and the deficit countries. The reason is that neither country deviates its growth trajectory much more extensively than the other. If these conditions are not satisfied, than the adjustment costs might be excessive in the international context. One reason why adjustment costs might be excessive is that the financial market might be inefficient, in that the interest rate differential would be larger than might be explained by the costs and risks associated with the movement of funds internationally. The risk of international investment would be over-priced. If private flows of capital are restrained, the case for flows of official capital is strong.

An alternative explanation for yield differentials which appear larger than would be consistent with market efficiency is that the goods market does not clear — the desire of investors to shift funds internationally to take advantage of the interest rate differential is forestalled because the appropriate current account balance cannot be generated. Thus the transfer problem appears — the current account is unable to adjust to the target level because the needed changes in relative prices and incomes cannot be effected. In this case, the stickiness in the goods market means that a yield differential persists in the financial markets. In effect, investors receive a 'rent' from the 'stickiness' in the goods market.

The implication of the argument is that if a disturbance causes the interest rates in the two areas to differ significantly, the capital market is not working efficiently. Frictions limit the flows of capital, with the consequence that the deficit country may incur excessively high adjustment costs. If the relationship between the interest rates in the two areas remains the same after the disturbance as before, the capital market is working efficiently. Even then, however, it may be concluded that the changes in the rate of growth of reserves are desirable to achieve the target rates of growth in the world price level. If the capital market is not working perfectly, then there is a strong case for official measures to reduce the adjustment costs. Thus if the necessary condition for the flow of capital to finance a payments deficit it the generation of an interest rate differential, the sufficient condition is that the flow of financial capital shall induce a current account surplus of the appropriate size, otherwise, the financial markets will be in disequilibrium – there will be apparent unexploited profit opportunities for the movement of financial capital. So if a yield differential persists, attention must be given to whether the cause is an inefficiency in the capital market or in the goods market. The case for official flows of funds – for financing rather than adjustment is stronger, the more convincing the evidence that the private capital market is inefficient. If the private capital market is efficient but the goods market is inefficient, the rationale for official capital flows appears weak.

The operational problem is to go from these general propositions to determining when payments imbalances, in effect current account imbalances, should be financed and when adjustment should occur. Current account imbalances may be due to monetary disturbances or to structural disturbances. Cyclical changes in income can be considered a form of a monetary disturbance.

Structural disturbances such as crop failures, new resource discoveries, changes in the terms of trade or monetary disturbances, such as a movement along the phases of the business cycle or a change in monetary policy, affect the current account balance. The question is whether the supply of finance is adequate so that the change in the current account balance from its pre-disturbance equilibrium level can be financed without excessive costs of adjustment.

Consider first the impact of a structural disturbance, such as crop failure or an increase in the price of imports, or the increased availability of exports. A crop failure is a non-repetitive event, in that a bad crop this year is likely to be followed by good crops or at least average crops in subsequent years. So on the theme of a time to save and a time to spend, the current account imbalance should be financed. In good crop years, holdings of international reserves should be increased, and external indebtedness should be reduced. In years of poor crops, reserves should be spent and external indebtedness increased. Over the crop cycle, from one year to the next, interest rates should vary pro-cyclically; interest rates should rise when crops are below average because the payments deficits leads automatically to a credit contraction, part of the financing of the increase in the current account deficit will be automatic. In contrast, in the surplus countries, interest rates should tend to fall. If the capital market is efficient, the need for official funds to finance the change in the current account balance might be trivial or non-existent; the case for official intervention is stronger, the higher the barriers to private flows.

Consider now an OPEC-type shock, defined to mean that the price of a major import is increased significantly. One of the major concerns in analysing the appropriate or policy-efficient response is whether the real price of oil will remain high indefinitely, or whether the real price of oil will decline, perhaps eventually (although not necessarily) to its pre-disturbance level. To the extent that the increase in the real price of oil is temporary, the analysis is similar to that of the crop failure; as far as possible, the oil-importers should finance the current account deficit rather than adjust to the deficit. In contrast, if the increase in the price of oil is believed permanent, an adjustment is necessary, and the key issue involves optimising the pace of the adjustment. One reason the speed of adjustment is important is that the ultimate balance of payments equilibrium will differ from the immediate post-disturbance balance of payments position because the amount of petroleum imported eventually will decline because of the price effect and the capital stock effect. There is always the problem that, when there is an increase in the price of oil, the authorities will not immediately be able to determine how much of the increase is permanent. So the argument for financing much of the initial increase in the current account deficit is strong. To some extent, financing will be automatic, since interest rates in the OPEC countries with large current surpluses will decline, while interest rates will rise in the deficit countries.

Consider an increase in its current account deficit caused by a surge in domestic income; imports increase and exports decline. Financing the current account deficit should tend to be automatic because interest rates will rise in the country with the current account deficit and fall in the countries with the current account surplus.

Finally, consider a change in monetary policy that leads to a change in the interest-rate relationship; assume for example, that one country pursues a more contractive monetary policy. If interest rates rise relative to the expected change in the exchange rate, capital will be attracted from abroad under a pegged exchange-rate system. Other countries will tend to be subject to capital outflows and their choice will be to adjust or to finance. Adjustment would involve an increase in the current account surplus so the increased capital outflow can be financed. Finance would involve either a reflective change in the monetary policy, in effect to neutralise the change in monetary policy of the first country, or official intervention to finance the capital outflow without a corresponding contraction in monetary policy, or with a smaller move toward contractive monetary policy. The argument for relying on official capital flows is that the trading partners are reluctant to permit their monetary policy to be 'set' abroad. The stronger the impacts of the change in the monetary policy in attracting capital from abroad, the stronger the evidence that the capital market is efficient.

If private capital flows respond to market-related changes in interest-rate differentials, the appropriate role of official flows becomes a major question — when should countries rely on official finance? In this context official finance might mean that the borrower is a government agency and that the lenders may be commercial banks, central banks or multinational institutions. Alternatively, official finance might mean that the lenders are public institutions rather than private institutions. One argument for official capital flows is that the lenders require excessively large payments for bearing the several risks of moving funds across the borders between currency areas and political jurisdictions when the borrowers are private; in this case, the distinctive risk associated with private borrowers is that of default. So the major argument for socialising external borrowing is that lenders charge excessive premiums for carrying the default risk. (From time to time, a secondary argument for socialising the borrowing is that the private lenders charge too high an exchange risk premium, although here the issue between a risk premium and an expected change in the exchange rate must be clarified.) The counterpart argument for socialising lending is that the private lenders charge too high a premium for carrying the political risk.

A second possible argument for official finance might involve cases where the non-interest element in the anticipated returns dominates the interest-rate element. Both borrowers and lenders may expect that the total return on assets denominated in the currency of the country with the payments deficit will prove too low because the currency will depreciate;

in this case the authorities may intervene in the foreign exchange market. In the previous case, the argument for official intervention was secular and based on the price of risk while in this case intervention would be sporadic and justified because the authorities believe that investors are excessively pessimistic (or optimistic) about the short-term outlook for the foreign-exchange value of the currency. A key argument for official intervention in the foreign-exchange market is that the investors have not correctly interpreted monetary policy and its impacts on anticipated exchange rates.

A third argument for official finance involves the lender-of-last-resort mechanism; official flows are undertaken to refinance private flows. Private international capital flows occur as investors move toward 'higher-quality' assets; in moments of concern or distress, the difference in risk dominates the differences in returns. Yet a concerted move toward a higher quality asset is impossible because of the fallacy of composition, for the relative supplies of higher quality and lower quality assets cannot change markedly. The abrupt shift out of lower quality assets raises their returns, and the suppliers or producers of the lower quality assets may encounter a solvency problem. The argument for official finance is that the adverse externalities from the solvency crises lead to costs to others – both to the community at large and to the producers of higher quality assets. Yet a distinction must be made between the general argument for a lender-of-last-resort argument for official finance and the application of the argument; at issue is whether the official lender provides credits to the borrowers or to the lenders.

III   THE FINANCING OF ADJUSTMENT IN THE 1970s

Four features stand out in reviewing the international monetary develop-ments of the 1970s – one is the highly variable OPEC current account surpluses; a second, the rapid growth of LDC external indebtedness; a third, the surge in the volume of the international reserves and the fourth, the variability of the foreign exchange value of the US dollar in terms of the German mark, the Swiss franc and other European currencies as well as the Japanese yen. The features are closely linked; in a crude sense, the counterpart to the OPEC current account surpluses was the LDC current account deficits. The accumulation of OPEC surpluses was the major com-ponent of the growth of international reserves. The variability of the foreign exchange value of the dollar may have been partly related to OPEC sur-pluses, on the argument that large OPEC surpluses might have meant a strong dollar because OPEC's demand for dollar securities dominated OPEC's demand for dollar goods.

Consider the OPEC surpluses as given, imposed on the international system by the price and output decisions of the oil exporters. The sharp increases in the price of oil in 1974 and again in 1979 and 1980 caused massive adjustment problems, because oil is so important in the import mix. Subsequently the less rapid surge in the exports to OPEC, and the reduction in OPEC's current account surpluses also led to adjustment problems, since non-OPEC surpluses must also have declined.

Consider first OPEC's own adjustment to the surge in its own export earnings; OPEC faced the 'finance or adjust' choice. The more rapid the growth in OPEC's imports, the smaller the deficits that oil-importers as a group had to finance. OPEC's adjustment involved the surge in imports of consumption goods, investment goods, military hardware and software and services. The less rapid the growth of these imports, the more rapid the accumulation of external assets by the OPEC countries. The equalisation-of-return norm leads to the question of whether rates of return on investments within the OPEC countries were as high as those on external assets. If not, then the OPEC countries may have invested too much at home and not enough abroad, given the level of their saving. (This might have happened if the surge in OPEC domestic investment had depressed the rate of return within the OPEC countries. The surge in OPEC domestic investment might have contributed to inflation within the OPEC countries; even though large payments surpluses are usually associated with deflationary pressures.)

The difficulty in assessing this argument is that the data are both bad and irrelevant. The surge in national incomes in the oil-exporting countries resulting from the improvement in their terms of trade, suggests that domestic rates of return are high, because rates of growth of national income have been high. For some countries, the combination of the importance of oil and the surge in its price meant that the growth in incomes was 20 to 30 per cent. Yet income grew rapidly only as long as the oil price was increasing, or oil production was increasing. At other times the high rates of return reflected scarcity rents as oil wealth was being converted into other forms of wealth. For the OPEC economies as a whole, productivity and real rates of return have been low. If the growth rates in the OPEC countries have been spuriously high, then the OPEC countries adjusted too rapidly; they should have invested more of the surge in their foreign exchange earnings abroad and less at home, even if individual investors may have been equalising rates of return on domestic securities and foreign securities. Yet the source of this misallocation – political pressures aside – is that the domestic rates of return in the OPEC countries on non-petroleum activities provided poor signals about the total return to the economy.

Consider now the 'adjustment or finance' choice in various oil-importing countries, especially in the oil-importing developing countries. While the usual story is that the surge in their external debt is a reflection of the increase in OPEC surpluses, and the sign of the argument is correct, the magnitudes are exaggerated, since this group of countries accounts for only 10 per cent of total world petroleum consumption. As a group, the LDCs did not 'adjust' to the sharp increase in the price of oil; instead their current account deficits increased by more than the increase in their oil-import bills. In effect, part of the OPEC surpluses were shunted to the developing countries; rather than adjust to a payments deficit, they 'adjusted' to payments surpluses and their currencies appreciated in real terms.

Currently, the debt-servicing problems of Mexico, Brazil, Argentina and other developing countries suggest they may have 'over-borrowed'. If so, the question raised is whether some allocative mechanism in the international system performed poorly. The story is that, given the surge in their OPEC deposits, the international banks set risk-adjusted loan rates in the form of mark-ups over London inter bank overnight rate (LIBOR) that led to the surge in the loans to the developing countries; LDC borrowers were better able to pay their (higher) mark-up than were borrowers in the industrial countries. So on a risk-adjusted basis, the LDC borrowers were more attractive. In this case, is the source of the problem that they borrowed too much because interest rates were too low? The competing explanation is that the lenders were engaged in a credit-rationing process, and that loans to LDC borrowers are not excessively large in relation to the size of the LDC economies.

Now the market value of loans to many of these countries is significantly below book value and many lenders would be willing to sell their loans at a discount. This phenomenon should not be surprising, for it is typical of this stage of the cycle. Yet the example demonstrates that these loans are effectively long-term loans, despite their short-term aspects.

The flow of funds to the LDCs demonstrates the effectiveness of the private capital market. The external savings of the OPEC countries were allocated to the borrowers with highest rates of return. This flow of funds cushioned the structural shock of the higher oil-price, and enabled the LDCs (or at least the credit-worthy LDCs) to delay their adjustment to the deficits. Yet some of these countries sought to delay eventual adjustment that must occur when OPEC surpluses decline and the oil-price falls. If the LDCs had adjusted continuously to the changes in the real price of oil (that is, if they had acted so that their current account balance had not changed) then they would have depreciated their currencies in real terms when the real price was declining. Private finance made it possible for these countries to avoid that trauma, and indeed to reverse part of the adjustment. When the real rates of interest fell, these countries increased their external loans. However, when the oil price fell, the OPEC surpluses evaporated, and the real interest rates rose, the borrowers were reluctant or unwilling to adjust. The appropriate policy would have been a real depreciation. That depreciation is now under way, in some cases with both economic and political trauma. It may be that the lenders will incur losses on these loans; such losses could be severe and point to the inadequacy of the risk premia. That concern should not detract attention from the effective allocation of saving and investment on a global basis.

Consider now the adequacy of finance for adjustment between the United States and other industrial countries in response to a monetary disturbance. The significant feature of this relationship has been the very sharp movements in exchange rates. These sharp movements in exchange rates are characteristic of excessive adjustment costs, for the current account had to adjust to finance the capital outflows. Usually the purpose of finance is to alleviate or lessen the changes in the exchange rates caused by changes in the current account balances where changes in the current account balance may result from crop failures, changes in the terms of trade, or cyclical changes in income. That is, the capital flows are supposed to dampen the shock – and that is the purpose of either private capital flows or public capital flows.

Yet in much of the last decade, changes in the current account balance have been induced by changes in interest rates and exchange rates; the current account balance has been obliged to finance the changes in the capital account balance. At an earlier stage such capital flows were considered destabilising. The pegged exchange rate counterpart of these changes would be a 'run' on a currency in anticipation of a devaluation or a revaluation, especially when the change in the exchange parity was not justified by the underlying economic situation. These flows demonstrate that national money markets are not sufficiently insulated from each other so that independent monetary policies are possible without effective real shocks.

IV   THE LENDER-OF-LAST-RESORT MECHANISM AND THE FINANCING OF IMBALANCE

The evidence of the last decade indicates that the availability of credits from private banks has enabled the developing countries to finance the adjustment problems that originated in the oil shock. Indeed these countries were able to increase their current account deficits by more than the increase in their oil-import bills. Some countries – fourth world countries as opposed to Newly Industrialised Countries (NICs) – might not be in this position. Because many countries have reduced their excess debt-servicing capacity and because the international banks are likely to be more cautious in their loans to developing countries in the future, the evidence of extensive availability of bank credits in the last decade does not mean that there will be an abundance of similar credits in the next decade. Even if the credits from the private banks in the next decade were only modest in magnitude in relation to the credits available in the last decade, the volume would almost certainly be large enough to finance the payments imbalances caused by structural shocks and monetary shocks. Such a judgement assumes that the magnitude of the structural shocks in the next decade will not be larger than the oil-price shocks.

The immediate major concern is the adequacy of lender-of-last-resort mechanism, and for three different types of problems. One is a run on a country's reserves evident in the Mexican case. A second is a run on particular institutions, or on the banks in a particular country; the Banco Ambrosiano case is relevant. The third is a shift away from off-shore deposits to domestic deposits. The common element is that for a relatively short period, interest-rate differentials appear small related to the risk of non-payment. So there is a shift toward higher quality paper or assets.

The need for a lender-of-last-resort mechanism reflects that lenders, depositors and financial intermediaries alter their asset preferences. The shift in asset preferences reflects that the premium associated with riskier financial and productive assets are inadequate, and so there is a shift to assets believed to be of higher quality. The shift may be from assets denominated in one currency to assets denominated in another currency, from offshore assets to on-shore assets, or from liabilities of secondary institutions to liabilities of primary institutions.

Borrowers and financial institutions maintain reserves or credit lines or other forms of liquidity to accommodate these shifts, yet from time to time the volume of these shifts may exceed the volume of their liquidity. In other cases the additional interest rates that must be paid exceed the return that the borrowers can earn, so a liquidity crisis becomes a solvency crisis.

A key general policy issue is how to structure the system to reduce the likelihood of a crisis – how much stability or safety to build into the system. There are numerous analogies – how much safety to build into aircraft, or into skyscrapers in earthquake zones, or into the braking systems of automobiles. Usually the trade-off involves low-probability high-cost events; the system or structure bears the costs of these safety characteristics.

The more specific policy issues for financial system involves the allocation of these costs among various groups. Consider the secondary banking crisis in Great Britain in the mid-1970s. A group of thirty or so financial intermediaries sold liabilities to the public and used the funds to buy liabilities issued by property developers; the interest rates paid by these banks exceeded those paid by the clearing banks. Then, as interest rates rose in a period of monetary contraction the fringe banks were squeezed by large loan losses attributable to falling property values and a loss of deposits as interest rates paid by the clearing banks increased. The liquidity of the fringe banks declined and some became insolvent. There was concern about the impacts of their failure on the banking system.

The public policy problem involved whether and how to provide assistance to these fringe banks and their depositors, creditors and shareholders. The depositors had benefitted from higher interest rates; should they also be saved – and if so, without penalty? Which fringe banks should be supplied with liquidity and how – from the clearing banks or from the central bank? Should 'insolvent' institutions be supplied with liquidity, if the insolvency was an aberration caused by the decline in property values? The usual argument is that the depositors in the banking system should be saved – even if not insured – while the managers of the institution should be replaced as a minimum requirement. Usually the owners or shareholders are not assisted directly, except as liquidity is supplied.

Consider now the external debt problems of the Latin American countries, especially in relationship to the major commercial banks. Consider the analogies with the British financial crises. These Latin American countries are the counterpart to the property developers; they borrowed short and invested long. Moreover these countries, like the property developers, were caught in a period of monetary contraction; the return on their equity investments declined while the real interest rate they had to pay on their debts increased. There are however, at least two important differences; one is that the borrowers are subject to an exchange risk, and the second is that the borrowers may not be insolvent – although some might be because of the exchange losses. (There is a quite separate issue of whether these exchange losses might be socialised.)

The counterpart to the fringe banks are the large international banks. It may be that these banks had anticipated the repayment problems of LDC borrowers in general and had priced their loans accordingly: it is unlikely that they anticipated the problems of particular borrowers. The scattered comments on increased mark-ups over LIBOR and the public concern suggests that the banks had not fully anticipated the risks. In a way, these banks got well beyond the 'point of no return' long before they had realised the severity of the liquidity problem which the borrowers might encounter.

The public policy problem involves whether external financial assistance should be provided and if so, to whom. The domestic analogy might suggest that liquidity be provided to stabilise the money supply – that any lender threatened by large loan losses would be merged with stronger financial institutions or nationalised; in the first case the national authority might bless the merger with a dowry. The domestic analogy would not suggest that the public funds be used to supply liquidity to the ultimate borrowers; that role would be reserved for the lenders, yet there are examples where the externalities resulting from the failure of a large firm might be so extensive that public intervention would be warranted; non-actuarial based disasters are an analogy.

The policy solution is to refinance the debts – for a lender with a higher credit-rating to provide credits or to recycle the funds. Commercial banks may re-finance non-bank lenders, and central banks may re-finance some commercial banks, although, on the international scene, some large commercial banks may re-finance some minor central banks. The International Monetary Fund may re-finance the external debts of some central banks, yet the IMF is a qualified lender-of-last-resort, and for two reasons. One is that the Fund does not issue any money; the Fund has no printing press of its own and no currency unit of its own. The second is that the Fund's holdings of various national currencies are limited by the capital subscriptions of its members and the currencies available under the 'General Arrangements To Borrow' and other credit lines. The Fund recycles the currencies of its members. From time to time, the Fund's holdings of useful currencies have been nearly exhausted. It seems unlikely that the Fund would ever have unlimited access to the currencies of its two or three largest members. The Fund's role would be that of a supplementary lender.

V   SUMMARY AND CONCLUSIONS

In this chapter I have discussed the effectiveness of private capital flows in financing the current account deficits of the developing countries. For countries, as for all other economic units, financing of deficits tends to be automatic, since interest rates tend to rise in the countries with payments deficits and fall in the countries with payments surpluses. The proposition that imbalances cannot occur unless they can be financed holds for countries. The key question is whether private capital flows will be adequate to permit the adjustment mechanism to work smoothly, or whether the pace of adjustment will be excessively rapid because of inability to finance a more extended deficit; the implication of the term 'excessively rapid' is that the costs of adjustment would be smaller if the payments imbalance might be reduced and eliminated over a more extended period.

If the source of the payments disturbance is cyclical, however, then the payments imbalance should induce changes in interest-rate differentials that should facilitate the financing of payments imbalances. If the payments imbalance is structural, then private capital flows also should help to finance the deficit – again, because of the disturbance, the deficit should be temporary. The major exception to the automaticity of financing the payments imbalances involves monetary disturbances, either changes in interest-rate differentials or in the expected change in the exchange rate, in the absence of official financing, the trade balance must adjust to finance the change in capital outflows. However, if investors or borrowers anticipate a non-trivial change in the exchange rate, the volume of capital flows undertaken to finance the current account deficits might diminish sharply because of the anticipated exchange loss.

The effectiveness of the market-induced flows of finance to facilitate the adjustment process has been illustrated by the ability of the oil-importing developing countries to finance the increase in their current account deficits attributable to the surge in the price of oil. Many developing countries, especially those with significant growth potential, were able to finance increases in their current account deficits much larger than those associated with the increase in their oil-import bills. Other developing countries, however, were judged less creditworthy, and required official finance to finance these structural deficits.

Now that Mexico, Brazil and Argentina have encountered debt-servicing crises, the automatic-financing mechanism has been faulted. These debt-servicing crises were triggered by a breakdown in the re-financing mechanism as borrowers anticipated a sharp increase in the price of the dollar in terms of their currencies; the borrowers wished to avoid revaluation losses associated with the shape increases in exchange rates. Because the volume of external debt appears to have ballooned relative to the national incomes, the inference is sometimes made that the banks have lent too much to these countries, or that the countries have borrowed too much. Several developing countries may have incurred too large a volume of external debt, given changed expectations about the real interest rate and the price of oil; if so, adjustments will be necessary in the volume of their external debt, for the problems of these countries represent the international counterpart of a domestic solvency problem.

For most developing-country borrowers, the current concern with the large volume of external debt involves a monetary problem comparable with a domestic liquidity problem. For many of these countries, their 'real' current account deficit has declined, after adjustment for the declines both in the interest rates on their external debt and the price of oil. Yet their external debt situation has worsened because many lenders are reluctant to re-finance the volume of external debt. For a while the financial flows are both destabilising and self-justifying; because certain lenders observe that the borrowers are finding it increasingly difficult to get some lenders to re-finance their credits, the self-interest of the original lenders requires that they 'follow the herd'. In these circumstances a public institution may be needed to re-finance some private loans.

REFERENCES

Robert Z. Aliber (1977) 'Living with Developing Country Debt', *Lloyds Bank Review*, October, pp. 34–44.

Robert Z. Aliber (1980) 'A Conceptual Approach to the Analysis of External Debt of the Developing Countries', Staff Working Paper No. 421, World Bank (Washington, DC).

Dragoslav Avramovic (1964) *Economic Growth and External Debt* (Baltimore: Johns Hopkins Press).

E. Bacha and C. Diaz Alejandro (1982) *International Financial Intermediation; A Long and Tropical View*, Essay in International Finance No. 147 (Princeton University).

P. K. Bardhan (1967), 'Optimal Foreign Borrowing', in K. Shell (ed.) *Essays on the Theory of Optimal Economic Growth* (Cambridge, Mass: MIT Press).

A. G. Barrett and A. L. Mayo (1978) 'An Early Warning Model for Assessing Developing Country Risk', in S. Goodman (ed.) *Financing Risk in Developing Countries* (New York: Praeger).

Pierre Dhonte (1975) 'Describing External Debt, a Roll-over Approach, *IMF Staff Papers*, March, pp. 159–86.

Pierre Dhonte (1979) *Clockwork Debt* (Lexington: Lexington Books).

Jonathan Eaton and N. Gersovitz (1980) 'LDC Participation in International Financial Markets: Debt and Reserves', *Journal of Development Economics*, February, pp. 3-21.

G. Feder (1979) 'Optimal International Borrowing, Capital Allocation and Creditworthiness Control', *Kredit and Kapital*, pp. 2, 207–20.

G. Feder (1980) 'Economic Growth, Foreign Loans, and Debt Servicing Capacity of Developing Countries', *Journal of Development Studies*, April, pp. 352–68.

G. Feder and R. Just (1977) 'A Study of Debt Servicing Capacity Applying Logit Analysis', *Journal of Development Economics*, March, pp. 25–38.

L. Franko and M. Seiber (eds.) (1979) *Developing Country Debt* (New York: Pergamon Press).

L. Goodman (1981) 'Bank Lending to non-OPEC LDCs: are Risks Diversifiable?', *Federal Reserve Bank of New York Quarterly Review*, Summer, pp. 10–20.

J. A. Hanson (1974) 'Optimal International Borrowing and Lending', *American Economic Review*, September, pp. 616–30.

H. R. Heller (1982), 'Country Risk and International Bank Lending', part of a panel discussion in Chapter 9 of P. Wachtel (ed.) *Crises in the Economic and Financial Structure* (Lexington: Lexington Books).

International Monetary Fund (1981) 'External Indebtedness of Developing Countries', IMF Occasional Paper No. 3 (Washington, DC).

G. Judge *et al* (1980) *The Theory and Practice of Econometrics* (New York: Wiley).

M. Katz (1982) 'The Cost of Borrowing, the Terms of Trade, and the Determination of External Debt', *Oxford Economic Papers*, July, pp. 332–45.

H. Kharas (1981a) 'The Analysis of Long-run Creditworthiness: Theory and Practice', Domestic Finance Study No. 73, World Bank (Washington, DC).

H. Kharas (1981b) 'On Structural Change and Debt Service Capacity', Domestic Finance Study No. 74, World Bank (Washington, DC).

H. Kharas (1981c) 'Constrained Optimal Foreign Borrowing by Less Developed Countries', Domestic Finance Study No. 75, World Bank (Washington, DC).

C. P. Kindleberger (1978a) 'Debt Situation of Developing Countries in Historical Perspective', in S. Goodman (ed.) *Financing Country Risk in Developing Countries* (New York: Praeger).

C. P. Kindleberger (1978b) *Manias, Panics and Crises* (New York: Basic Books).

B. King (1968) 'Notes on the Mechanics of Growth and Debt', *World Bank Staff Occasional Papers*, No. 6 (Baltimore: Johns Hopkins Press).

J. E. Leimone (1979) 'The Growth of Commercial Bank Lending to Non-Oil LDCs: Some Analytical Issues', paper given to XVI Meeting of Technicians of Central Banks of the American Continent (San Jose, Costa Rica).

C. Loser (1977) 'External Debt Management and Balance of Payments Policies', *IMF Staff Papers*, March, pp. 168–92.

J. McCabe and D. S. Sibley (1976) 'Optimal Foreign Debt Accumulation with Export Revenue Uncertainty', *International Economic Review*, October, pp. 675–86.

J. Sachs (1981) 'The Current Account and Macroeconomic Adjustments in the 1970s', *Brookings Papers on Economic Activity*, pp. 1, 201–68.

J. Sachs (1982) 'LDC Debt in the 1980s: Risk and Reforms', in P. Wachtel (ed.) *Crises in the Economic and Financial Structure* (Lexington: Lexington Books).

J. Sachs and D. Cohen (1982) 'LDC Borrowing with Default Risk', Working Paper No. 925, National Bureau of Economic Research (Cambridge, Mass.).

K. Saini and D. Bates (1978) 'Statistical Techniques for Determining Debt Servicing Capacity for Developing Countries: Analytical Review of the Literature and Further Empirical Results', Research paper No. 1718, Federal Reserve Bank of New York.

N. Sargen (1977) 'Economic Indicators and Country Risk Appraisal', *Economic Review of the Federal Reserve Bank of San Francisco*, Autumn, pp. 19–35.

Y. Tagaki (1981) 'Aid and Debt Problems in Less Developed Countries', *Oxford Economic Papers*, pp. 324–37.

J. Thornblade (1978) 'A Checklist System, a First Step in Country Evaluation', in S. Goodman (ed.) *Financing Country Risk in Developing Countries* (New York: Praeger).

I. Walter (1981) 'Country Risk, Portfolio Decisions and Regulation in International Bank Lending', *Journal of Banking and Finance*, March, pp. 77–92.

B. Wasow (1979) 'Savings and Dependence with Externally Financed Growth', *Review of Economics and Statistics*, February, pp. 150–4.

P. A. Wellons (1977) *Borrowing by Developing Countries on the Eurocurrency Market* (Paris: OECD).

M. S. Wionczek (1982) *LDC External Debt and the World Economy* (Mexico City: Il Colegio de Mexico).

2 The Role of Financial Institutions

GEOFFREY W. MAYNARD

The increase in the relative importance of financial institutions, particularly banks, in the international transmission of capital and the financing of balance of payments deficits in recent years is brought out in Tables 2.1 and 2.2.

Table 2.1 shows that the volume of business conducted in international financial markets, which are usually taken to include the Foreign Bond sector of domestic markets as well as the more truly international Eurobond and bank credit markets located 'offshore', rose almost twentyfold in the course of a decade. Eurocurrency bank credits increased more than twice as fast as lending through bonds, so that by 1981 bank credits were two thirds of the total. The seminal event underlying the expansion of the Euro-markets was the imposition by the US of capital and credit market controls in the mid 1960s (that is, the Interest Equalization Tax, the Voluntary Foreign Credit Restraint Programme, and Regulation Q) which effectively shifted a large proportion of US money and capital markets abroad, where they have stayed (despite abolition of the controls in 1974) because of tax considerations and freedom from regulatory requirements existing in domestic markets. More fundamentally, however, the expansion of the international financial market in general can be attributed to a number of long-term factors – the general restoration of currency convertibility at the end of the 1950s, the growth of world trade and multinational enterprise, and technological innovations affecting information and communications, all of which speeded up the integration of the world economy. By creating massive payments disequilibria between oil-consuming and oil-producing nations, the quadrupling in oil prices in 1973–4 and further doubling in 1979 provided a further massive fillip to the markets – the most notable features of the expansion subsequent to 1973–4 being

TABLE 2.1 International financial flows, 1971–82 (US $million)

	1971	1972	1973	1974	1975	1976	1977	1978	1979	1980	1981	1982 1st half
Total international credit	10247	16544	29689	36120	40903	61365	75741	104299	123390	119312	186339*	89778
Euro-currency bank credits	3963	6796	21851	29263	20992	28849	41765	69919	82430	77392	133354*	46624
International bonds	6284	9748	7838	6857	19911	32516	33976	34380	40960	41920	52985	43154
Euro-currency bank credits												
Industrial countries	2601	4097	13783	20683	7231	11254	17205	27380	26030	39100	86022	20821
Developing countries	1286	2414	7288	7318	11098	15017	20976	38612	48600	35054	45239	25279
Communist countries	66	285	779	1238	2597	2503	3394	3767	7525	2809	1791	374
International organisations	10	0	0	24	65	74	190	160	275	429	302	150
International bonds												
By currency												
US dollars	3325	5261	3466	4287	10198	19727	19055	13085	17050	19856	33382	28317
Other	2959	4487	4372	2570	9713	12789	14921	21295	23910	22064	19603	14837
By borrower:												
Industrial countries	4930	7415	5829	5390	15214	24200	23851	24821	31856	32732	40978	34054
Developing countries	98	564	664	263	585	1595	3421	4501	3093	2485	4769	3264
Communist countries	25	50	0	40	239	96	248	0	75	65	75	65
International organisations	1231	1719	1345	1165	3873	6626	6454	5058	5936	6638	7163	4587

* Inflated by about $45 billion stand-by and other credits raised by US corporations in the Euromarkets for the attempted purchase of Conoco.

SOURCE Morgan World Financial Markets.

first the increased role played by private banks operating in the Euro-Credit markets, and second, substantial shifts in the pattern of lending. Before 1973 industrial countries were virtually the only borrowers in financial markets with most of the borrowing being done by private borrowers, mainly business corporations; after 1973, developing countries had growing access to the markets, and public sector borrowers began to displace private sector ones in relative importance. Thus, whereas at the beginning of the 1970s, developing countries were negligible borrowers in international markets, by the end of the decade they were responsible for almost 30 per cent of the off-take from the markets, largely in the form of bank credits. Industrial countries remained the principal borrowers in the bond markets.

Table 2.2 shows how the current account balance-of-payments positions of the main groupings of countries behaved through the 1970s; and also their net borrowing through international capital markets. Net borrowing grew roughly in line with the sum of the current account deficits.[1] The association between the two is a good deal closer in the case of the non-oil developing countries (namely the newly industrialised countries and oil-producing but non-capital-surplus countries) and the centrally planned economies, largely because the actual running and size of the deficits depended quite crucially on the availability of finance. This of course is not the case for the industrial countries whose participation in the international capital markets reflects an intermediary role in the channelling of oil exporters' balance-of-payments surpluses to non-oil developing countries as well as among themselves.

I COMMERCIAL BANK INVOLVEMENT

Commercial bank involvement in international financial markets goes back well before the oil-price shock of 1973–4. Although national regulations differ – for example, US and Japanese banks are not allowed to engage in underwriting activities – banks operate in primary and secondary security markets on a significant scale, buying and selling securities on behalf of clients and of themselves, in addition to conducting their normal deposit-taking and lending business. Their participation has certainly contributed to geographical and sector integration of financial markets, thereby bringing borrowers and lenders closer together and reducing the gap between the risk-adjusted rate of return on investment and the rate of return to savers, allowing for the latter's risk and liquidity preference. In other words, their growing involvement has contributed to the efficiency of financial markets.

TABLE 2.2 Balance-of-payments deficits, 1971–82 ($ billion)

	1971–3 (annual average)	1974	1975	1976	1977	1978	1979	1980	1981	1982e
i) Sum of current account deficits	18	76	78	73	76	85	93	153	n.a.	n.a.
ii) Current A/C Balances[1]										
Non-oil developing countries	-12	-37	-46	-32	-28	-37	-57	-86	-99	-97
Oil exporting developing countries	–	-5	-10	-8	-6	-8	-8	-11	-21	-23
OPEC	+4	+68	+35	+40	+32	+3	+70	+115	+71	+25
Industrial countries	+18	-14	+18	-3	-6	+30	-10	-45	-4	+11
Centrally planned economies	–	-2	-6	-5	-2	0	1	2		
Net borrowing through international capital markets[2]	19	36	41	61	76	104	123	117	186	
of which:										
(a) From banks	11	29	21	29	42	70	82	77	133	
by										
non oil developing countries	9	15	8	11	13	26	35	23	33	
Centrally planned economies	2	4	3	3	3	4	7	3	2	
Industrial countries	16	22	7	11	13	29	27	39	86	
OPEC		3	3	4	7	11	13	11	12	
(b) From bond market	8	10	20	32	32	34	41	42	53	
by										
Industrial countries	5	5	15	24	22	25	32	33	41	
Other	3	5	5	8	10	9	9	9	12	

e = estimate.
NOTE 1 Negative sign equals deficit; positive sign equals surplus. Total deficits and total surpluses do not balance owing to statistical and timing errors.
All figures rounded.
2 Columns do not add up owing to double counting and unallocated.
3 Although reliable when this paper was written, the figures in this table are subject to frequent revision and should be used with care.
SOURCE World Bank, IMF, Morgan Guaranty World Financial Markets and T. Rybzynski (unpublished paper).

The increasing dominance of these banks in the markets in the 1970s may have had something to do with the acceleration of inflation and subsequent rise in interest rates which followed the oil-price shocks: potential investors in bonds may have been reluctant to increase their portfolios. More likely, however, the greatly increased role of the banks in channelling finance to developing countries, which is perhaps the most significant feature, can be attributed first to the asset preferences of the OPEC lenders who placed a substantial proportion (probably a third) of their surplus oil revenues as short term deposits in the Euro-banks, and second, to the greater experience and capacity of the banks in the assessment and pricing of both commercial and sovereign country risk. Moreover the banks were quickly able to develop instruments such as the syndicated Euro-credit which effectively shared country risk among them, which would not have been possible for non-bank lenders. The relative shift in the pattern of lending away from lending to private sector borrowers to lending to public sector ones mentioned earlier, was largely due to the negative economic impact of the oil-price rise on private corporate activity and to the policy response of governments. The oil-price rise seriously reduced economic activity and profits in the private sectors of the oil-consuming countries, creating serious recession subsequent to both 1973–4 and 1979. Governments responded by running larger public sector deficits which they financed by borrowing from banks.

Against this historical and descriptive background, a number of questions arise. Two are very familiar: how far has the growing involvement of banks in international financial intermediation and the consequent enormous expansion of Euro-currency markets led to the creation of excess liquidity and therefore to inflation? How far has the increasing integration of world financial markets, in which, as indicated, banks have played a major role, imposed serious and growing constraint on national economic policy-making? Neither of these questions will be pursued here since they have already attracted much attention. Instead, I shall comment first on the question: 'how well have banks, and indeed international financial markets generally, coped with monetary squeeze, high real and nominal interest rates and unstable exchange rates now affecting the world economy?' and second, on the question whether the international banks have over-extended their lending to developing countries so that the viability and security of the system is now greatly at risk.

II VULNERABILITY OF THE BANKS TO A MONETARY SQUEEZE

Clearly, unexpected changes in interest rates and exchange rates impose risks on both bond holders and issuers, as well as on financial intermediaries.

Bond holders suffer when interest rates rise or the currency in which their bonds are denominated depreciate whilst bond issuers gain; and vice versa. Because of this, bond markets can dry up when interest rates and exchange rates are highly volatile either because of reluctance of lenders to buy bonds or because of a reluctance of borrowers to issue them. But bond markets can adapt (and have adapted) to this situation by inventing new security instruments. Thus we have seen the introduction of *Floating Rate Notes* (FRNs) to meet the problem of interest rate fluctuations, and *Currency Options* to meet the problem of currency fluctuations. FRNs are usually issued in relatively small denominations ($1000), with medium term maturity (5–7 years), and carry an interest rate which is usually adjusted at six-monthly intervals in line with the London interbank offer rate (LIBOR). Thus to a large extent both borrowers and lenders are protected against unexpected interest rate changes. Although FRNs were issued and bought in the early 1970s, they were only issued on an appreciable scale in the late 1970s when interest rate fluctuations became most violent. In 1980, Euro-FRNs represented about 19 per cent of all Euro-bonds issued in the market (and probably more than that in 1981) as compared with about 9 per cent in 1977 (Table 2.3). Currency option bonds are issued in one currency but carry an option for the investor to take payments of interest and capital in another currency. Usually the exchange rate is fixed in advance so that these options put the exchange risk on the borrower which may explain why the issue of such bonds has been rather limited. However, there have been one or two issues which stipulate a floating exchange rate so enabling the exchange risk to be shared between borrower and lender. Thus, despite widely fluctuating and rising

TABLE 2.3 *Euro-bond borrowing by instrument, 1977–80 ($ billion and percentage)*

	1977		1978		1979		1980	
	$	%	$	%	$	%	$	%
Straight	15.7	94.4	11.1	69.6	11.1	62.5	14.2	64.1
Convertible and warrants	1.2	6.0	1.3	8.2	1.6	9.1	2.6	11.7
Special placement	0.8	3.7	0.8	5.3	0.8	4.7	0.9	4.5
Floating rate notes	1.8	9.4	2.6	16.3	4.2	23.6	4.2	19.1
Other and unknown	neg.	0.2	0.1	0.2	–	–	0.1	0.5
Total	19.5	100	15.9	100	17.8	100	22.1	100

SOURCE World Bank

interest rates in the last few years, the bond market has continued to channel substantial flows of funds from lenders, although, as Table 2.1 shows, the increase in those flows has been proportionally much less than in the case of the Euro-credit markets. As one would expect, issues denominated in US dollars declined relatively to issues denominated in other currencies in 1978–80 when the dollar was weak, but recovered strongly in 1981 and 1982 as the dollar became strong. Clearly it is the supply side, not the demand side, that dominates the market. Currency cocktail issues have been less in vogue than their supporters might have expected.

Banks operating in Euro-credit markets are faced with *maturity transformation and foreign exchange risks* and also *prudential* risks. Since banks tend to borrow short and lend long, and issue liabilities in one currency and acquire assets in another they are exposed to interest rate and exchange rate fluctuations. However Euro-banks are substantially protected against interest rate fluctuations since their loans are typically in the form of roll-over credits on which the interest rate is adjusted every six months: they rely on their Treasury departments to fund themselves defensively during the six months they are at risk, and also to match or hedge their foreign exchange exposure. Since Herstatt, commercial banks are not great position-takers in either money or foreign exchange markets. It is often suggested that banks underestimate the difficulties they could experience in funding themselves in the interbank market at a time of liquidity crisis and in the absence of a lender of last resort. Certainly, there have been times when money markets have become tight and smaller banks have had to pay a premium over the price available to larger banks; profits no doubt suffer: but there have been very few occasions in the last few years, during which Euro-rates have been forced to very high levels owing to monetary squeeze in the US market, when even the smallest bank found it impossible to fund its assets. Of course the matter might be different in the case of debt defaults which put a particular bank's capital at risk, for then funding might not be available whatever price was offered. In recent months, one or two banks in highly exposed positions, have suffered a cut back of interbank lines of credit available to them. It is in the area of debt default, rather than in maturity transformation and foreign exchange exposure, that the more serious problems facing the banks could be found; and it is to this that we now turn.

Monetary stringency and high nominal and real interest rates have adverse direct and indirect effects on borrowers in international financial markets, and therefore affect the stability and fragility of those markets.

The *direct* effect arises in respect of the debt-service burden borne by the major borrowers in the market; and of most concern here are the dozen or so developing countries which have accumulated substantial external debt during the last decade. At the end of 1982 total LDC external debt amounted to more than $500 billion so that a rise of 1 per cent in nominal interest rates increases debt service by about $5 billion. Although attention is usually focused on the external debt-service ratio which includes amortisation payments of the developing countries, of more significance in our present context is the ratio of net foreign interest payments to the export of goods and services. This ratio has doubled in the last six years (from 6.5 to 13 per cent), largely although not wholly because of the world-wide rise in interest rates. The rise in interest payments clearly represents a massive extra burden on the major borrower countries impairing their development prospects as well as their ability to repay on time.

The *indirect* effect arises through the impact of restrictive monetary policies and high interest rates on world economic activity in general. World economic recession depresses the export markets of the developing countries for both commodities and manufactured goods, so impairing the ability of the borrowing countries to earn the foreign exchange revenue necessary to service external debt. Clearly there is an increase in risk of default or enforced re-scheduling which can undermine confidence in the market. The spread of protectionism, not far away, would add to the difficulties. On the other hand we should take a favourable consequence of high interest rates into account, namely the consequential fall in real oil-price which to some extent alleviated the burden on the balance of payments.

III   BANK LENDING TO DEVELOPING COUNTRIES

These considerations bring us to our second question, namely whether the international banks have over-extended their lending to developing countries and are now vulnerable to monetary squeeze, massive default and consequent failure.

The statistics may seem daunting. Briefly: medium-term Euro-bank credits to non-OPEC LDCs have risen by over $200 billion since 1973 to a total of around $250 billion and now represent about 50 per cent of the total of medium- and long-term credit. The ratio of external debt to the GNP of the developing countries has risen to over 40 per cent, and although the ratio of debt to exports has remained fairly stable, the external debt service ratio (i.e. the ratio of debt service to export revenue) has risen from around 15 per cent to 25 per cent. As indicated before, these figures apply to a very limited number of developing countries: indeed eight countries — Brazil, Mexico, Korea, Philippines, Algeria, Indonesia, Venezuela and Argentina — account for over 60 per cent of total LDC public sector debt to the banks. Within this total, Mexico, Brazil and Argentina with external public sector debts of the order of $65 billion, $55 billion, and $35 billion respectively, clearly stand out. It is possible to be horrified by such statistics and to take a sombre view of the prospects, particularly for the banks, but perhaps we should stand back a bit and take a calmer view.

It is clear that the role of the international banking system has changed significantly since the oil-price shock of 1973. In the 1950s and 60s the function of the banks was to provide temporary financial facilities for *private borrowers* — mainly multinational corporations for the purpose of financing their investment and trading activities — and a temporary haven for the assets of *private* lenders. Today, banks get a much larger proportion of their resources from public sector depositors, largely OPEC, and they devote a much larger part of their lending to meeting the balance-of-payments and development-financing needs of developing countries channelled through *public sector* agencies. In providing balance-of-payments finance on longer terms than the IMF (and with less conditionality) and putting less emphasis on project finance than does the World Bank, the banks are increasingly occupying a role somewhere between that of the IMF and the World Bank. Thus it might be thought that not only are the banks exposing themselves more to political pressure than was the case a decade ago, but they can also be accused of paying less attention to the end-use of the funds they lend than they did earlier; to put it bluntly, they are financing consumption rather than investment, thereby prejudicing the *reversibility* of financial intermediation which is its essential characteristic. At best, the structure of banks' balance sheets is becoming increasingly predetermined, and bankers' freedom of action accordingly circumscribed.

However, questions have to be posed. Suppose the banking system had not been willing or able to recycle the financial surplus of OPEC? Would the world economy be in a better or worse condition than it is today? That oil-importing countries had to adjust to higher oil-prices there can be no doubt, but should they have been forced to do so more quickly? Would it have been better to have allowed earlier and deeper world recession to cap the rise in real oil-price so as to prevent, or at any rate limit, the massive real investment in the Middle East (probably uneconomic from an international point of view) and build-up of OPEC financial claims on Western banks? Would international financial markets be less fragile than they are today? Leaving aside these questions, did the international financial system fail quite as badly as some people think in fulfilling its major function of channelling saving into productive investment?

While it is impossible to trace many details of the end-use of funds channelled through international financial markets and the banks, there is some evidence that not all has been dissipated in consumption. To begin with, it is interesting to note that some of the large developing countries succeeded in borrowing back from international capital markets a substantial proportion of (in some cases even more than) the real income they lost as a result of the rise in oil-price and worsening terms of trade (Table 2.4). This was true for example of Brazil, Korea and the Philippines. It is also interesting to note that middle-income oil importing countries as a group succeeded in maintaining their economic growth rate following the oil-price crisis better than did the industrial countries as a group (Table 2.5). Thus, in the case of the industrial countries, GDP growth averaged about 3.2 per cent per annum in the decade of the 1970s as compared with 5 per cent in the 1960s. For the middle-income countries the comparable figures are 5.5 per cent and 6.1 per cent, indicating a very small decline in growth rates, given the severe worsening in their terms of trade. Some countries, including the ones mentioned above, even raised their growth rates, at any rate prior to the second oil shock in 1979. Perhaps it can be inferred that this external borrowing was not altogether wasted.

Some support for this latter conclusion can be drawn from statistics relating to capital formation in these countries. Thus in the case of a number of them, investment as a proportion of GDP rose in the years following the oil-price (Phillipines, Korea, Taiwan and, understandably, the oil-producers generally) whilst in other countries it was at least maintained (Table 2.6). Given that worsening terms of trade would have lowered

TABLE 2.4   *Ratio of incremental borrowing to incremental oil bill, 1973–9*

	Total external borrowing*	Commercial borrowing*
Brazil	1.13	1.01
Korea	0.90	0.67
Philippines	1.04	0.73
Morocco	3.54	2.38

* Incremental gross disbursements of external public debt

SOURCE   World Bank; US Government National Foreign Assessment Center.

Table 2.5   *GDP growth rates, 1960−81* (per cent per annum)

	1960−70	*1970−79*	*1980−81*
Industrial countries	5.1	3.2	1.3
Low-income countries (excluding India, China)	4.3	3.8	
Middle-income countries			
Oil exporters	6.5	5.5	
of which: Nigeria	3.1	7.5	
Algeria	4.6	5.8	
Mexico	7.2	5.1	
Oil importers	5.9	5.5	
of which: Brazil	5.4	8.7	
Philippines	5.1	6.2	
Korea	8.6	10.3	
Taiwan	9.2	8.0	
Morocco	4.2	6.1	
All developing countries	5.8	5.0	3.6

SOURCE World Bank *World Development Report.*

TABLE 2.6   *Investment/GNP ratio, 1973−81*

	1973	1974	1975	1976	1977	1978	1979	1980	1981
Middle Income Countries									
Brazil	0.23	0.24	0.26	0.24	0.23	0.22	0.21	0.22	0.20
Korea	0.24	0.26	0.26	0.24	0.26	0.31	0.33	0.33	0.28
Philippines	0.15	0.19	0.24	0.25	0.24	0.24	0.26	0.26	0.26
Taiwan	0.26	0.29	0.30	0.28	0.26	0.26	0.28	0.30	0.29
Morocco	0.14	0.14	0.23	0.28	0.32	0.25	0.23	0.21	
Algeria	0.41	0.36	0.43	0.46	0.48				
Indonesia	0.19	0.18	0.21	0.21	0.21	0.22	0.23	0.23	
Mexico	0.20	0.21	0.22	0.22	0.22	0.22	0.24	0.25	
Venezuela	0.27	0.19	0.26	0.32	0.39	0.42	0.32	0.25	
Nigeria	0.17	0.19	0.13	0.25	0.29	0.31			
Industrial Countries									
Belgium	0.21	0.22	0.22	0.21	0.21	0.21	0.22	0.23	
Denmark	0.26	0.25	0.24	0.23	0.23	0.23	0.21	0.19	0.16
France	0.23	0.24	0.23	0.23	0.22	0.21	0.21	0.22	
Italy	0.20	0.22	0.20	0.20	0.19	0.18	0.19	0.20	0.20
Germany	0.25	0.22	0.21	0.21	0.21	0.21	0.22	0.23	0.23
Sweden	0.22	0.22	0.21	0.21	0.21	0.20	0.20	0.20	0.19
UK	0.19	0.20	0.19	0.19	0.18	0.18	0.18	0.18	

SOURCE IMF *International Financial Statistics.*

real national income relatively to GDP, some of the heavy borrowers actually succeeded in raising the proportion of their real national income invested in real capital; in other words, the increase in net external indebtedness was matched at least to some extent by a rise in net worth at home. A contrast can be drawn with industrial countries. In many of these the ratio of investment to GDP fell, suggesting that although the industrial countries adjusted their current account balances-of-payments more quickly to the oil-price shock, they did so more by reducing real investment than by reducing real consumption. No doubt, the decline in real investment that took place can be related to the sharp fall in the rate of profit on capital that occurred in industrial countries in the 1970s[2] which, in turn, was related to the failure of real wages to adjust downwards in line with worsening terms of trade. We do not have similar statistics for developing countries, but given less organised and less trade-union dominated labour markets in developing countries as compared with the industrial ones, it seems possible that the returns to capital were better maintained. If so, it is an intriguing possibility that international capital markets did a better job at redistributing world savings to areas where the real return on capital remained relatively high than they have been given credit for so far.

IV   VULNERABILITY OF THE BANKING SYSTEM

What do we conclude from the foregoing? It can hardly be denied that the massive expansion and the character of international lending during the last decade or so has left international financial markets somewhat more vulnerable than they were in the 1960s; or that high and unstable interest rates create problems for fund borrowers and lenders, and intermediaries. But it seems that the maturity transformation and foreign exchange risk problems have been relatively well handled. This is not to deny that some smaller banks at some time or another may well be faced with embarrassing liquidity squeezes, but the system as a whole is hardly likely to founder on it. As for the volume and direction of lending, I do not believe that the surge of bank lending to a limited number of developing countries represented simply an unthinking accommodation to a sudden increase in demand for loans. In the main it reflected a market view that the developing countries share of the overall supply of 'bankable' projects had increased. Moreover, banks now devote much more time and effort to analysing and monitoring the creditworthiness of countries than they ever did before: quite simply, banks know much more about the economies of the developing countries than they did in the past.

This is not to suggest that no problems will arise. The next few years are bound to be difficult ones for the financial markets with some debtors finding it difficult to meet their maturing obligations. Admittedly the recent fall in the nominal and real price of oil has relieved the balance-of-payments position of the oil-consuming countries: OPEC's balance-of-payments surplus disappeared in 1982 and a moderate deficit seems likely through 1983 and 1984; but the gain will be felt mainly in the balances of payments of the industrial countries. Developing country deficits will remain very large and will have to be financed. These countries are suffering acutely from world recession, in the form of declining commodity prices and contracting export markets, and also of course from the unnaturally high level of interest rates. Indeed, interest payments on existing debt will probably amount to more than half of the total current account deficit of those seven or eight developing countries which have been large external borrowers in recent years. In addition to these short-run factors, developing countries are faced with the further problem that substantial amounts of medium-term debt incurred in the second half of the 1970s have become due for repayment. It has been estimated[3] that one third of the total external debt of, and more than 40 per cent of the debt owed to banks by, major developing countries fell due in 1982. Thus, although international lending continued to grow strongly in 1982 and may do so in 1983, we shall almost certainly see a substantial acceleration in the recent tendency for *net* flows of finance to developing countries to decline relatively to *gross* flows. Indeed, because of increasing risk and pressure on commercial bank capital-asset ratios, *net flows* of finance to developing countries have been falling in absolute as well as relative terms since 1978. This trend seems likely to continue unless there is a substantial change in market environment.

The increasing riskiness of bank lending and the plight of the developing countries have led to calls both for more explicit central bank lender-of-last-resort facilities for the banks and the international inter-bank market; and for an IMF safety net that would meet the needs of developing countries facing short-run liquidity problems. The two together, so it is argued, would restore confidence to the market and encourage banks to maintain their lending.

Certainly there is need to increase the resources of the IMF so that the short-term liquidity needs of developing countries can be met; and the recent decision to increase IMF quotas is a step in the right direction. Also, it is vital that the increased riskiness of commercial bank lending should not lead to a drying up of new money to developing countries: without significant net new lending the economic adjustment required of them would be catastrophically abrupt and would put further at risk existing bank debt. Even so, banks should not be encouraged to lend unwisely or at relatively low spreads by the thought that they will be bailed out if difficulties arise; and countries should not be encouraged by the availability of low-priced credit to avoid necessary adjustments.

The world's financial problems (which can be handled if the world's financial lenders keep their cool) arise basically from the world's real problems, and although these look serious enough (in 1982) they will not be with us permanently. High real and nominal interest rates are the result of a restrictive stance of monetary policy in the US and of a crisis of confidence in capital markets, largely engendered by events in the 1970s, not likely to be repeated in the 1980s. Inflation in 1982 is a good deal lower than a year ago and capital markets have notoriously short memories. Real and nominal interest rates have recently fallen substantially and will continue to do so: moreover, nominal and real oil-price is likely to fall significantly in the course of 1983; the world economy will pick up. The problems of the borrowing countries will ease, and the immediate difficulties of the international capital market will be relieved by a return to a more stable and expanding world environment.

NOTES

1. The assymmetry between total deficits and total surpluses is due to statistical errors and omissions and timing asymmetries in recording.
2. T. P. Hill, *Profits and Rates of Return*, (Paris: OECD 1979).
3. Morgan Guaranty, *World Financial Markets* (New York).

3 Modelling International Banking Flows: an Analytical Framework

DAVID T. LLEWELLYN

A major feature of the international monetary system of the 1970s was the increasing role of international banking generally and in particular the shift in the balance of roles of the official and private sectors. In terms of the provision of liquidity, the financing of the transfer of real resources and balance-of-payments financing, the private international banking sector (measured in terms of on-shore and off-shore external lending of private banks) substantially increased its role both absolutely and relatively to the traditional official sector (governments, central banks and official multi-national development and financing organisations). This development was manifest in terms of the substantial increase in the volume of external assets of banks in major financial centres (Tables 3.5–3.8), the rise in the proportion of external assets and liabilities in banks total balance sheet positions, the relative shift from trade financing to more direct balance of payments financing, and the substantial rise in the number of banks participating in international lending business. The World Bank estimates that in 1978 the number of banks participating in the syndicated Euro-credit market was ten times that in 1972. Earnings from international business became increasingly significant over the decade. The range of nationality of banks participating on a significant scale in international lending was also extended.

In general, the international banking sector has operated in a competitive environment of greater intensity than in many purely national banking systems. Nevertheless, market conditions (in terms of volume and borrowing terms) in the syndicated Euro-credit sector changed frequently during the course of its rapid expansion during the 1970s. Goodman (1980) identifies four sub-periods characterised in terms of a 'lenders' market' (1970 to late 1972 and mid-1974 to mid-1977) and a 'borrowers' market' (late 1972 to mid-1974 and mid-1977 to 1980). The analysis in a later section of this Chapter indicates that changes in market conditions are associated in part with the observed alteration in the leadership of the market by different nationalities of banks in turn associated with differences in banks' portfolio objectives and constraints.

The syndicated Euro-credit market is a substantial part of what is defined here as the international banking sector, but the international banking sector and the volume of international bank lending are defined more widely than financial and credit flows through the Euro-currency market. Lending to non-residents in domestic currency, particularly by banks in the United States, Germany, Switzerland, France and Japan, is an integral part of the international banking sector. While the focus of analysis is frequently on the Euro-currency part of the market, external assets in domestic currency represented over 25 per cent of total external lending in 1980 against less than 10 per cent in 1971 (columns (7) and (8) of Table 3.6). More detail is given in Table 3.8 which indicates that external assets of banks in America account for around 54 per cent of identified external domestic currency assets of the international banking sector.

In this context, and in the light of possible future constraints to the role of the international banking sector (Llewellyn, 1982), the object of this Chapter is twofold. Firstly to consider the role of the international banking sector in the world economy. Secondly to indicate a possible broad analytical framework for modelling international banking flows (at the firm and industry level) in terms of an integration of flow of funds analysis and the role of the international banking sector as providing financial intermediary services on a global basis.

An indication of the size and growth of the international banking sector is given in Tables 3.4 to 3.10. At the end of 1980 the volume of cross-border domestic and Euro-currency assets of banks in the BIS reporting area amounted to $1323 billion (against $126 billion in 1971, Table 3.6). Some indication of the currency structure is given in Table 3.4. On the basis of BIS estimates of double-counting associated with inter-bank redepositing, the volume of net international bank credit outstanding is given as $810 billion at the end of 1980 (Table 3.4). The geographical disposition of net international bank credit is given in Table 3.5 which indicates that around 33 per cent was against Eastern Europe and non-oil developing countries.

TABLE 3.1 Summary of payments balances on current account, 1973–82¹ (in billions of US dollars)

	1973	1974	1975	1976	1977	1978	1979	1980	1981	1982²
Industrial countries	17.7	-13.9	17.9	-2.6	-5.7	29.8	-10.2	-44.8	-3.7	11.0
Canada	–	-1.6	-4.6	-4.0	-4.0	-4.0	-4.3	-1.9	-5.8	-5.0
United States	9.1	7.6	21.2	7.5	-11.3	-10.9	4.9	8.4	11.0	5.0
Japan	0.1	-4.5	-0.4	3.9	11.1	18.0	-8.0	-9.5	6.2	13.5
France	-0.1	-4.9	1.0	-4.9	-1.6	5.2	3.0	-6.3	-6.6	-6.5
Germany, Fed. Rep. of	7.1	13.0	7.6	7.7	8.5	13.4	0.1	-8.8	-1.0	10.5
Italy	-2.2	-7.6	-0.2	-2.6	3.1	7.9	6.4	-9.5	-7.3	-6.5
United Kingdom	-1.3	-7.2	-2.9	-0.6	1.5	4.5	1.3	11.5	19.8	12.5
Other industrial countries	5.0	-8.7	-3.9	-9.6	-12.9	-4.3	-13.7	-28.7	-20.0	-12.5
Developing countries										
Oil-exporting countries³	6.7	68.3	35.4	40.3	30.8	2.9	69.8	115.0	70.8	25.0
Non-oil developing countries³	-11.6	-37.0	-46.5	-32.0	-28.3	-39.2	-58.9	-86.2	-99.0	-97.0
By analytical group										
Net oil exporters	-2.6	-5.1	-9.9	-7.7	-6.5	-7.9	-8.5	-11.0	-20.6	-23.0
Net oil importers	-9.0	-31.9	-36.6	-24.3	-22.8	-30.6	-48.8	-72.7	-80.5	-74.0
Major exporters of manufactures	-3.7	-19.1	-19.6	-12.2	-7.9	-9.9	-21.5	-32.4	-36.0	-31.5
Low-income countries	-4.0	-7.5	-7.5	-4.1	-3.6	-7.5	-10.0	-14.5	-14.3	-15.0
Other net oil importers	-1.3	-5.2	-9.5	-7.9	-11.3	-13.2	-17.4	-25.8	-30.2	-28.0
By area										
Africa⁴	-2.1	-3.5	-6.9	-6.1	-6.6	-9.0	-9.7	-12.7	-13.3	-13.0
Asia	-2.4	-9.6	-8.9	-2.6	-1.6	-6.1	-12.6	-22.5	-24.8	-27.0
Europe	0.3	-4.3	-4.7	-4.1	-7.6	-5.2	-8.5	-10.9	-7.9	-6.0
Middle East	-2.6	-4.5	-7.0	-5.4	-5.2	-6.5	-8.5	-7.8	-9.0	-12.0
Western Hemisphere	-4.7	-13.5	-16.4	-11.9	-8.7	-13.2	-21.3	-33.1	-41.5	-35.5
Total⁵	12.8	17.4	6.8	5.7	-3.2	-6.5	0.7	-16.0	-31.9	-61.0

1. On goods, services, and private transfers.
2. Figures are rounded to the nearest $0.5 billion.
3. The People's Republic of China, which is both a net oil exporter and a low-income country, is included in the total (from 1977 onward) but not in the subgroups.
4. Excluding South Africa.
5. Reflects errors, omissions, and asymmetries in reported balance-of-payments statistics on current account, plus balance of payments with other countries (mainly the Union of Soviet Socialist Republics and other non-member countries of Eastern Europe and, for years prior to 1977, the People's Republic of China).

SOURCE IMF World Economic Outlook, 1982.

TABLE 3.2   Non-oil developing countries: current account financing, 1973–82[1] (in billions of U.S. dollars)

	1973	1974	1975	1976	1977	1978	1979	1980	1981	1982
Current account deficit[2]	11.6	37.0	46.5	32.0	28.3	39.2	58.9	86.2	99.0	97.0
Financing through transactions that do not affect net debt positions	10.1	13.0[3]	11.8	12.0	14.9	17.2	23.0	24.1	26.3	27.8
Net unrequited transfers received by governments of non-oil developing countries	5.4	6.9[3]	7.1	7.4	8.3	8.2	10.9	12.3	12.9	13.6
SDR allocations, valuation adjustments, and gold monetisation	0.4	0.7	-0.6	-0.2	1.3	2.1	2.8	1.8	-0.2	—
Direct investment flows, net	4.3	5.3	5.3	4.7	5.3	6.9	9.2	10.0	13.6	14.1
Net borrowing and use of reserves[4]	1.5	23.9[3]	34.7	20.1	13.4	22.0	35.9	62.1	72.7	69.2
Reduction of reserve assets (accumulation)	-9.7	-2.4	1.9	-13.8	-12.4	-15.8	-12.4	-4.9	-1.6	-4.0
Net external borrowing[5]	11.2	23.3[3]	32.9	31.2	25.8	37.8	48.4	67.1	74.3	73.2
Long-term borrowing	11.7	19.5[3]	26.6	27.9	26.5	35.3	37.9	45.5	55.8	59.4
From official sources	5.4	9.3[3]	11.4	10.8	12.6	14.2	15.4	20.5	20.2	22.3
From private sources	8.3	13.7	15.3	19.3	23.0	27.9	33.1	31.4	37.0	38.5
From financial institutions	7.1	12.6	13.8	17.0	19.4	23.9	32.4	30.1	35.5	37.0
From other lenders	1.2	1.1	1.5	2.4	3.6	4.0	0.8	1.3	1.5	1.5
Residual flows, net[6]	-2.0	-3.5	-0.1	-2.3	-9.2	-6.9	-10.6	-6.4	-1.4	-1.4
Use of reserve-related credit facilities[7]	0.2	1.7	2.5	4.4	-0.1	0.5	-0.6	1.7	5.4	6.0
Other short-term borrowing, net	0.2	5.2	6.4	12.2	0.8	4.7	10.5 }	19.9	13.1	7.8
Residual errors and omissions[8]	-0.8	—	-2.7	-11.2	-1.1	-2.5	0.5 }			

[1] Excludes data for the People's Republic of China prior to 1977.

[2] Net total of balances on goods, services, and private transfers, as defined in the Fund's *Balance of Payments Yearbook* (with sign reversed).

[3] Excludes the effect of a revision of the terms of the disposition of economic assistance loans made by the United States to India and repayable in rupees and of rupees already acquired by the U.S. Government in repayment of such loans. The revision has the effect of increasing government transfers by about $2 billion, with an offset in net official loans.

[4] That is, financing through changes in net debt positions (net borrowing, less net accumulation – or plus net liquidation – of official reserve assets).

[5] Includes any net use of nonreserve claims on nonresidents, errors and omissions in reported balance of payments statements for individual countries, and minor deficiencies in coverage.

[6] These residual flows comprise two elements: (1) net changes in long-term external assets of non-oil developing countries and (2) residuals and discrepancies that arise from the mismatching of creditor-source data taken from debt records with capital flow data taken from national balance of payments records.

[7] Comprises use of Fund credit and short-term borrowing by monetary authorities from other monetary authorities.

[8] Errors and omissions in reported balance of payments statements for individual countries, and minor omissions in coverage.

TABLE 3.3   Financing requirement and financing of non-oil developing countries, 1973–82 ($ billion)

	1973	1974	1975	1976	1977	1978	1979	1980	1981	1982	1973–82
(A) Financing Requirement											
(1) Current Account	11.6	37.0	46.5	32.0	28.3	39.2	58.9	86.2	99.0	97.0	535.7
Plus (2) Increase in Reserve Assets	9.7	2.4	-1.9	13.8	12.4	15.8	12.4	4.9	1.6	4.0	75.1
Less (3) Net Direct Investment	4.3	5.3	5.3	4.7	5.3	6.9	9.2	10.0	13.6	14.1	78.7
Equals (4) Total Financing Requirement	17.0	34.1	39.3	41.1	35.4	48.1	62.1	81.1	87.0	86.9	532.1
(B) Financing account											
(5) *Non-Debt Transactions*	5.8	7.6	6.5	7.2	9.6	10.3	13.7	14.1	12.7	13.6	101.1
(i) Net unrequited transfers	5.4	6.9	7.1	7.4	8.3	8.2	10.9	12.3	12.9	13.6	93.0
(ii) SDR allocations etc.	0.4	0.7	-0.6	-0.2	1.3	2.1	2.8	1.8	-0.2	–	8.1
(6) *Net External Borrowing: Non-Banks*	4.2	13.8	19.0	16.3	6.6	14.0	16.0	37.0	38.8	36.2	201.9
(i) long term from official sources	5.4	9.3	11.4	10.8	12.6	14.2	15.4	20.5	20.2	22.3	142.1
(ii) From non-bank private sources	1.2	1.1	1.5	2.4	3.6	4.0	0.8	1.3	1.5	1.5	18.9
(iii) Use of reserve-related credit[1]	0.2	1.7	2.5	4.4	-0.1	0.5	-0.6	1.7	5.4	6.0	21.7
(iv) Other (including errors and omissions)[2]	-2.6	1.7	3.6	-1.3	-9.5	-4.7	0.4	13.5	11.7	6.4	19.2
(7) *Net External Borrowing: Banks*	7.1	12.6	13.8	17.0	19.4	23.9	32.4	30.1	35.5	37.0	228.8
(8) Total Financing	17.1	34.0	39.3	40.5	35.6	48.2	62.1	81.2	86.8	85.8	531.8

[1] Use of IMF credit and short-term borrowing by monetary authorities from other monetary authorities.
[2] Errors and Omissions in balance-of-payments accounts and minor omissions in coverage together with (i) net changes in long term external assets of non-oil LDCs and (ii) residuals and discrepancies arising from mismatching of creditor-source data taken from debt records with capital flow data from balance-of-payments records.

SOURCE Table 3.2.

TABLE 3.4 *External assets and liabilities of banks reporting to the BIS, 1979–81 ($ billion)*

Banks in	European reporting countries						United States	Canada	Japan	Offshore branches of US banks[1]	Grand Total	Net international bank credit[2]	Memo. item: Non-reporting banks in offshore[3] centres
	Domestic currencies					Total foreign and domestic currency							
	Total	France	*of which* Germany	Switzer-land	United Kingdom								
							Assets						
Amounts outstanding													
1979 Dec	136.3	23.2	47.6	27.2	15.5	776.0	136.3[4]	25.6	45.5	127.6	1,111.0	665	135
1980 March	132.0[5]	21.5	45.6	27.8	15.9	775.2	134.7[4]	28.9	49.8	129.9	1,118.5	680	142
June	148.8[5]	25.1	51.5	29.9	18.6	840.3	152.6[4]	30.5	51.3	131.5	1,206.2	745	154
Sept	149.6	25.3	49.8	30.5	20.5	849.9	164.8[4]	32.9	60.1	140.4	1,248.1	775	165
Dec	151.7	24.4	51.8	29.5	22.7	902.9	176.8[4]	35.5	65.7	141.0	1,321.9	810	175
1981 March	145.4	23.3	47.7	29.0	23.3	907.2	183.8[4]	33.9	74.8	147.1	1,346.8	820	189
							186.6[4]				1,349.6		
June	134.7	21.5	42.7	28.4	20.7	884.7	201.0[4]	36.7	70.3	154.0	1,346.7	825	201
Sept	139.4	22.9	43.6	29.0	21.0	920.6	214.0[4]	38.1	82.4	167.7	1,422.8	875	219
Changes[6]													
1980 Q3	*3.8*	*0.9*	*−0.2*	*1.1*	*1.7*	*17.5*	*12.2[4]*	*2.5*	*8.5*	*8.9*	*49.6*	*35*	*..*
1981 Q1	*5.0*	*1.0*	*−0.6*	*1.9*	*2.0*	*31.6*	*7.0[4]*	*−1.4*	*10.1*	*6.1*	*53.4*	*30*	*..*
Q2	*5.7*	*1.3*	*0.8*	*1.1*	*0.6*	*18.1*	*14.4[4]*	*3.1*	*−2.8*	*6.9*	*39.7*	*35*	*..*
Q3	*3.0*	*0.8*	*−0.4*	*−0.1*	*1.7*	*30.5*	*13.0[4]*	*1.4*	*12.6*	*13.7*	*71.2*	*45*	*..*

Liabilities

Amounts outstanding												
1979 Dec	111.4	6.6	54.3	7.4	19.2	777.2	130.1[7]	32.8	50.5	128.8	1,119.4	665	125
1980 March	103.3	7.3	46.5	7.4	19.5	779.3	132.6[7]	35.4	57.8	131.5	1,136.8	680	133
June	125.4[5]	8.7	53.5	9.7	23.9	853.9	131.1[7]	37.2	67.7	133.5	1,223.4	745	143
Sept	128.9	9.4	52.2	11.6	26.2	870.8	132.6[7]	39.4	75.1	142.3	1,260.2	775	153
Dec	127.9	8.6	50.7	12.0	27.7	928.4	139.3[7]	43.6	80.2	143.0	1,334.5	810	164
							133.4[7]				1,347.1		
1981 March	120.3	8.0	48.1	12.0	26.7	929.5	133.6[7]	47.2	87.1	149.9	1,347.3	820	177
June	107.1	6.1	41.6	11.5	24.9	899.0	141.2[7]	56.4	86.5	157.6	1,340.7	825	188
Sept	108.4	5.5	42.1	12.2	25.2	929.6	154.4[7]	59.6	97.3	172.8	1,413.7	875	206
Changes[6]												
1980 Q3	*5.9*	*0.9*	*0.2*	*2.0*	*2.0*	*24.3*	*1.5[7]*	*2.3*	*7.2*	*8.8*	*44.1*	*35*	*..*
1981 Q1	*1.7*	*0.2*	*0.9*	*1.0*	*0.7*	*27.6*	*-5.9[7]*	*3.7*	*7.9*	*6.9*	*40.2*	*30*	*..*
Q2	*1.1*	*-0.8*	*-0.7*	*0.2*	*1.8*	*9.6*	*7.6[7]*	*9.5*	*0.9*	*7.7*	*35.3*	*35*	*..*
Q3	*0.9*	*-0.7*	*-0.7*	*0.4*	*2.1*	*26.7*	*13.2[7]*	*3.2*	*11.0*	*15.2*	*69.3*	*45*	*..*

[1] In the Bahamas, the Cayman Islands, Panama, Lebanon, Hong Kong and Singapore.

[2] 'Grand total' adjusted on a partly-estimated basis to exclude double-counting resulting from redepositing among the reporting banks.

[3] Estimates for non-reporting banks in offshore centres mentioned under footnote 1 and all banks located in Bahrain and the Netherlands Antilles.

[4] Excluding all custody items.

[5] Including for the first time positions of banks in Ireland. At the end of June 1980, these domestic currency positions amounted to $0.1 billion on the assets side and to $1.8 billion on the liabilities side.

[6] Computed for non-dollar positions at end-period exchange rates.

[7] Excluding all custody items except negotiable US bank certificates of deposit held on behalf of non-residents.

SOURCE *BIS Press release.*

I   THE ROLE OF INTERNATIONAL BANKING

The development of international banking over the 1970s took place in the context of substantial changes in the world economy with the simultaneous development of inflation and recession, greatly increased payments imbalances between countries, the structural aspects of two sharp rises in the price of oil, and sometimes volatile exchange rates and interest rates. Trends and developments in international banking interact with the world economy with causality working in both directions. Developments in the world economy impinge upon the international banking sector through their effect upon confidence, the supply and demand for the intermediation services of international banking, and through interest rate implications. The rise in the absolute size of international payments imbalances (Table 3.1) and the structural change in financing (Tables 3.2 and 3.3) were major factors in the development of the international banking sector. Over the period 1973–82 (Table 3.1) industrial countries in aggregate had a cumulative deficit of only $4.5 billion though it ranged from a deficit of $45 billion to a surplus of $30 billion. The cumulative OPEC surplus of $465 billion had, as a counterpart, an aggregate deficit of $536 billion for non-oil-exporting developing countries.

With respect to the financing of LDC deficits in the 1970s and early 1980s, four features are worth highlighting. First, the deficits were increasingly financed through borrowing rather than use of reserves. Second, non-debt forms of financing (aid and autonomous capital inflows) declined in relative importance. Third, the proportion of debt incurred against banks rose sharply over the decade as the private sector came to displace the traditional official sector in balance of payments financing. Finally, in real terms the flow of aid declined markedly. At the same time international bank lending tended to shift from private to public sector borrowers, from short- to long-term assets and from trade-related to balance-of-payments financing.

The total financing requirement of non-oil exporting LDCs, (NOLDCs), is adapted in Table 3.3 from the presentation given by the IMF in Table 3.2. The *total financing requirement* is given as the current account deficit, plus the rise in external reserves, minus (assumed autonomous) net direct investment flows. The financing account is divided into: (i) non-debt transactions, (ii) external borrowing from non-banks, and (iii) net external borrowing from the international banking sector. To the extent that borrowing from this sector is a residual (perhaps questionable relative to borrowing from the IMF), and on the assumption that the current account deficit and rise in reserves was not limited by any financing constraint, the

TABLE 3.5 *'Net' external bank lending, 1975–80 ($ billion: end-year)*

| | | International Bank Credit Against | | | | | |
| | Reporting area | Other developed | Eastern Europe | OPEC countries | Other developing | Other and unallocated | Total net external claims |
	(1)	(2)	(3)	(4)	(5)	(6)	(7)
1975	114.6	40.8	21.6	14.3	63.0	5.0	260
1976	135.0	54.5	28.8	24.1	80.9	6.1	330
1977	189.1	55.5	38.3	39.1	98.7	9.3	430
1978	232.3	63.9	47.5	56.4	120.8	14.1	535
1979	297.6	72.4	55.9	64.1	157.1	17.9	665
1980	378.4	85.6	59.8	70.0	195.0	21.2	810

(7) = (1) + (2) + (3) + (4) + (5) + (6)

SOURCE BIS *Press release*, various issues.

TABLE 3.6 Components of the international lending market, 1971–80 ($ billion: end-year)

	European Reporting Area					Full Reporting Area					
	Cross border foreign currency claims	Cross border domestic currency claims	External bank lending (total cross-border claims)	Domestic foreign currency claims	International lending market (total claims)	Cross border foreign currency claims	Cross border domestic currency claims	External bank lending (total cross-border claims)	International lending market (total claims)	External bank lending	International lending market
	(1)	(2)	(3)	(4)	(5)	(6)	(7)	(8)	(9)	(10)	(11)
1971	100	12	112			114	12	126			
1972	132	13	145			150	13	163			
1973	187	21	208			247	49	296			
1974	215	32	247	24	271	282	79	361	384		
1975	258	39	297	89	387	343	99	442	532		
1976	305	48	353	102	455	418	130	548	650		
1977	385	81	466	129	595	514	176	690	819	767	896
1978	502	109	611	156	767	659	233	893	1049	1000	1156
1979	640	136	776	196	972	829	281	1111	1307	1246	1442
1980	751	152	903	255	1158	981	342	1323	1578	1498	1753

(3) = (1) + (2); (5) = (3) + (4); (8) = (6) + (7); (9) = (4) + (8).

SOURCE BIS *Press Release*, Various Issues.

TABLE 3.7   External assets of banks in domestic currency, 1973–81 ($ billion)

	Austria	Belgium/ Luxembourg	France	Germany	Italy	Netherlands	Switzerland	UK	Canada	Japan	US	Total
						Banks resident in:						
1973		1.2	1.9	8.1	0.8	0.9	7.3	1.4	0.4	0.8	26.0	48.8
1974		1.6	1.1	14.2	0.6	2.7	9.2	1.9	0.4	1.4	45.0	78.1
1975		1.7	1.2	21.0	0.4	3.5	9.1	1.7	0.5	1.5	58.3	98.9
1976		2.4	1.5	25.9	0.3	4.2	10.9	1.8	0.5	2.1	79.3	128.9
1977	2.0	3.2	11.5	31.5	0.3	5.2	14.5	12.2	0.4	3.6	90.2	174.6
1978	2.9	3.9	18.2	40.3	0.6	8.5	19.3	14.7	0.5	8.0	115.7	232.6
1979	4.2	4.7	23.2	47.6	1.3	11.4	27.2	15.5	0.6	11.4	133.6	280.7
1980	4.8	4.6	24.4	51.8	1.0	11.3	29.5	22.7	0.6	17.0	172.7	340.4
1981	5.2	4.0	23.0	51.1	0.7	12.3	31.7	23.2	1.1	21.0	250.0	422.7

SOURCE BIS Annual Reports.

TABLE 3.8 External bank positions against country groups, 1975–80 ($ billion: end-year)

	Full[1] reporting	Offshore centres	Other[3] developed countries	Eastern Europe	OPEC countries	Other developing countries					Total
						Latin America	Middle East	Asia	Africa	Unallocated	
Claims											
1975	235.1	61.9	40.8	21.6	14.3	43.5	3.3	12.9	3.3	5.0	441.7
1976	269.5	83.5	54.5	28.8	24.1	57.4	4.4	14.7	4.4	6.1	547.4
1977	349.9	98.9	55.5	38.3	39.1	65.9	5.2	20.5	7.1	9.3	689.7
1978	466.9	123.5	63.9	47.5	56.4	79.9	6.5	23.1	11.3	14.1	893.1
1979	587.7	155.6	72.4	55.9	64.1	103.5	8.2	31.1	14.3	17.9	1110.7
1980	704.0	187.5	85.6	59.8	70.0	130.2	9.8	38.9	16.1	21.2	1323.1
Liabilities											
1975	270.1	40.8	33.2	6.3	51.8	16.3	6.0	10.6	4.1	7.9	447.1
1976	319.6	56.0	35.0	7.6	64.2	22.3	7.3	14.9	5.3	11.3	543.5
1977	408.5	71.5	28.1	8.4	77.9	25.2	10.0	20.1	6.7	15.6	672.0
1978	533.5	96.3	38.1	10.6	82.5	33.2	13.8	22.2	7.4	18.1	856.3
1979	685.7	139.2	46.1	15.4	120.3	38.4	15.9	26.0	9.3	23.0	1119.3
1980	823.7	164.6	50.1	15.6	159.7	36.3	18.9	27.5	10.0	28.2	1334.6
Net position											
1975	−35.0	+21.1	+7.6	+15.3	−37.5	+27.2	−2.7	+2.3	−0.8	−2.9	−5.4
1976	−50.1	+27.5	+19.5	+21.2	−40.1	+35.1	−2.9	−0.2	−0.9	−5.2	+3.9
1977	−58.6	+27.4	+27.4	+29.9	−38.8	+40.7	−4.8	+0.4	+0.4	−6.3	+17.7
1978	−66.6	+26.6	+25.8	+36.9	−26.1	+46.7	−7.8	+0.9	+3.9	−4.0	+36.8
1979	−98.0	+16.4	+26.3	+40.5	−56.2	+65.1	−7.7	+5.1	+5.0	−5.1	−8.6
1980	−119.7	+22.9	+35.5	+44.2	−89.7	+93.9	−9.1	+11.4	+6.1	−7.0	−11.5

+ = Net Bank Claims.

[1] Excluding the offshore centres.

[2] Other countries in Western Europe and Australia, New Zealand and South Africa.

SOURCE BIS *Press Release*, various issues.

demand for banking sector finance may be derived in terms of constraints on the supply of alternative financing mechanisms including aid and concessionary borrowing from the official sector. Over the period 1973–82, of the total *ex post* financing requirement of $532 billion non-debt forms contributed 19 per cent; non-bank financing 38 per cent and banking sector financing a total of 43 per cent. Reserve-related credit facilities (IMF credit and inter-central-bank arrangements) contributed 4 per cent over the period as a whole. This represents a marked change compared with the 1960s when direct investment, concessionary capital flows and use of reserves provided the bulk of current account financing.

II INTERNATIONAL FINANCIAL INTERMEDIATION

The international banking sector has intermediated between financial surpluses and deficits in the world on a substantial scale over the 1970s. While the focus is on the international dimension, the efficiency of the market also means that at times domestic financial intermediation has been displaced with domestic surpluses and deficits also intermediated externally. To the extent that the international banking sector is more 'efficient' (in terms of offering a higher deposit interest rate and lower lending rate, and meeting the maturity preferences of deficit and surplus units) than some domestic banking systems, and assuming that exchange control does not prevent surplus and deficit units from choosing the most efficient form of intermediation, internal deficits and surpluses within a country may be intermediated by the international banking sector. Net external saving of a country (current account surplus) is identically equal to the net positive sum of individual internal units' gross savings in excess of investment, and similarly for the measurement of a country's aggregate external financing requirement. A given aggregate current account deficit or external financing requirement can co-exist with an infinite combination of internal surpluses and deficits. Given the option of internal versus external financial intermediation mechanisms, the focus of attention with respect to analysing international banking flows should be the evolution of internal, rather than purely international, surpluses and deficits. Except where governments are directly involved it is not countries as such which borrow internationally (or make deposits in the international banking sector) but those internal agents that are in deficit. In many cases individual agents in deficit have the option of financing either from domestic institutions or nationally. Similarly, those in surplus have the option of making deposits at either domestic or international financial institutions. Residents

TABLE 3.9 *Supply and absorption of external bank funds by region, 1974–80 ($ billion; end-year)*

	Full reporting area[1]		*Other developed countries*	*Eastern Europe*	*Middle-east*	*Latin America*	*Caribbean area*	*Singapore*	*Others*	*Unallo-cated*	*Total group*[1]
	(1)	*(2)*	*(3)*	*(4)*	*(5)*	*(6)*	*(7)*	*(8)*	*(9)*	*(10)*	*(11)*
1974	+3.4		+4.9	+1.1	−18.9	+3.2	+1.9	+1.1	+2.2	−2.3	−1.1
1975	−8.1		+4.0	+5.7	−3.7	+1.5	+3.5	+1.0	+1.1	−1.1	+5.0
		Offshore centres			*OPEC countries*	*Latin America*	*Middle East*	*Asia*	*Africa*		
							Developing Countries				
1976	−15.1	+6.4	+11.9	+5.9	−2.6	+7.9	−0.2	−2.5	−0.1	−2.3	+9.3
1977	−8.5	−0.1	+7.9	+8.7	+1.3	+5.6	−1.9	+0.6	+1.3	−1.1	+13.8
1978	−8.0	−0.8	−1.6	+7.0	+12.7	+6.0	−2.5	+0.5	+3.5	+2.3	+19.1
1979	−31.4	−10.2	+0.5	+3.6	−30.1	+18.4	−0.4	+4.2	+1.1	−1.1	−45.4
1980	−21.7	+6.5	+9.2	+3.7	−33.5	+28.8	−1.4	+6.3	+1.1	−1.9	−2.9

− Net supply of funds by region.

+ Net absorption of funds by region.

[1] For an interpretation of positions against the reporting area and the Total group position see Llewellyn (1979).

SOURCE Calculated as changes in net positions from Table 3.8.

TABLE 3.10 Supply and absorption of external bank funds (intra-group positions), 1974–80 ($ billion: end-year)

	Austria	Belgium/ Luxembourg	Denmark	France	Germany	Ireland	Italy	Netherlands	Sweden	Switzerland	UK	Canada	Japan	USA	Total intra- group
	(1)	(2)	(3)	(4)	(5)	(6)	(7)	(8)	(9)	(10)	(11)	(12)	(13)	(14)	(15)
1974[1]	—	+2.1	—	-1.9	-1.5	—	+2.1	-0.9	+0.2	-6.7	+1.0	-0.4	+7.1	+2.3	+3.4
1975[1]	—	+1.8	—	+0.5	-1.5	—	-1.3	-0.7	+0.7	-4.1	-0.5	-0.2	+2.5	-5.3	-8.1
1976	—	+0.3	—	-1.0	+2.7	—	+2.5	-1.7	+1.2	-4.1	-4.2	-0.4	+1.1	-11.6	-15.1
1977[2]	+0.9	+6.0	+5.6	-1.1	+5.3	+0.9	+1.0	-1.9	+2.1	-13.9	-2.6	+2.5	-1.6	-11.3	-8.5
1978	+0.6	+5.1	+1.8	+0.3	+10.9	+0.2	-1.6	-0.4	+1.3	-11.7	-4.6	+0.8	+4.3	-14.5	-8.0
1979	+1.5	-1.7	+2.0	-2.0	+4.8	+1.4	-1.5	-3.9	+1.4	-24.3	-23.8	+1.3	+6.7	+6.9	-31.4
1980	+1.2	+7.9	-0.1	+1.1	+1.6	+0.4	+8.4	-7.0	+2.5	-15.1	-1.1	-1.0	+8.9	-29.1	-21.7

[1] Data for 1974 and 1975 are for external foreign currency positions only.
[2] Due to the extension of the Reporting Group, the supply and absorption of funds by Austria, Denmark and Ireland is calculated from 1977 on the assumption that a net position of zero applied in the previous year.

SOURCE BIS Press Release, various issues.

of a country may be both making deposits and borrowing from the international banking sector. For instance, because domestic financial institutions are not fully developed, surplus agents in some developing countries (including OPEC) make deposits in the Euro-currency market while simultaneously deficit agents in the same country are borrowing in the market.

The displacement of domestic primary financing and of the domestic banking system by the international banking sector is not confined to developing countries where domestic financial systems may be comparatively under-developed. Because of the structure of dollar interest rates in New York and London it may be profitable for corporations in the US to utilise financial surpluses in the Euro-dollar market while other US corporations in financial deficit may borrow marginally more cheaply in this sector. This is true particularly when dollar interest rates are high as the effective 'tax' on domestic bank intermediation resulting from interest-free reserve requirements is increased. Such off-shore displacement is not uncommon within the US banking system and was particularly substantial in 1979 and 1981 (both years of unprecedentedly high domestic interest rates and reserve requirement 'tax'). In the third quarter of 1981 alone, non-banks in the US borrowed in excess of $4 billion from the Euro-dollar market but also contributed around $1 billion of funds to the market.[1]

It follows that the aggregate balance sheet of the international banking sector may expand independently of the size of balance of payments surpluses and deficits. In principle the focus of analysis should be on: (i) the pattern of internal surpluses and deficits, (ii) the portfolio preferences of domestic agents who have the option of either domestic or external institutions and (iii) the relative efficiency (and willingness) of the international banking sector to provide intermediation services. Exclusive orientation around the pattern of *national* balance of payments surpluses and deficits is clearly not appropriate as three broad patterns of financial flows through the international banking sector may be identified: (i) between surplus and deficit *countries*: (ii) between surplus and deficit *sectors* or agents within a country, and (iii) between surplus and deficit sectors in different countries with neither country in aggregate being in balance of payments surplus or deficit. There is little correlation, year by year, between the volume of international banking flows and the pattern of international payments imbalances. As surplus and deficit sectors in different countries have different portfolio preferences and constraints, changes in the structure of international payments imbalances may affect the volume of international banking flows.

Despite the large cumulative OPEC surplus, and the small deficit of

TABLE 3.11   *Recycling of OPEC funds through the reporting banks to other outside-area countries: 1974–6 and 1979–81 (in \$ billions, at constant end-period exchange rates)*

Year	Net identified inflows (+) from OPEC countries (1)	Net identified outflows (−) to other outside-area countries (2)	Total identified net outflows (−) of funds from the reporting area (3) = (1) + (2)
1974	+24.0	−20.0	+4.0
1975	+2.5	−23.5	−21.0
1976	+3.0	−21.5	−18.5
1979	+29.9	−25.8	+4.1
1980	+33.9	−50.8	−16.9
1981 (1st 9 months)	+4.6	−39.8	−35.2

SOURCE BIS *Press Release.*

industrial countries, OPEC countries have not been the dominant net suppliers of funds. Industrial countries have been more substantial net suppliers of international banking funds. Table 3.11 indicates virtually no correlation between the identified net inflows of OPEC funds to the international banking sector in the reporting area and the identified net outflows (lending) of funds to countries outside the reporting area. More generally, Table 3.13 below identifies the broad pattern of flow of funds through the international banking sector over the period 1976–80. The data is based on BIS reports summarised in Tables 3.4 to 3.7. The net absorption and supplies of funds are defined in Tables 3.9, 3.10 and 3.13 in terms of changes in the banks' net position against identified areas. Thus if either the banks' assets rise or liabilities fall against an identified country or group of countries, the country is defined as a net absorber of funds. Conversely, for the measurement of net supplies of funds. Table 3.13 indicates that, over the period 1976–80, NOLDCs (Latin America, Asia and Africa) absorbed \$82.7 billion and developed countries outside the reporting area were net absorbers of \$27.9 billion. Eastern Europe also absorbed \$28.9 billion. The dominant net suppliers were surplus sectors in the Reporting Group itself (\$78.6 billion)[2], and OPEC (\$52.2 billion).

III ALTERNATIVE THEORETICAL APPROACHES

In modelling and analysing international banking flows and behaviour, three alternative analytical approaches have been adopted: (i) a pure flow of funds framework; (ii) a portfolio approach to banking behaviour, and (iii) multiplier models. Each has an analogy with similar approaches to analysing domestic banking flows.

The first concentrates on the pattern and volume of non-bank supplies and demands for international banking funds. In its extreme form, banks are viewed as largely passive in the process of accepting deposits from surplus sectors and financing the deficits of deficit sectors. In these models banks implicitly have no portfolio objectives or constraints, and the supply of intermediation services is infinitely elastic. Attention is therefore focus-·sed upon the structure of balance-of-payments imbalances in the world economy. Within this approach alternative presentations postulate the volume of international banking flows as being either supply- or, more usually, demand-determined. Heller (1979) adopts the latter approach with respect to the Euro-currency market observing that the supply of Euro-dollars is demand-determined and that lending is not limited by constraints determined by the supply of reserves. The analysis is of limited

TABLE 3.12   Medium-term projections of payments balances on current account

	1972	1977	1982	1986 A	1986 B	1986 C
				(In billions of US dollars)		
Industrial countries	16.2	−5.7	11	55	98	14
Developing countries						
Oil exporting countries	2.9	30.8	25	15	15	25
Non-oil developing countries	−10.6	−28.3	−97	−120	−163	−89
Net oil exporters	−2.3	−6.5	−23	−28	−37	−25
Net oil importers	−8.3	−21.8	−74	−93	−127	−64
Major exporters of manufactures	−2.4	−7.9	−32	−37	−56	−23
Low-income countries	−2.8	−5.3	−11	−16	−18	−13
Other net oil importers	−2.4	−11.3	−28	−33	−43	−23
Total[1]	8.5	−3.2	−61	−50	−50	−50
				(In per cent of exports of goods and services)		
Industrial countries	4.1	−0.6	0.6	2.1	3.8	0.5
Developing countries						
Oil exporting countries	11.5	18.7	8.5	3.6	3.6	5.7
Non-oil developing countries	−12.1	−12.9	−20.1	−14.7	−20.7	−10.5
Net oil exporters	−21.3	−20.2	−27.9	−20.6	−27.0	−17.5
Net oil importers	−10.8	−12.3	−18.5	−13.7	−19.4	−9.0
Major exporters of manufactures	−6.8	−7.7	−13.4	−9.0	−14.2	−5.4
Low-income countries	−45.2	−41.7	−58.2	−50.3	−60.0	−40.9
Other net oil importers	−11.1	−20.7	−25.9	−18.7	−25.5	−17.3
Total[2]	1.7	−0.2	−2.3	−1.3	−1.3	−1.3

[1] On goods, services, and private transfers. The People's Republic of China and India are not included in the subgroup of low-income countries but are included in the group totals, net oil-importers and non-oil developing countries. However, the People's Republic of China is excluded from the data for 1972.

[2] Reflects errors, omissions, and asymmetries in reported balance of payments statistics, plus balance of listed groups with other countries (mainly the Union of Soviet Socialist Republics, other non-members of Eastern Europe and, in 1972, the People's Republic of China).

SOURCE IMF *World Economic Outlook*, 1982.

TABLE 3.13   *Net supplies and absorption of funds through the international banking sector: 1976—80[1] (S billion)*

	1976—80
Net Supplies: Countries in:	
OPEC	52.2
Other Middle East	6.4
Others	4.1
Reporting Area	78.6
Total	141.3
Net Absorption:	
Offshore financial centres	1.8
Other developed countries	27.9
Eastern Europe	28.9
Latin America	66.7
Asia	9.1
Africa	6.9
Total	141.3

[1]   The particular classification of groups of countries was changed in 1976 and similar data is not identifiable for the period before 1976.

SOURCE   BIS *Banking Reports.*

relevance here in that it focusses upon one component of international banking (the Euro-market) rather than the broader market of international bank lending.

The second approach, based largely on credit-rationing models, considers the objectives, constraints and costs of banks providing financial inter-mediation services. The focus of attention is upon the profit-maximising and risk-minimising strategies of banks. Banks determine the terms upon which services are provided and these in turn affect the volumes and pattern of international banking flows. Johnston's (1980) study takes non-bank supply and demand for funds and borrowing and lending conditions in national banking systems as exogenously determined, and the analysis focusses upon the supply of intermediation services. The limitations of the third approach, which seeks to explain the volume of Euro-market flows in terms of internal dynamics of the market, have been outlined elsewhere (Llewellyn, 1980).

With respect to supply factors, a necessary distinction is between the supply of non-bank funds to the international banking sector (e.g. OPEC deposits at banks in America or in the Euro-currency market), and the supply of funds and international intermediation services made available at the initiative of banks. To the extent that banks are free to switch funds from domestic sources, the volume of funds made available internationally may be totally independent of external funds made available by non-residents. In Table 3.4, for instance, non-residents increased their deposits at banks in America by $24.3 billion while the banks' external assets were increased by $77.7 billion (December 1979 – September 1981). In this sense banks in America were a net provider of 'international funds' as well as an entrepôt mechanism between non-residents.

In the portfolio approach, banks are not passive agents in the international flow of funds. They have balance sheet objectives and act aggressively to secure them. Subject to official regulations, banks have a choice over the total size of the balance sheet, over the sources of funds and the geographical structure of assets. They must be presumed to seek to balance the risk-adjusted marginal rate of return on domestic and external assets and to obtain funds in the cheapest markets. The supply and demand for international banking funds ceases to be exogenous and independent of banks' own portfolio behaviour. The volume of demand which the banks are prepared to meet will be determined by their own objectives and constraints and this determines the price at which intermediation services are supplied. Total planned assets (domestic and external) are funded at the lowest price though the banks' liability management will itself determine deposit interest rates. In this sense it is not appropriate to postulate OPEC deposits as funding bank lending to oil importing countries as if the volume of OPEC deposits was independent of the terms offered by banks. These terms are important and determined by objectives with respect to the acquisition of external assets. OPEC has a range of options other than bank deposits. In this sense a more appropriate description is that banks, being motivated ultimately by the desire to acquire earning assets, fund loans rather than lend autonomous deposits.

The limitation of the pure non-bank supply and demand versions (flow of funds approach) can be seen in terms of their implications. A pure supply-side approach implies an infinite elasticity of demand, and banks lend what they receive irrespective of the terms. Conversely, an exclusive demand-side orientation postulates an infinite elasticity of supply which in turn implies that banks are pure liability managers and indifferent as to the cost or source (bank versus non-bank) of funds. This has been questioned empirically by Johnston (1980).

An integrated approach, which does not emphasise exclusively supply or demand factors or the exclusive role of non-banks or banks, is more likely to be the most appropriate framework of analysis. The pattern and volume of flow of funds of non-banks must be considered as banks cannot determine the volume and price of lending independently of the portfolio preferences of non-banks. But similarly, the banks are not passive in the process of international financial intermediation and their own portfolio objectives and constraints are relevant in determining the volume and terms of international lending and borrowing.

IV   AN INTEGRATED FRAMEWORK

An integrated framework for analysing and forecasting international banking flows and the terms on which they are offered incorporates three fundamental elements:

1. Flow of funds analysis which identifies the pattern of financial surpluses and deficits in the world economy. This is more complex than simply analysing balance-of-payments surpluses and deficits though these are clearly important. Flow of funds analysis focusses upon: (i) the pattern of financial surpluses and deficits, and (ii) the preferred structure of the assets and liabilities of surplus and deficit units.
2. The second element views the international banking sector as performing financial intermediation services on a world-wide scale similar to that conducted within domestic financial systems. The focus is therefore upon the general principles of financial intermediation.
3. The third element is that international banking involves banks in making portfolio adjustments (on both sides of their external balance sheet) with a view to maximising profits subject to risk constraints.

The factors incorporated within an integrated approach are summarised in Figure 3.1. The flow of funds component includes: (i) the structure of financial surpluses and deficits (both within countries and for countries as a whole), and (ii) the portfolio preferences of surplus and deficit sectors. The factors influencing the supply of financial intermediation services are divided between (i) efficiency considerations, (ii) the portfolio objectives and preferences of financial institutions, and (iii) their portfolio constraints.

A payments imbalance creates two portfolio requirements with respect to the disposal of the surplus and the financing of the deficit. The nature of countries' demand for international bank credit is reasonably unambiguous. At one level it can be viewed as being determined predominantly by the aggregate external financing requirement adjusted for the availability of alternative financing mechanisms. The notion of an autonomous 'supply' of non-bank funds is less acceptable given that banks have a wide range of options in funding the acquisition of external assets, the inter-bank market is able to redistribute liquidity, and banks have a choice over the terms offered to depositors. The supply of international banking funds is determined in part by the portfolio preferences of non-bank depositors determining the terms (interest rate) at which external and domestic loans are made. But to the extent that the elasticity of demand for international bank loans is at all interest-sensitive, the portfolio preferences of surplus sectors will influence not only the terms but also the volume of international banking flows. Banks are viewed in this framework as bidding for deposits to meet the external and internal lending business they are prepared to meet. The supply of non-bank deposits becomes largely endogenous. Surplus sectors maintain bank deposits if they are made attractive, but this is an option of the banks and determined predominantly by their asset objectives.

To the extent that a decision is made to maintain bank deposits, one particularly significant portfolio choice of surplus countries is with respect to the domestic or Euro segment of the banking system. If a deficit agent (outside the US) opts for borrowing from the US banking system two immediate outcomes are possible: (i) if the corresponding surplus sector (in the US or elsewhere) chooses to repay US bank credit there is no net excess demand for bank credit and banks are not constrained by capital or reserves considerations; (ii) if there is no corresponding repayment of bank credit an excess demand for credit emerges. In this case, and on the assumption that banks operate with zero excess reserves, the resultant bidding for reserves by US banks induces a rise in dollar interest rates the extent of which is determined by the elasticity of supply of reserves (Fed's monetary policy) and the elasticity of demand for bank credit (domestic and external). Alternatively a decision of the surplus sector to hold the dollar bank deposit in the Euro-market increases the lending capacity of the dollar banking system. The lending capacity of the Euro-market is not constrained by the supply of Federal funds and a new deposit increases the lending capacity of the Euro-market without reducing that of the American banking system (Llewellyn, 1980). If the deficit sector seeks funding in the Euro-market international financial intermediation can be conducted at lower interest rates as there is no immediate excess demand for bank credit.

```
(A)  FLOW OF FUNDS FACTORS

1.  Structure of financial surpluses and deficits

    (i)  Internal, i.e. within the country .
    (ii) Aggregate, i.e. balance of payments

2.  Portfolio preferences of surplus and deficit sectors

    (i)   direct versus indirect intermediation options
    (ii)  maturity preferences
    (iii) choice of institutions
    (iv)  choice of currency
    (v)   choice of instruments

(B)  SUPPLY OF FINANCIAL INTERMEDIATION SERVICES

1.  'Efficiency' of the international banking sector, e.g. as
    determined by controls and regulations

2.  Portfolio preferences of financial institutions

    (i)   growth of balance sheet objectives
    (ii)  the balance of domestic and external assets and
          liabilities
    (iii) relative demand for domestic versus external credit
    (iv)  degree of risk aversion
    (v)   relative profitability and risk

3.  Portfolio constraints on financial institutions

    (i)   capital constraints
    (ii)  exposure limits
    (iii) regulation requirements
```

FIGURE 3.1   *International banking flows: analytical framework*

V   FLOW OF FUNDS: BALANCES

The main potential non-bank supply and demand factors for international banking funds may be identified as follows:

1. **Supply**

(i) The aggregate surpluses of those *sectors* in the world economy which have access to the international banking sector for the investment of financial surpluses. The focus should, in principle, be upon *sectors* or agents within countries rather than countries in aggregate. Only to the extent that a country's aggregate payments surplus reflects a constant structure of internal surpluses and deficits (or that the portfolio preferences of different internal sectors are not significantly different) is it legitimate to focus upon the balance of payments of *countries*.

(ii) The US balance of payments position may have a unique effect upon the supply of international banking funds by virtue of the reserve currency role of the dollar (see Inoue, 1980). In addition to the mechanism described in Inoue, a US deficit may induce a net creation of financial assets following official intervention in the foreign exchange market in that financial aggregates rise in the corresponding surplus country but do not fall in the US. In order to maintain balance in portfolios, a proportion of the net creation of financial assets is likely to be placed directly in the international banking sector. Central banks may also swap dollars against domestic currency, with the banks induced to place the funds internationally. This technique has been used by the Swiss, German and Japanese monetary authorities. To the extent that any net creation of reserves (the reserve currency mechanism) is held by central banks who invest in the Euro-dollar market, the supply capacity of this sector is increased. In addition, arbitrage funds may flow to the Euro-dollar market to the extent that foreign exchange market intervention induces a fall in surplus countries' interest rates.

But for reasons noted earlier, the role of 'autonomous supply factors' is questionable except to the extent of their contribution to determining the terms on which banking funds are made available. Demand factors are likely to be more central.

2. Demand

(i) The sum of sectoral deficits in the world economy is central to the analysis with the same aggregation qualification as noted when considering the corresponding supply factors.

(ii) The demand for reserves – augmentation adds to financing requirements. Table 3.3 shows that NOLDCs' reserves rose in each year except 1975 in the period 1973–82. To the extent that a borrowing country adds to reserves and invests the proceeds in the Euro-dollar market, the net cost of the operation is approximately equal to the lending margin on syndicated Euro-credits plus management fees. Such demand might therefore be sensitive to changes in borrowing conditions. The IMF (1982) notes the tendency for the real value of NOLDCs' reserves to decline (despite net nominal rises) and observes that the ratio of reserves to imports declined to 17 per cent in 1981 compared with 26 per cent in 1978 and 32 per cent in 1973.

(iii) The need to re-finance maturing debt (and hence the maturity profile of external debt) is a further factor in the demand for gross borrowing, though it is not a factor increasing banks' exposure to borrowers. While maturity transformation by banks has been a feature of international lending in the 1970s and early 1980s, the IMF (1982) notes that

> the banks' preference for short horizons has been reinforced by persistent and erratic inflation in the central currency used for international payments. Therefore, the maturity transformation that banks can be expected to perform will remain limited . . . (maturity transformation) cannot be said to be optimal.

While the last point is questionable, and almost denies the *raison d'être* of financial intermediation, the structural shift from official to private sector financing has had the effect of shortening the average maturity of outstanding aggregate external indebtedness. Inflation has also had the effect of shortening average real maturities relative to nominal maturities. Re-financing requirements will remain strong over the coming years and this increases the vulnerability of NOLDCs to shifts in the portfolio objectives and constraints of the international banking sector.

(iv) Internal factors such as the evolution of large scale investment projects and budget deficits in an environment of domestic financial constraints have also affected the demand for international bank credit.

(v) To the extent that trade flows (independently of the evolution of current account balances) are financed through the banking sector, the rate of growth of world trade can be a factor increasing the demand for short-term trade-related bank finance.

(vi) Expectations of deteriorating borrowing conditions have also, at times, influenced NOLDCs' borrowing strategy. It is not unknown for debt to be repaid and re-financed at more advantageous terms.

Balance-of-payments data record *ex post* transactions and partly reflect the relative ease of financing. On the basis of *ex post* observations, an analysis by Fleming (1981) traces the supply and demand factors for LDC borrowing year by year for the period 1977 to 1981. Plausible explanations for year by year variations in borrowing and the movement of the margin are offered albeit on the basis of *ex post* observation. At a minimum the analysis suggests that the basic supply and demand factors identified do have some bearing on the pattern and volume of international banking flows.

VI   PORTFOLIO PREFERENCES

The portfolio preferences of both surplus and deficit sectors, and the availability and terms of alternative options for financing deficits and disposing of surpluses, are central influences on the volume and terms of international banking flows. Portfolio preferences may change because of structural changes within countries' domestic financial systems. For instance, in 1981 the very sharp acceleration (from $9.6 billion to $31.2 billion) in new international bank deposits by US non-banks (despite a slightly lower Euro-dollar differential against money-market rates in the US) was associated with the growing role in the US of Money Market Mutual Funds and their facility for absorbing small savings and investing in national and international money markets which are not available to their own depositors.

The major issues with respect to surplus sectors are the choices between: (i) *primary* versus *secondary* assets (a choice between direct or indirect financing of deficit sectors),[3] (ii) marketable versus non-marketable assets, (iii) public sector versus private sector assets, and (iv) domestic versus Euro-market bank deposits if the choice is to acquire bank deposits. The choices will also be determined by factors influencing maturity preferences. The advantages of indirect mechanisms (meeting different maturity preferences etc.) are as well established in the international sector as they are within domestic financial systems. There has been a clear tendency over the 1970s for the banking sector to displace borrowing through the international bond markets, though this has been associated partly with interest-rate trends. OPEC, for instance, while making some direct investment abroad and loans to developing countries, invested close on 40 per cent of its current account surplus in bank deposits over the period 1974–81. The decision as between the US banking system and the Euro-dollar market is significant in that, as described earlier, in the latter case the total lending capacity of the international banking sector is increased while it remains constant in the former.

A distinction should be drawn between positive wealth effects and wealth-distribution effects. It was argued earlier that a US balance of payments deficit overall can be a factor inducing a rise in world financial assets (some of which would likely be reflected in the Euro-dollar market). But a US current account deficit causes a shift in wealth from US residents to the rest of the world, and this will induce a net change in the volume of Euro-dollar deposits only to the extent of different portfolio preferences of US and non-US residents. Frydl (1982) correctly establishes that 'whether a shift of wealth arising from US current account deficits was a force behind high Euro-dollar growth is an empirical question that can be answered correctly only by a detailed model of world-wide portfolio behaviour'.

In the case of the redistribution of wealth associated with oil, it is likely that the differences in portfolio behaviour have been sufficiently significant to be a factor in the growth of the Euro-dollar market. This is partly because OPEC's tradition of high liquidity preference can be met more readily in the Euro-dollar market than the US banking system.

While OPEC has tended to have a high liquidity preference, there has also been a tendency to diversify among more countries and currencies, and to lengthen the maturity of assets. The diversification has involved increased investment in equities, bonds and government securities as well as the acquisition of real assets. While the bulk of placements remain within a limited number of industrial countries, and in the Euro-currency markets, there was some tendency over the 1970s to reduce the proportion of placements in bank deposits. There seems to be a tendency for bank deposits to absorb a high proportion immediately after a sharp rise in the OPEC investible surplus but to decline gradually thereafter.

On the demand side, the portfolio preference of deficit sectors is determinded by: (i) the availability of alternative sources of funding, (ii) the cost of the alternatives (in various dimensions) and (iii) the balance sheet structure of the corporate sector. One of the factors behind the NOLDCs' strong demand for bank financing over the 1970s has been the slow growth of alternative financing options (aid, direct investment flows and the lending capacity of development institutions) relative to the sharp rise in the total external financing requirement (Tables 3.2 and 3.3). One of the major elements with respect to the 'cost' of alternatives is not the interest cost (borrowing from the international banking sector is frequently the most expensive financing mechanism) but the 'conditionality' cost. Given the small amounts (relative to financing requirements) that can be borrowed from the IMF, and that the conditions are often resisted, the Fund has tended to be used as a lender-of-last-resort even though the interest cost is markedly lower. Those countries with access to the international banking sector can borrow substantially more there than from the IMF and without policy conditionally provisions. Thus the lending capacity and the nature of conditionality provisions of the IMF are likely to influence the demand for bank credit. Over the 1970s, not only did the lending capacity of the IMF not keep pace with the sharp rise in financing demand, but the Fund was usually lending below its full capacity. This reflected a portfolio decision of borrowers.

Corporations in the industrial countries also have the option of financing through the international banking sector. This was the main factor behind the sharp rise in US borrowers' use of the syndicated Euro-credit market in 1981. This is somewhat artificial in that a large proportion represented stand-by facilities (which were not drawn down) mostly in connection with takeover moves within the US oil industry. The individual amounts negotiated were massive and required a wider syndication group than could be arranged within the United States. Corporate sector demand is influenced largely by the same considerations that determine the structure of its domestic financing, and has much to do with balance sheet structures.

VII FINANCIAL INTERMEDIATION SERVICES

Figure 3.1, which summarises an integrated approach to the analysis of international banking flows, identifies the flow of funds and the provision of financial intermediation services. The latter considers: (i) the question of 'efficiency' of the international banking sector; (ii) the portfolio objectives and preferences of financial institutions and (iii) the constraints on financial institutions.

Efficiency considerations relate mainly to the imposition of controls or regulations which inhibit the conduct of international financial intermediation. They constrain the banks' balance sheet relative to the objectives set by the banks. It follows that if, after a period of control, the control mechanisms are lifted, it is likely that banks would make an immediate but finite stock-adjustment to secure the desired, but previously constrained, portfolio objective. Similarly, bank regulators or governments can impose balance sheet requirements (for example, capital ratios related to world consolidated balance sheet positions) which may limit the expansion of banks' balance sheet positions in general and the acquisition of external assets in particular. The issue of 'efficiency' (for example, through reserve requirements on banks' domestic liabilities) is also relevant to the ability of the international banking sector to displace domestic intermediation mechanisms by providing intermediation services between surplus and deficit agents within the same country.

The main considerations with respect to the portfolio objectives and preferences of financial institutions are summarised in Figure 3.1 above. The presumption must be that the banks, when in effect allocating capital to competing ends (lending activities), seek to equalise the risk-adjusted marginal rate of return. Whether this is done in the short run as well as the long run is debatable. The evidence noted later suggests that banks take a long-run view when making judgements about the structure of balance sheets as between domestic and external assets. There is a similar presumption in favour of portfolio diversification in order to minimise risks both between domestic and external assets in aggregate but also within each. International lending is itself part of a process of portfolio diversification which increases the range of lending opportunities especially as, in some industrial countries, risks on domestic assets have increased. To the extent that such general portfolio diversification reduces total balance sheet risks, a lower capital—assets ratio is appropriate. Overall, in the 1970s the loan loss-record on international business was lower than on domestic lending which, in itself, would justify lower lending margins.

In the final analysis, institutions' portfolio decisions relate to the desired growth of the total balance sheet, and the distribution of the total between, for instance, domestic and external assets. Decisions with respect to the former are presumably determined predominantly with reference to overall risk-adjusted rates of return, capital constraints and managerial potential. The balance, and changes in the balance between domestic and external assets, would be expected to be determined by: (i) requirements of risk-minimisation through portfolio diversification; (ii) perceptions of relative risk between domestic and external assets, (iii) relative rates of return and (iv) relative demand for loans.[4] The estimation of absolute and relative risk is a complex procedure undertaken with varying degrees of precision and sophistication between different banks. The main considerations in determining perceived risk in external lending have been summarised by Maynard (1982) in terms of the debt-capacity of borrowing countries:

1. relative importance of the foreign trade sector
2. vulnerability to external shocks
3. compressibility of imports
4. level of foreign exchange reserves
5. degree of diversification and structural balance of the economy
6. quality of economic management and ability and willingness to undertake adjustment policies
7. political stability.

Morgan Guaranty (1982) recently observed a slowdown in banks' international lending, and a widening of margins, reflecting a general assessment that risks in international lending have increased. The factors noted include:

1. general developments in the world economy
2. the high level of dollar interest rates which have increased debt servicing burdens
3. the high volume of maturing debt in 1982 which increases the vulnerability to disruptions in their access to credit markets
4. international political developments
5. the growing credit difficulties being experienced by some of the banks' *domestic* customers. This last mentioned is presumably a factor restraining the growth of banks' total balance sheet.

In a recent Group of Thirty study bankers were surveyed about risks and margins. The majority (62 per cent) believed that lending margins would widen but 70 per cent also replied that this would not increase lending. The majority believed that wider margins would not compensate for higher risks. In the same survey bankers listed credit-risk, capital adequacy problems and relative profitability of lending as the three most important constraints then currently emerging. Maynard (1982) also gives details of the decline in the capital—assets ratio of major banks conducting international business.

An implication of the framework established earlier is that, while the size of financial imbalances and the portfolio preferences of surplus and deficit sectors are important, analysis of international banking flows must also incorporate portfolio objectives and constraints of banks. Several strands of evidence support various aspects of this broad approach. For instance, evidence supports the stock-adjustment effect following the imposition or lifting of controls. This was seen clearly in the case of banks in America after the abolition of US capital controls in February 1974, when external assets of banks in America more than doubled in 1974 and 1975. Similarly, Japanese banks made a substantial stock-adjustment towards the acquisition of external assets following the lifting in 1977 of official restraints on participation in syndicated Euro-credits. There was also a sharp and immediate rise in the volume of external lending in sterling of banks in the UK following the abolition of exchange control in 1979. This suggests that banks have a view about the balance of their domestic and external assets and move quickly towards the desired portfolio structure following the removal of officially imposed constraints.

There is also some impressionistic evidence that banks respond to trends in domestic demand for credit by switching funds between domestic and international lending. The slower rise in external assets of banks in America in 1977 and 1978 at a time when international lending in general was rising sharply (Tables 3.6 and 3.7)[5] was associated in part with a stronger trend in domestic demand for bank credit. Wigny (1982) suggests that the sharp decline in the share of LDC lending given by American banks between 1976–7 and 1978–9 (46 per cent to 15 per cent) was also associated with a portfolio adjustment following three years of sharp expansion in external assets, capital constraints and the dynamic entry to international banking markets of banks from other countries, again associated in part with weak domestic demand for bank credit in industrial countries (see also Fleming, 1981).

The experience of banks in America since 1973 may be applied to illustrate these diverse consideration in portfolio management. The exceptionally strong expansion in US banks' external lending after 1973 and deceleration in 1977 and 1978 may be accounted for largely by the simultaneous effects of the abolition of US capital controls at the beginning of 1974 together with slack domestic demand for bank credit in the US in 1975 and 1976 and subsequent revival during 1977 and 1978. Four separate phases may be identified in the post-1973 period:

1. An immediate stock adjustment effect in 1974 and 1975 following the removal of capital controls that had been enforced over ten years.
2. A further sharp expansion in 1976 associated in part with slack domestic demand for bank credit in the US.
3. A retrenchment in 1977 and 1978 as domestic demand for credit became more buoyant.
4. A period since 1978 when US banks have tended to adopt a somewhat lower profile in international lending (certainly compared with, say, Japanese and European banks) preferring not to change substantially the proportion of external to total bank assets.

These phases may be explained largely in terms of traditional portfolio balance theory of financial intermediaries where banks are assumed to have a desired balance in their total portfolio as between domestic and external assets. Figure 3.2 represents a profile of external lending of banks in America.

In the absence of capital controls (that is, when banks are free to choose the balance between domestic and external lending) and assuming a steady expansion in total business, it might be expected that external lending would be on a steadily rising trend (*AA* in Figure 3.2). The trend of

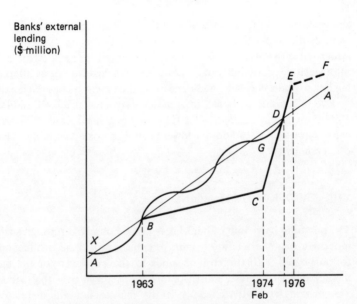

FIGURE 3.2   *US banks' portfolio adjustment*

domestic and external assets would not necessarily be the same as, given general trends in the world economy (expansion of world trade and multinational corporations etc.), external business would be expected to represent a rising share of total bank lending even on a trend basis. The actual course of lending (*XG*) would be likely to fluctuate around this trend due to cyclical changes in the relative demand and/or profitability of domestic and external lending. However, the imposition of capital controls in 1963 forced bank external lending along a lower trend (*BC*). With the abolition of controls an immediate and substantial stock-adjustment would be expected as external lending was adjusted to the desired (unconstrained) position that might have been expected in the absence of the controls. This is represented by the trend *CD*. This once-for-all portfolio adjustment by the banks might take, say, eighteen months and during that period an exceptionally rapid growth in external lending would be expected. However, during 1976 domestic demand for bank credit was weak and hence the rapid expansion in external lending (represented by *DE*) continued in 1976 taking it above the trend line *AA*. As domestic demand revived in the following year the expansion in external lending moderated (*EF*). Thus to a large extent the particularly sharp expansion in external lending of US banks in the period 1973–6 was due to the combined influence of the abolution of US capital controls and the weakness in domestic demand for bank credit in the US. The deceleration in 1977 and 1978 was in turn associated with the revival in US domestic demand for bank credit; a change in the relative profitability of domestic and external lending as international lending margins narrowed and concern at the extent of sovereign exposure.

External assets of banks in America expanded relatively modestly in 1979 though they accelerated in 1980. But in general since 1978 American banks have tended to adopt a lower profile compared with banks based in other countries.

VIII   EVIDENCE ON MARGINS

The portfolio behaviour of banks may also be observed through analysis of movements in the lending margin or spread. Most bank lending-rates are formula-based with the cost of funds to the borrower comprising: (i) a market rate of interest, and (ii) a margin or spread over the market rate. The margin is usually fixed while the market rate fluctuates over the maturity of the loan. The margin over LIBOR on syndicated Euro-credits is clearly not a measure of 'profits' as banks may fund at a lower cost than LIBOR (particularly if they have direct access to non-bank deposits) and for the major banks associated fee income can be substantial (Davis, 1979). Wallich (1979) has suggested that to cover costs and capital, and without contributions to overheads, at a LIBOR of 10 per cent a margin of around 1½ per cent is required if funding is made at LIBOR. Competition has kept the margin for prime-borrowers well below this level for many years.

While the borrower is ultimately concerned with the total cost of borrowing, the two elements of interest cost (the market rate and the margin) must be separated for analytical purposes as they measure different concepts and are determined by different sets of factors. Dollar LIBOR, for instance, is ultimately determined by the total demand for dollar bank credit (domestic and international) and the supply of reserves made available by the Federal Reserve. Given arbitrage between the domestic and Euro-market components of the dollar money-market, LIBOR is determined ultimately by monetary policy in the United States. It is a reflection of the total demand for dollar bank credit in relation to the supply capacity determined by the availability of reserves. On the restrictive assumption that the cost of funds to banks in the syndicated Euro credit market is in fact LIBOR, the margin is the supply price of intermediation and, as such, should be determined by : (i) the cost of providing intermediation services, (ii) the opportunity cost (e.g. the interest rate differential between the cost of funds to banks and, say the government bond yield), (iii) the perceived risk of external lending, and (iv) the degree of risk aversion of banks. Thus, LIBOR is a reflection of liquidity conditions but the margin reflects the supply price of intermediation. While the *volume* of international lending may be influenced by liquidity conditions (to the extent that the demand for funds may be interest-sensitive), the margin should not be so influenced. Neither should 'liquidity conditions' influence the interest rate differential between the domestic and external components of money markets. Thus, a fall in the domestic demand for bank credit in the US, even though it might induce a portfolio shift towards international lending, and a larger volume of loans, should not *in itself* induce any change in either the international lending margin or the differential between domestic and Euro-dollar interest rates or margins.[6] Arbitrage determines the interest rate differential, the cost of intermediation, etc. determines the margin in a highly competitive market, and the total demand for dollar bank credit together with the monetary policy stance of the Fed determines the absolute level of interest rates.

A useful representation of the determination of LIBOR and the margin is given by Davies (1982) on the basis of a perfectly competitive market. The margin reflects marginal costs of intermediation which are given as capital, operating costs and opportunity costs. This framework predicts that a rise in the demand for syndicated loans induces a rise in LIBOR (and in the volume of loans), while an increase in the supply of Euro-dollar deposits causes LIBOR to fall (and the volume of loans to rise). Under the conditions postulated, the effect upon the margin is indeterminate and determined by the cost conditions of the industry, (i.e. whether marginal costs are rising, constant or falling). In this representation, concepts of 'excess liquidity' (often applied in commentary on the markets) would be irrelevant to the determination of the level of margins unless the industry is characterised by falling costs. The model would also predict a rise in margins in the face of a rise in the opportunity cost of lending (e.g. rise in the bond yield).

Several variables have been incorporated by different analysts in models of the prime margin including: (i) the level of LIBOR, (ii) the volatility of interest rates, (iii) proxies for lending risk, (iv) the number of banks in the market, (v) movements in the domestic demand for bank credit in industrialised countries and (vi) industrial production in major countries. The level of interest rates might operate through the 'tax' effect of reserve requirements (causing the opportunity cost of reserve requirements to rise) and high interest rates imply a higher rate of return on capital. Volatile interest rates increase the banks' risk of maturity transformation within roll-over periods and hence might cause the margin to widen. The number of banks could be a relevant variable if (i) there was previously an element of imperfection and monopoly profits in the market, (ii) new entrants are prepared to take a longer-term view of profitability and might be willing to undertake business at a loss in the short run in order to establish themselves in the market, or (iii) if firms in the industry operate with rising marginal costs. The last point is relevant to the extent that, with more banks, the same volume of business is spread among a larger number of institutions. Industrial production is included by Brittain (1982) who finds the margin to be more closely linked with industrial activity than with liquidity conditions in the US. Brittain's analysis concentrates on risk factors and the interpretation is that, through the effect on international trade, rising industrial production in their export markets reduces the risk of lending to developing countries.

Goodman (1980) finds the level and variability of LIBOR to be significant: a 1 per cent change in LIBOR induces a 7 basis points fall in the margin, and a 0.01 per cent rise in the quarterly standard deviation. Davies (1982) finds opportunity costs to be a powerful influence but, as predicted in the model, there is no statistically significant result from the volume of lending. The number of banks (the number of foreign banks directly represented in London) does not seem significantly to affect the margin in the syndicated Euro-credit market.

Several studies indicate a significant inverse relationship between the level of LIBOR and the margin (see also Fleming and Howson 1980) and, given the 'tax' effect of reserve requirements, this seems theoretically reasonable. The margin has been cyclical and generally in line with the cyclical variability of LIBOR, though the relationship has been less clear-cut since 1979.

Johnston (1980) finds no significant relationship between the level of LIBOR and the margin but, as should be expected, perceived default risks (positive) and the banks' capital assets ratio (negative) are both found to be significant influences. The level of domestic margins is also found to be a factor determining international lending margins, again confirming the importance of opportunity costs and the rationality of banking strategies based upon portfolio maximising strategies. Johnston also finds that the ratio of bank liabilities against non-banks to total liabilities is a significant influence with a rise in the proportion inducing a fall in the margin. This is interpreted as banks not being indifferent with respect to the structure (bank versus non-bank) of their liabilities, believing non-bank funding to be less risky (more stable) than funding through the inter-bank market. This result also confirms that banks are not passive agents adjusting the supply of funds to demand at constant margins, but that they incorporate their own portfolio objectives and constraints into the conditions under which intermediation services are supplied.

There is also evidence of discrimination between borrowers as, at any one time, margins vary between countries, groups of countries (industrialised versus developing), and also between different borrowers in the same country. This again argues against a pure supply- or demand-determined model of international bank lending. Brittain (1982) notes that borrowers in countries with a high debt—GNP ratio tend to have to concede wider margins and a similar result is found by Angelini (1979).

Overall, the evidence argues against the volume of international bank lending being exclusively demand- or supply-determined. Banks respond to credit risks and their portfolio objectives and constraints are important factors in the market. Notions of 'excess liquidity', 'borrowers' market' etc. are at best ill-defined but frequently meaningless unless strongly qualified. The margin on syndicated lending has been cyclical but also on something of a downward trend over the 1970s with some evidence of a slight reversal in 1982. It may be that the increase in the number of banks active in the market has been a factor in the downward trend for reasons indicated earlier. In particular, the distinction between short-run and long-run portfolio behaviour is significant when new nationalities of banks enter the market. It is largely in this sense that the next section argues why there might be a downward bias to lending margins in international lending and why a distinction needs to be drawn between the behaviour of banking 'firms' and the 'industry'.

IX THE INDUSTRY AND THE FIRM

The number of banks active in the international lending market in general, and the syndicated Euro-credit market in particular, increased substantially over the 1970s. This may have been a factor behind the apparent secular decline in lending margins suggesting either a degree of market imperfection in the early 1970s, though since competed away (Inoue, 1980) or a willingness of new entrants to take a longer term view of profitability. This increasing number and nationality of banks active in the market may impose something of a downward bias to margins in this sector to the extent that the terms are set by marginal banks. At any one time banks in different countries have different interests in the market. Changes in regulations can cause an upsurge in international lending by banks in a particular country; this stock adjustment effect has been noted for Japanese banks and also for American banks after the abolition of capital controls in 1974. New entrants to a market, keen to develop new business, may take a longer-term view of profitability and may be prepared in the short run, to write loans at unsustainable margins. Banks in different countries may face different risks on domestic business. Banks in different countries start with different portfolio mixes, and some may be prepared to develop international growth strategies rather than concentrate on immediate profitability. In a Group of Thirty survey Mendelsohn (1981) noted that banks whose international assets had grown at a relatively fast pace in the years up to 1978 (notably American banks) tended to expect a somewhat slower growth in subsequent years than those banks which had lagged at an earlier stage. He judged that the era of rapid international expansion for large US banks had passed. In contrast, he noted that bankers in Japan, whose proportion of international business was then relatively small, expected a large increase in their international business 'providing it is permitted by official guidance'. But Japanese bankers believed international business would continue to be subject to official 'guidance' and that this made it almost impossible to develop long-term strategic plans. This similarly makes it difficult to forecast Japanese banks' international lending. Conventional capital ratios also vary substantially between banks in different countries, and the dynamism is sometimes made by those banks with particularly low capital—asset ratios compared, for instance, with US banks.

To the extent that terms are determined by those banks which at a particular time are most aggressive in the market, and that the factors mentioned are not synchronised between banks of different nationality, a downward bias is imposed on margins. It is well-established that the leadership of the syndicated Euro-credit market alternates between countries because of the factors peculiar to that country at the time.

For these reasons, forecasting the behaviour of international banking *aggregates* on the basis of a framework applicable to the banking firm is hazardous. The 'leadership' of the market has changed frequently because of the non-synchronisation of portfolio objectives and constraints as between banks in different countries. American banks certainly dominated the syndicated Euro-credit market throughout the 1960s and early 1970s. European and Japanese banks entered in a big way in the early 1970s though the latter withdrew after 1974 but re-entered in 1978. Since then the share of American banks has declined markedly. Since 1979 OPEC financial institutions have become significant participants; the IMF (1982) estimates that in 1981 one-quarter of syndicated Euro-credits were lead-managed by OPEC banks.

Casual observation might suggest that the supply of international intermediation is infinitely elastic in that volumes have increased sharply while the terms have tended to ease. While this may be partly accounted for by changes in the nationality of borrowers, and possibly by different perceptions of risk by different banks, the major factor is probably the different portfolio objectives and constraints of different nationality of banks. For reasons noted elsewhere (Llewellyn, 1982) banks in aggregate are 'locked-in' to LDC debt. This is not a picture recognised by bankers who see loans being repaid. But this is effectively being done by passing the debt on to other banks who, so far, have been prepared to absorb it. Debt has been re-financed by other banks with different objectives and constraints and this is possible while there are others to absorb it.

X CONCLUDING REMARKS

Both theory and the limited systematic empirical evidence suggest that an integrated approach to the analysis of international banking flows is likely to be the most fruitful. Such an approach focuses upon the pattern of surpluses and deficits, their portfolio preferences and the objectives and constraints of banks in providing international financial intermediation services. As in many cases domestic agents have a choice between domestic and external intermediation mechanisms, in principle the focus with respect to surpluses and deficits should be on agents within countries rather than the balance of payments of countries. International banking flows are not dependent upon *international* payments imbalances, and a given volume of *international* imbalances is consistent with an infinite range of volumes of international banking flows determined by: (i) the pattern of internal surpluses and deficits, (ii) the portfolio preferences of these internal agents and (iii) the objectives and constraints of institutions providing international financial intermediation services.

There is also a serious aggregation problem in the analysis of international banking both with respect to surpluses and deficits, and with the financial institutions making the market. This is a major problem in forecasting. While the banking sector has been able and willing to provide intermediation services, volumes of international lending have been largely demand-determined. The pattern and portfolio preferences of surplus sectors are of second-order importance except in so far as they determine the terms under which banks can provide funds. To the extent that there is any elasticity in the demand for funds, the portfolio preferences of surplus sectors may also influence the volume of international banking flows.

A distinction has also been drawn between the firm and the industry. Hitherto the supply of intermediation services seems to have been highly elastic. But this is probably associated with different portfolio objectives and constraints of different nationalities of banks rather than a reflection of the behaviour of a constant structure of firms in the industry. This could prove to be a particularly significant issue in the context of the currently-projected substantial external financing requirements of oil-importing developing countries.

NOTES

1. BIS data identifies that in the first quarter of 1979 the US was a substantial net absorber of $10.2 billion following net supplies of £11.9 billion in the final quarter of 1978. Within this total US banks borrowed $7.8 billion from the Euro-dollar market. The broad picture with respect of changes in the banks' position against the US may be summarised: (i) the US was in total a net absorber of $10.2 billion; (ii) US banks borrowed heavily in the Euro-dollar market, and (iii) non-banks in the US were net *suppliers* of funds (around $9 billion!) to the international banking sector outside the US. In effect, the international banking sector (and the Euro-dollar market in particular) intermediated between surplus and deficit sectors *within the US*. The complex opposing financial flows (simultaneously to and from the US) were related to the same basic factors: (i) the lifting in 1978 of US reserve requirements on funds borrowed by US banks from external sources, (ii) a rise in reserve requirements on domestic CD issues, and (iii) the repayment of about $11.5 billion by banks elsewhere in the reporting area of their debts to banks in the US due to the unwinding of speculative positions taken up in the final months of 1978.
2. Table 3.10 indicates substantial differences in the pattern as between countries in the Reporting Area. Switzerland and the US were notable net suppliers of funds.
3. Direct loans to deficit units or purchase of financial assets issued by deficit units.
4. The theory and evidence on this is ambiguous. If the banks' total assets are constrained by any factor (e.g. capital) in the short run the acquisition of domestic and external assets are alternatives. If there is no constraint on the total balance sheet position, banks are free to meet any and all profitable demand for loans and the two are not competitive. In this case there would be no presumption of a negative correlation between the two. Although analysts, including bankers, the BIS and the IMF, have argued that a particular fast growth of external assets has been due to slack domestic demand for credit, the precise empirical evidence and theoretical foundation is not clear.
5. This is not seen for 1978 in Table 3.7 as there was a sharp rise (22 per cent) in the final quarter of the year.

6. Unless, for instance, the reduced demand for bank credit reflects a shift by borrowers to alternative forms of funding because of an uncompetitively wide bank margin maintained by imperfect competition.

REFERENCES

A. Angelini, *et al.* (1979) *International Lending, Risk and the Euromarket* (London, Macmillan).

B. Brittain (1982) 'US Monetary Policy and Falling Spreads on Internationally Syndicated Bank Loans', in D. E. Fair and L. de Juvigny (Eds) *Bank Management in a Changing Domestic and International Environment* (The Hague, Martinus Nijhoff).

P. Davies (1982) Appendix to 'Evolving Problems of International Financial Intermediation', in D. E. Fair and L. de Juvigny (eds.), *Bank Management in a Changing Domestic and International Environment* (The Hague, Martinus Nijhoff).

S. Davis (1979) 'Techniques in International Banking', in S. Frowen (ed.) *Framework of International Banking* (Guildford Educational Press).

A. Fleming (1981) 'Private Capital Flows to Developing Countries and Their Determination', World Bank Staff Working Paper, No. 484, dated August 1981.

A. Fleming and S. Howson (1980) 'Conditions in the Syndicated Medium Term Euro-Credit Market', *Bank of England Quarterly Bulletin*, September 1980.

E. J. Frydl (1982) 'The Eurodollar Conundrum', *Federal Reserve Bank of New York*, Quarterly Review, Spring 1982.

L. S. Goodman (1980) 'The Pricing of Syndicated Eurocurrency Credits', *Federal Reserve Bank of New York, Quarterly Review*.

R. Heller (1979) 'Assessing Euromarket Growth: Why the Market is Demand Determined', *Euromoney*, February 1979.

IMF (1982) *World Economic Outlook* (Washington DC: IMF).

K. Inoue (1980) 'Determinants of Market Conditions in the Eurocurrency Market: Why a Borrowers Market?' BIS *Working Paper* No. 1.

R. B. Johnston (1980) 'Banks International Lending Decision and the Determination of Spreads on Syndicated Medium Term Euro Credits', *Bank of England Discussion Paper*, No. 12.

D. T. Llewellyn (1979) 'International Financial Intermediation' in S. Frowen (ed.), *Framework of International Banking* (Guildford Educational Press).

D. T. Llewellyn (1980) *International Financial Intermediation* (London: Macmillan).

D. T. Llewellyn (1982) 'Avoiding an International Banking Crisis', *National Westminster Bank Review*, August 1982.

G. Maynard and P. Davis (1982) 'Evolving Problems of International Intermediation'. In D. E. Fair and L. de Juvigny (eds) *Bank Management in a Changing Domestic and International Environment* (The Hague: Martinus Nijhoff).

M. C. Mendelsohn (1981) *Outlook for International Bank Lending* (New York: Group of Thirty).

Morgan Guaranty (1982) *World Financial Markets*, August.

H. Wallich (1979) 'Developments in International Banking', *mimeo*.

D. Wigny (1982) 'Evolving Problems of International Financial Intermediation', in D. E. Fair, and L. de Juvigny (eds) *Bank Management in a Changing Domestic and International Environment* (The Hague: Martinus Nijhoff).

4 On the Theory of International Money

K. ALEC CHRYSTAL*

The international monetary literature of the 1950s and 1960s was dominated (or so it now seems) by the institutionalist. Of central concern was the position of central banks (especially with regard to 'liquidity') and how they related to one another. The past decade has seen a major shift of emphasis towards the private sector of the system. Partly this has taken the form of spillover from macro-economics especially in the form of the monetary approach to the balance-of-payments and exchange rates, but to a lesser extent this has also been due to a new interest in the international context of what is in reality a highly developed monetary system. The Eurocurrency system has obviously been an object of great curiosity though only recently has the analytical literature on this subject penetrated the surface in important ways (see Niehans and Hewson, 1976; and McKinnon, 1977). McKinnon has long been a pioneer in discussions of the private sector of the system, and his recent book (McKinnon, 1979) makes a major contribution to increasing our grasp in this neglected field.

The present author has already attempted to apply the macro-economic notions of 'demand for money' in the international economy (Chrystal, 1977, 1978; Chrystal, Wilson and Quinn, 1983. However, the purpose of the current paper is to take a rather more abstract or micro-economic look at the role of 'money' in the international economy with particular emphasis on the role of 'money' in foreign exchange markets.

There has already been a steady trickle of literature, over the last decade or so, concerned with justifying the existence of 'money' in abstract general equilibrium models of closed economies. The need for such a

* I am grateful to Ross Starr for advice at an early stage in the preparation of this paper.

demonstration was clearly established by Hahn (1965) who showed that in the standard tâtonnement models, a 'non-monetary' solution could easily exist. One possible way out of this corner was investigated by Ostroy (1973) and Ostroy and Starr (1974). They consider the role of money in sequential trading economies. A further important contribution is that of Jones (1976) who analyses the way in which the use of a medium of exchange may evolve. The importance of these questions is clear once it is seen that, since monies obviously exist and play an important role in modern economies, models which cannot handle the existence of money must be of limited significance (at least in an immediate policy sense).

In what follows, an analytical investigation is undertaken of an additional dimension of 'money'. This arises because of the self-evident existence in the international economy of monies which fulfil functions similar to those more familiar in a domestic context. The formal theoretical literature to date has been concerned almost exclusively with 'single money, multiple goods, multiple trader' economies. In the international economy there are many potential monies for use in trade, so which of these is used is very much a matter of choice. In other words, a substantial volume of transactions takes place in the 'multiple money, multiple goods, multiple trader' world. The principles involved in the choice of international money should be well-known in other contexts, but the international economy offers interesting new dimensions to a familiar problem.

The plan of this chapter is as follows: first, it will outline an earlier approach to this issue and discuss some stylised facts which have recently emerged, second, it will analyse the emergence of 'international monies' and third, it will investigate trader balances of foreign currencies.

I   INVENTORY MODELS AND FOREIGN EXCHANGE HOLDINGS

The first formal attempt to analyse international money was by Swoboda (1968, p. 39) who made a direct application of the Baumol–Tobin transactions demand inventory model. If an importer must meet a stream of foreign-currency payments M evenly over a period, and he withdraws cash in discrete lumps from domestic bonds, then his optimal average foreign cash balance will be

$$F = \sqrt{\frac{aM}{2r}} \tag{1}$$

where a is the brokerage cost of moving from bonds to foreign cash (per transaction), and r is the interest rate on domestic bonds.

Now consider the problem of trading with n different currency areas. There will be n different expenditure streams, $M_1, M_2 \ldots M_n$. So the importer will have to hold balances of n different currencies $F_1, F_2, \ldots F_n$. His total foreign currency balances will be

$$\sum_{i=1}^{n} F_i = \sum_{i=1}^{n} \sqrt{\frac{aM_i}{2r}} \quad i = 1, \ldots, n \tag{2}$$

However, if payments could be rearranged so that all were made in a single currency, there would be a considerable saving of foreign cash balances. This would mean that more resources could be held in interest-bearing bonds. Assuming for simplicity that $M_1 = M_2 = \ldots = M_n$, then the saving in cash balances would be

$$(n - \sqrt{n})\sqrt{\frac{aM_i}{2r}} \tag{3}$$

This expression is definitely positive so long as $n > 1$ and $a, M_i, r > 0$. Swoboda concludes that 'This establishes the proposition that there are economic advantages to be derived from the use of vehicle currencies' (p. 41).

This is an important result because it breaks the common presumption that actors will only wish to hold working balances of either the money of the currency area in which they live or the money of an area with which they are actively trading. It would be quite rational to organise trade such that the settlement medium used over large areas of international trade was not the domestic money of either party to the trade. Helpful as it is, however, to establish this simple point, the above analysis is now recognised to be deficient for a number of reasons. These deficiencies have emerged both from empirical studies of the method of finance in foreign trade and from an increased understanding of the structure of foreign exchange markets.

The most important single piece of information arises from studies of the currency of invoice of foreign trade (Grassman, 1973, 1976; Page, 1977; Carse, Williamson and Wood, 1980; Magee and Rao, 1980). The greater part of trade in manufactured goods between developed nations is invoiced in the currency of the exporter. Of the remainder the bulk is invoiced in the currency of the importer. Only a small proportion (probably less than 5 per cent) is invoiced in third party currencies. Grassman regarded this evidence as a death-blow to the vehicle currency hypothesis and argued that the international monetary system was, after all, symmetrical in the sense that no single currency fulfilled the role of international medium of exchange. The remainder of this chapter is devoted to demonstrating that, while Swoboda's analytical framework is certainly inadequate in the light of the evidence, there is an important role for 'international money' irrespective of the evidence on invoicing patterns.

Even the invoicing evidence suggests some role for international monies. In particular, it is clear that much of the external trade of 'Third World' countries, especially trade in homogeneous primary commodities, is invoiced in third party currencies – notably the dollar. However, the most important datum which has to be incorporated into any relevant analysis of international monies is the fact that foreign exchange markets are almost entirely intermediated. Goods traders do not buy or sell currencies directly in foreign exchange markets, rather this is done by the specialist foreign exchange divisions of commercial banks. The existence of universal intermediation presents prima facie evidence of significant non-convexities (Heller and Starr, 1976) in transactions technology which could obviously be related to the economies of scale evident in Swoboda's model. However, the very existence of intermediation means that the foreign exchange market can be analysed at two distinct levels – the level of the goods trader and that of the foreign exchange dealer. Of central concern for the present work is the holding of (international) money balances as media of exchange by these two groups of actors. There are in reality three major areas worthy of enquiry:

1. First, there is the important question of the choice of currency in terms of which firms set their prices. McKinnon (1979) suggests it is rational for differentiated manufactures to be priced in local currency while homogeneous commodities are priced in terms of an international money. There must, however, be a margin of choice at which enconomic analysis becomes appropriate, though this issue will not be pursued here. Further discussions is also available in Magee and Rao.
2. For any given pricing and payments pattern, traders still have to decide the size and composition of their money balances. All traders will presumably hold working balances of the local currency. The issue is the extent to which they will wish to hold balances of international money. There are two aspects to this – transactions demand and speculative demand. With regard to transactions demand, McKinnon argues that traders will in general have a 'preferred monetary habitat' in the local currency. Traders would only buy foreign exchange immediately

prior to making payments and sell it immediately after receipt. It will be argued below that this will not always be the case.

There has recently been a growing literature pointing to the speculative demand for foreign exchange (Calvo and Rodrigues, 1977). This arises because citizens of high inflation countries will substitute into holdings of foreign currency at the margin. While it has been demonstrated that there is significant substitution between international monies (Chrystal, 1977; Chrystal, Wilson and Quinn, 1983), it is not clear that high inflation countries are substantial holders of foreign exchange (Chrystal, 1979). The reason for this is that high inflation countries, for this very reason, impose severe foreign exchange controls.

A more fundamental problem with the currency substitution literature, however, is that the analysis should apply *mutatis mutandis* to all foreign-currency-denominated assets and not just to 'money'. The peculiarities of that literature arise from the fact that choice is restricted to two non-interest-bearing moneys. If the menu of assets available were broader a domestic resident would never choose foreign money for speculative purposes if there was an interest-bearing asset of the same denomination available. In other words speculative arguments *per se* are not a sufficient explanation for holdings of foreign money. Some additional story is required about transactions costs or liquidity services, etc. On the other hand, once interest-bearing assets are entertained, the novel properties of currency-substitution models disappear or at least merge into the more familiar capital-flows literature. Accordingly, the speculative approach to international money holdings will not be pursued here, though its potential importance should not entirely be ignored.

3. The final important area relates to the organization of the foreign exchange markets themselves. McKinnon argues that even if international monies, such as the dollar, are not the settlement media in manufactured goods trade (apart from where the US is a party to the trade), they (especially the dollar) are used as media of exchange in the foreign exchange markets. Forward markets, in particular, are universally structured with the dollar as settlement medium. The vast bulk of trade in spot markets is also done through the dollar though here a number of cross-markets do exist between major currencies — notably within Europe (including Japan).

Accordingly, the two topics that will now be investigated further are, first, the use and evolution of media of exchange within the market made up by foreign exchange dealers alone and, second, the reasons why goods traders may hold balances of international monies irrespective of invoicing patterns.

II   THE EMERGENCE OF INTERNATIONAL MONIES

The analysis of this section makes liberal use of the analysis applied by Jones (1976) to the emergence of media of exchange in goods markets. However, some aspects of this analysis seem even more appropriate when transformed to foreign exchange markets. What follows differs from the approach of Krugman (1980) who discusses the use of vehicle currencies in financing trade imbalances. Here trade is presumed to be in basic balance.

The foreign exchange market is presumed to be made up of a large number of individual foreign exchange dealers sitting by telephones but otherwise isolated. Each trader has a given order for various quantities of different currencies to be purchased within a given period. This demand is a derived demand, coming from the needs of goods traders. However, the dealer does not merely transfer each order directly into the market. Rather, he will go to the market with lumps of orders. The reason for this is that, although market clearing-prices are presumed to be known, there still exists a significant set-up cost for each exchange. The intuition of this is that, even though exchange rates are known to a close approximation, a dealer wishing to sell currency A for currency B has to telephone other dealers using expensive lines until he finds another dealer wishing to make the opposite exchange. It is cheaper to do this for a small number of large deals than for a large number of small deals. For the problem to be non-trivial, it is necessary to assume that dealers do not have complete prior information about other dealers' demands and supplies. However, they do have some subjective notion, based upon experience, of the relative scale on which various currencies are traded. For example, they know that the number of dealers selling dollars for sterling on a particular day is likely to be much greater than the number selling drachmas for cruzeiro.

What makes the problem interesting is that dealers who can be presumed to conduct their affairs so as to minimise expected costs of any ultimate exchange, may choose to structure their transactions via an intermediate currency — drachmas for dollars, dollars for cruzeiro, rather than drachmas for cruzeiro. It is the potential use of this intermediate currency that is of particular interest.

The trading space is presumed to contain n currencies and a large number of individual dealers. Currency units are defined so that all exchange rates are unity and quantities exchanged in each trade are presumed to be all of equivalent value (for example, 1 million dollars' worth per transaction). To accomplish any given exchange, say of currency i for currency j, a dealer searches randomly for another dealer who wishes to exchange j for currency i. The transactions-cost to the individual dealer is assumed to be proportional to the time spent searching for a complementary trade. The dealer will seek to structure his trades so as to minimise this cost. His trading strategy will be chosen prior to entering the market (that is, before picking up the telephone) on the basis of his beliefs about the probabilities of finding takers for various deals. These beliefs are derived from his previous experience in the market whereas the true probabilities are the fractions of traders offering to buy or sell each currency.

It is assumed that the subjective probability, P_i, that any randomly encountered dealer will want to buy currency i, is equal to the probability that he will want to sell currency i. In other words each dealer believes that currency markets will clear at the known prices on each and every day. Each dealer also assumes that the currency supplied by each other dealer is independent of the currency demanded. For example, sellers of dollars are not more likely to demand sterling than sellers of Deutschmarks. This allows us to state the subjective probability of another dealer wishing to trade currency i for currency j as P_iP_j. The objective of each dealer is to achieve a given ultimate exchange in the minimum time, that is, with a minimum number of telephone calls. If he does this by direct exchange, the expected number of telephone calls is:

$$\frac{1}{P_iP_j} \tag{4}$$

If he does this by indirect exchange, whereby i is traded for k and k for j, the expected number of telephone calls is:

$$\frac{1}{P_iP_k} + \frac{1}{P_kP_j} \tag{5}$$

The optimising dealer will obviously choose as his intermediary currency one with the highest expected probability of being bought and sold. Define P_n as $\text{Max}(P_k)$, then indirect exchange will be used as long as:

$$\frac{1}{P_iP_n} + \frac{1}{P_nP_j} < \frac{1}{P_iP_j} \tag{6}$$

Two other propositions immediately follow. First, the choice of currency

n is independent of i and j. This follows from the assumed independence of currencies demanded and supplied, so P_n is invariant to the ultimate deal desired. Second, there is no longer transactions chain preferable to (5). This is because:

$$\underset{k,l}{\text{Min}} \quad \frac{1}{P_iP_k} + \frac{1}{P_kP_l} + \frac{1}{P_lP_j} = \frac{1}{P_iP_n} + \frac{1}{P_nP_n} + \frac{1}{P_nP_j} \tag{7}$$

This involves a trade of currency n for itself which is redundant.

To summarise so far, the use of a medium of exchange in currency markets is not hard to envisage. It could arise in the above model whenever $P_n > P_i + P_j$. In the real world it means that, since the market for dollars is clearly substantially larger than that of other currencies, the dollar could reasonably be a candidate for medium-of-exchange in currency markets irrespective of the evidence on invoicing patterns.

What then will the equilibrium trading structure look like if we allow the system to evolve from an initial position of total direct trade (barter)? Intuitively, the evolution is quite simple. If $P_n > P_i + P_j$ for any pair (i, j), indirect trade using currency n will be adopted. This will raise P_n and lower all other $P_i(i \neq n)$. This will increase the number of deals for which $P_n > P_i + P_j$, and the process will continue. Where will it stop? Some more analytical apparatus is required to answer this question:

Definitions

$P = (P_1, \ldots, P_n)$ is vector of subjective probabilities of a randomly chosen dealer wishing to sell each currency $i = 1, \ldots, n$.

$q = (q_1, \ldots, q_n)$ is the actual proportion of dealers selling currencies $i = 1, \ldots, n$.

s is the fraction of ultimate exchanges executed indirectly using currency n as medium of exchange.

m is the constant number of individuals entering the market each 'day' to initiate a given ultimate exchange. Those using indirect exchange complete the second deal the next day.

$U = (u_{ij})$ is matrix of fraction of dealers entering who wish *ultimately* to exchange currency i for currency j. U is constant and

$$u_i = \sum_{j=1}^{n} u_{ij} = \sum_{j=1}^{n} u_{ji}$$

is the fraction of new entrants ultimately demanding and supplying the ith currency.

$$u = (u_1, \ldots, u_n)$$

It follows from the definitions of s and u and from the previous argument that $0 \leqslant s \leqslant 1 - u_n$. This is because an ultimate demand for currency n will be achieved directly.

The total number of dealers in the market on a particular day is $m + ms$ (new entrants + those completing indirect exchange from previous day). The number of dealers demanding the nth currency is $mu_n + ms$. So

$$q_n \approx \frac{mu_n + ms}{m + ms} \approx \frac{u_n + s}{1 + s} \tag{8}$$

where $\approx$ arises from the fact that s today is only approximately equal to s yesterday. It is assumed that (8) holds with equality.

The number of dealers demanding currencies $i = 1, \ldots, n - 1$ is mu_i. So

$$q_i = \frac{mu_i}{m + ms} = \frac{u_i}{1 + s} \qquad (i = 1, \ldots, n - 1) \tag{9}$$

(8) and (9) may be rewritten as:

$$q = u + \frac{s}{1 + s} \, (e_n - u) \tag{10}$$

where $e_n = (0, 0, 0, \ldots, 0, 1)$.

The dynamic adjustment of the system is determined by the assumption that P is revised each day in proportion to its distance from q.

$$\Delta P_t = \lambda(q_t - P_t) \qquad 0 < \lambda < 1 \tag{11}$$

The complete system is now described by equations (10) and (11) with the addition of the definition of s which is:

$$s = \sum_x u_{ij} \qquad (x = i, j, \ldots P_n > P_i + P_j) \tag{12}$$

The existence of a solution to this system is easy to establish. The u_{ij} are parametric. In equilibrium, $P_i = q_i \; \forall \; i$. Any q is associated with some value of s. The domain of q (and P) is a compact convex set with lower and upper bounds of u and $u + (e_n - u) (1 - u_n)/(2 - u_n)$. From any initial value P always approaches q. So an equilibrium will always exist even if only at the boundary. However, an analytical solution for s cannot be obtained owing to the discontinuity of (12). This discontinuity arises from the fact that the addition of another currency whose trade is inter-mediated involves a discrete jump. So even though P is continuous, s will not be. The possibility of multiple locally stable equilibria may, however, be illustrated by defining an arbitrary s^e. This is the value of s that is consistent with any given value of the P vector and is defined by:

$$P = u + \left(\frac{s^e}{1 + s^e} \right) (e_n - u) \tag{13}$$

Analytically, the role of s^e is as of the expected value of s, though no such direct expectations are held by the actors. The value of this, however, is that the system can now be reduced to a relationship between s and s^e (Jones, 1976, p. 770). As s^e rises, s moves up in steps. This corresponds to discrete increases in the number of currencies for which $P_n > P_i + P_j$. For given initial conditions s^e always adjusts towards s. Both s and s^e are bounded below by 0 and above by $1 - u_n$ and in equilibrium $s = s^e$. $s = 1 - u_n$ whenever $s^e > u_i + u_j - u_n \; \forall \, i \neq n, j \neq n$. These conditions determine only that a locally stable equilibrium will exist whenever $s = s^e$. Possible solutions are illustrated in Figure 4.1.

Starting at an initial point such as X, with $s^e = 0$, the function $s = (u, s^e)$ moves upward in steps until it reaches point B. At B all dealing is through an intermediary currency. However, *whenever* the function crosses the diagonal, there is a locally stable equilibrium such as at A. In principle, there may be a multiplicity of points such as A or there may be none at all. For domestic goods trade there can be a strong presumption that monetary exchange becomes almost universal, and once it is so, it is seldom reversed. In foreign currency dealing, there can be no such presumption. The possibility of the system being in a point such as A and occasionally moving would seem quite strong. Let us return to the realities of the environment within which foreign exchange dealers exist.

Consider the world economy as it existed in the 1950s. The role of the dollar under the Marshall Plan for the reconstruction of Europe has been outlined by McKinnon (1979, chapter 11). It is clear that during that period, not only was the US by far the largest economy in world trade but also other central banks were committed to using dollars to peg exchange rates. At this time the above analysis would suggest that the dollar would become the intermediary currency *par excellence*. The only obvious exception to this was the use of sterling among sterling area countries, though it is not clear to what extent sterling was used as an intermediary

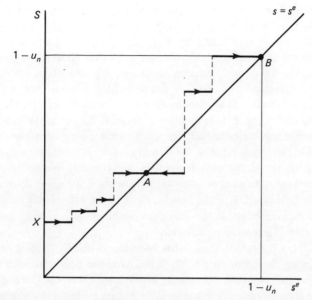

FIGURE 4.1 *Equilibrium in the use of intermediary currency*

as opposed to a reserve asset. If it were used in the former capacity, it could only have been because of a violation of the assumption that the currency ultimately demanded is independent of the currency initially supplied.

However, over the past two decades three important changes have taken place. Two have been gradual, one relatively sudden. First, the structure of world trade has changed. Clearly the share of the US in world trade has declined. It is less clear that dollar-dominated trade has reduced in share, particularly if capital markets are included. None the less, it is probably true that currencies like the Deutschmark and yen are closer substitutes for the dollar (in some sense) now than they were twenty-five years ago. In effect, there are now deep and active markets in many currencies other than the dollar. Some evidence on the declining relative use of the dollar is given by Magee and Rao. Second, the information systems available to foreign-exchange dealers have changed considerably, especially in the last decade. The Visual Display Units (VDU) with which every dealer is now equipped, permit him to get prices currently quoted for the major currencies from any other major bank in the world. At present banks are not committed to deal at these prices, but it is understood that in the near future they will come to represent a binding commitment. In other words, the price at which a deal is actually made can still only be established by a telephone call and presumably where bargaining is involved this will continue to be true. However, it does mean that, within the group of major currencies, the role of an intermediary currency is largely redundant. A dealer wishing to trade, say sterling for Deutschmarks, may do so directly in a well-developed market. The virtual certainty of finding a taker quickly at no great discount makes the use of an intermediary step through the dollar unnecessary. However, outside the major currencies (say, of the Group of Ten) it is still quite likely that the role of the dollar as intermediary is extremely important. This is reinforced by the fact that many currencies are still pegged to the dollar. However, it is not difficult to imagine rivals to the dollar being established. The Deutschmark within the European countries is an obvious candidate for the role of intermediary currency.

The third important change has been the switch to floating exchange rates among the major currencies. If this had been associated with a major decline in the use of the dollar as an intervention currency, this could have reduced the use of the dollar as an intermediary currency, by changing the U matrix in the foregoing analysis. It is not clear to what extent such a decline in dollar intervention actually took place, though presumably the probabilities of such intervention have changed.

In summary, there is a good case for thinking of the dollar as an intermediary currency in world exchange markets, though if anything the changes of the last two decades should have reduced the relative importance of that role rather than enhanced it. This decline may, of course, be related to the apparent decline of the dollar as an invoicing currency but clearly the relationship is quite loose.

III   TRADER BALANCES OF FOREIGN CURRENCY

This chapter has established a reason why foreign exchange dealers may give currencies like the dollar a special role in their activities. From this it is safe to presume that dollars will occupy a greater proportion of dealers' portfolios than would otherwise be necessary. In effect, this establishes the demand for dollar balances in bank's portfolios for other than purely speculative purposes. The question now to be considered is whether this intermediary role of the dollar could also make it more desirable in the portfolios of goods traders. McKinnon presumes that it does not. He takes it as given that goods traders will have a 'preferred monetary habitat' in their own local currency. In contrast, we have already seen that the inventory model applied to this area by Swoboda, does indicate the possibility of foreign currency holdings, though these are directly related to the invoice pattern of trade payments. The dollar would only have a special role in traders' portfolios to the extent that the dollar had a special role in ultimate payments. Let us, therefore, consider if there could be other reasons for a goods trader to hold a bank account in dollars even though he is neither a US resident nor about to make a *known* payment in dollars. Purely speculative motives for such holdings will continue to be disregarded.

Consider, say, a UK importer resident in the UK. He is presumed to hold a sterling bank account and to own sterling-denominated interest-bearing assets. In the process of making trade payments, he will obviously obtain foreign exchange and be seen to hold it for a short time until a final settlement is made. However, this is not particularly interesting. What is of concern is whether he is ever likely to find it beneficial to open up a bank account as an ongoing operation and hold in it balances of the intermediary currency, i.e. dollars. If he is to do so, it must depend upon the costs of alternative ways of organising his affairs.

Notation

Let there be $n + 1$ currencies with sterling denoted 0, and the dollar denoted n.
Let C_{ij}, $ij = 0, \ldots, n$ be the cost per unit of converting currency i into currency j.
Let r be the interest rate on domestic bonds.
Let S_i, $i = 0, \ldots, n$ be the cost per unit per period for holding a bank account in currency i as compared to r.
Let P_i, $i = 1, \ldots, n$ be the proportions of import payments made in currency i.

$$\sum_{i=1}^{n} P_i = 1$$

Notice first that by assuming a constant unit cost of converting one currency into another, which corresponds to the practice of a standard bid ask spread, we are avoiding the *raison d'être* of Baumol-type cash inventories. A number of cases can be identified.

Case 1

$$C_{ij} = C_{jk} \ \forall \ i,j \quad S_i = S_j \ \forall \ i,j; \quad P_i \gtreqless P_j \ \forall \ i,j$$

If exchange costs and service charges are the same for all currencies, then *whatever the trade pattern*, there is no net benefit to holding a dollar bank account, or indeed, any bank account other than in sterling. The only justification for holding onto a foreign currency deliberately is if the trader has both *receipts* and *expenditures* in that currency. This, of course, does not generate balances of the intermediary currency except in so far as that trade is dollar-denominated (where the dollar is the intermediary currency). Rather, currency balances would be related to net trade payments in a multitude of currencies.

Case 2

$$C_{in} < C_{ij} \ \forall \ i,j; \quad S_i = S_j \ \forall \ i,j; \quad P_i \gtreqless P_j \ \forall \ i,j$$

If the dollar is the intermediary currency (to some extent) for exchange dealers, and they 'pass on' the lower cost of dollar transactions to a significant degree, this alone could justify dollar holdings irrespective of the pattern of trade. If receipts accrue in sterling, then transaction costs through dollars must be less than half those between other currencies to justify converting sterling into dollars and the dollars into other currency. However, if receipts are in other currency, and payments are in different (and perhaps uncertain) other currencies, then a rather smaller transaction-cost differential could justify holding dollars if the choice is between dollars and sterling.

Case 3

$$C_{ij} = C_{jk} \ \forall \ i,j,k; \quad S_n < S_j \ \forall \ i,j; \quad P_i \gtreqless P_j \ \forall \ i,j$$

If dollar banking is for some reason more competitive so that the real return on deposits is greater than in other currencies, clearly this benefit could make it optimal to hold deposits in dollars as opposed to domestic currency. The interest differential would, however, have to be sufficient to compensate for the extra transactions costs.

Case 4

$$C_{in} < C_{ij} \ \forall \ i,j; \quad S_n < S_j \ \forall \ i,j; \quad P_n > P_j \ \forall \ i,j$$

In reality, it is safe to presume that no exchange cost is lower than that for the dollar, no denomination of banking is more competitive (vis Euro-dollars), and the dollar has the greatest probability of being the currency of ultimate payment and receipt (especially when financing is included). Swoboda (1969), for example, points to transactions costs vis a vis dollars being as little as one tenth of those *vis-à-vis* other currencies. Under these circumstances, it is not hard to see that it may be rational for goods traders to hold active balances of dollars (or perhaps one of the other major currencies) as an integral part of his operations in addition to the currency of the country in which he is resident, and to some degree at least inde-pendent of the direction and denomination of ultimate payments. Specu-lative and or portfolio diversification arguments can only be expected to increase the likelihood of signficant holdings of major currencies. So the presumption of a 'preferred monetary habitat' in local currency is one that should be applied with caution.

IV SUMMARY

Foreign exchange markets are largely intermediated. An analysis has been presented suggesting a possible role for an intermediary currency like the dollar in the market made up of professional foreign-exchange dealers. It is suggested that, if anything, the relative importance of this role may be declining. It is also demonstrated that goods traders may hold working balances of dollars, even though they do not reside in the US, depending upon the structure of transactions costs, service charges and ultimately, though not directly, upon the pattern of trade payments. The point of the analysis is to demonstrate that the role of 'international money' may be greater than the mere denomination of trade payments would indicate.

REFERENCES

G. A. Calvo and C. A. Rodriguez (1977) 'A Model of Exchange Rate Determination under Currency Substitution and Rational Expecta-tions', *Journal of Political Economy*, vol. 85, pp. 617–25.
S. Carse, J. Williamson and G. Wood (1980) *The Financing Procedures of British Foreign Trade* (Cambridge University Press).
K. A. Chrystal (1977) 'Demand for International Media of Exchange', *American Economic Review*, vol. 67, pp. 840–50.
K. A. Chrystal (1978) 'International Money and the Future of the SDR', *Princeton Essays in International Finance*, p. 128.

K. A. Chrystal (1979) 'Some Evidence in Defence of the Vehicle Currency Hypothesis', *Economic Letters*, vol. 3, pp. 267–70.

K. A. Chrystal, N. D. Wilson and P. Quinn (1983) 'Demand for International Money, 1962–77', *European Economic Review* vol. 21, pp. 287–98.

S. Grassman (1973) *Exchange Reserves and the Financial Structure of Foreign Trade* (London: Saxon House).

S. Grassman (1976) 'Currency Distribution and Forward Cover in Foreign Trade', *Journal of International Economics*, vol. 6, pp. 215–21.

F. Hahn (1965) 'On some Problems of Proving the Existence of Equilibrium in a Monetary Economy', in F. Hahn and F. P. R. Brechling (eds) *The Theory of Interest Rates* (London: Macmillan).

W. P. Heller and R. M. Starr (1976) 'Equilibrium with Non-convex Transactions Costs', *Review of Economic Studies*, vol. 43.

R. A. Jones (1976) 'The Origin and Development of Media of Exchange', *Journal of Political Economy*, vol. 84, pp. 757–75.

P. Krugman (1980) 'Vehicle Currencies and the Structure of International Exchange', *Journal of Money, Credit and Banking*.

S. P. Magee and R. K. S. Rao (1980) 'Vehicle and Non-vehicle Currencies in International Trade', *American Economic Review*, vol. 70, pp. 368–73.

R. I. McKinnon (1977) 'The Eurocurrency Market', *Princeton Essays in International Finance*, p. 125.

R. I. McKinnon (1979) *Money in International Exchange* (Oxford University Press).

J. Niehans and J. Hewson (1976) 'The Eurodollar Market and Monetary Theory', *Journal of Money, Credit and Banking*, pp. 3–27.

J. M. Ostroy (1973) 'The Informational Efficiency of Monetary Exchange', *American Economic Review*, vol. 69, pp. 597–610.

J. M. Ostroy and R. M. Starr (1974) 'Money and the Decentralization of Exchange', *Econometrica*, vol. 42, pp. 1093–114.

S. A. B. Page (1977) 'Currency of Invoicing of Merchandise Trade', *National Institute Economic Review*, pp. 77–80.

A. K. Swoboda (1968) 'The Euro-dollar Market: an Interpretation', *Princeton Essays in International Finance* 64.

A. K. Swoboda (1969) 'Vehicle Currencies and the Foreign Exchange Market: The case of the Dollar', in R. Z. Aliber (ed.) *The International Market for Foreign Exchange* (New York: Praeger, 1969).

5 Loan Capital in Development Finance, the Role of Banks, and Some Implications for Managing Debt

NICHOLAS C. HOPE
AND DAVID W. McMURRAY*

I INTRODUCTION

The rapid growth of developing countries debt and the even faster growth of their borrowing from the commercial banks have been highly publicised outcomes of the economic turmoil that marked the 1970s. Less well publicised is the accompanying growth – at least up to 1980 – in most countries' debt-servicing capacity. Also few commentators have noted the substitution of debt for equity in the external liabilities of developing countries, which has meant that the rising obligations of debt service as a share of export earnings have been offset partly by a fall in the share of export earnings required to service direct investment. One careful assessment of the data up to 1980 concluded that there was 'no evidence of a

* This chapter depends heavily on the work of staff of the External Debt Division of the World Bank. Particular contributions were made by Barbara Schwartz and Iveta Hagelis, with computer assistance from Vilas Mandlekar and secretarial support by Sally Heycox and Lan Ha Ly. Helpful comments were received from Graeme Dorrance, Gershon Feder, Helen Hughes, David Llewellyn, and Adrian Wood. The views and interpretations are those of the author(s) and may not be attributed to the World Bank or its affiliated organisations.

93

systematic deterioration in the external position of developing countries during the decade'.[1] In a later piece using different data and estimates for 1981, the OECD reached similar conclusions, finding that the situations calls for 'neither complacency nor alarm'.[2]

More recent developments in the financial markets, the prolonged slump in the industrial countries and the rash of (mainly multilateral) debt re-schedulings that saw a record number of Paris Club agreements in 1981–2 have cast doubt on these conclusions and have provoked an emphasis on the perils, rather than the benefits, of international lending. The perils are seen to be two. For the creditors – the prospect of substantial loan losses, with the burgeoning importance of flows through the financial markets meaning that the soundness of lending by banks is questioned seriously. For the debtors – a heavy burden of debt-service obligations, which can be met, if at all, in a world of record real interest rates and sluggish export growth, only by heavy doses of deflation. Put simply and in extreme form, critics of the evolution of international lending and borrowing are arguing two cases:

1. the process of international financial intermediation is destabilised by and some intermediaries are threatened with collapse because of lending to developing economies;[3] and
2. the developing countries' economic advance is threatened by their obligations to service their external liabilities.

Policy recommendations would appear to be that (private) lenders should avoid loans to developing countries, which in turn should avoid accepting them.

If not exactly a pair of straw men, this rendering of the concerns of many responsible commentators on financial developments does border on caricature. It is, perhaps, an over-reaction to the excessive emphasis on the risks in international lending, and the consequent tendency to overstate the potential costs and to understate the benefits it conveys. For private creditors, lending to developing economies has offered a welcome oppor-tunity for portfolio diversification and, at least in the stage of explosive growth of bank lending in the mid-1970s, for ensuring higher returns than were available on domestic loans. As well, bank lending has supported the activities of clients interested in exporting to, or investing in, developing countries; and has introduced the banks to longer-term markets for their services, as many developing economies are in the financial markets to stay.

For developing countries, the benefits from foreign borrowing have been analysed more closely. Eaton and Gersowitz[4] have identified four benefits from external capital inflow: (i) eases adjustment (to permanent income loss) (ii) supplements investment (iii) smoothes income cycles and (iv) meets the transactions needs of trade. Each of these uses of loan finance has different implications for developments in a country's debt. Financing adjustment to a once-for-all income-loss results in an increase in debt to the extend that the income loss is deferred, at the cost of future income foregone through service payments. The increase in debt will not necessarily add to a country's external liabilities in the longer term. Supplementing investment with foreign resources can lead to the well-known long cycle of debt accumulation, as a country first imports capital then accumulates external assets as it matures into a capital exporter. A country can continue to add to its net liability position for very long periods provided that the return on the investment of foreign capital exceeds its costs. Smoothing income cycles, or compensating for temporary fluctuations in income from internally or externally induced shocks, should have no longer-term effects on external indebtedness. Finally, financing trade should cause (mainly short-term) external liabilities (and assets, including reserves) to grow steadily with trade growth. A presumption is that so long as a country's imports exceed its exports its current trade-related liabilities should exceed its current trade-related assets, but ultimately the size of assets and liabilities should be comparable. Clearly, benefits from each of these uses of foreign capital will vary between countries depending on, among other things, the efficiency of their investment, their capacity for good economic management, their susceptibility to internally and externally generated shocks and their reliance on international trade.

For each use of foreign capital, but especially for the last two, the presumption is that once a country enters the financial markets it is there for the long haul. An integral part of the development process is the transformation of a developing economy from one dependent for its external capital on official aid to one that has free access to, and is creditworthy to borrow from, the financial markets. In the interim stages, countries depend to greater or lesser degrees on direct investment, on non-concessional official capital and on officially-supported flows from private creditors. Most countries reveal a preference for financial credits from the commercial banks, or — even better — from the bond markets. Financial credits are an indicator of financial maturity and a strong credit standing; and, more important, they are flexible (they are finance debt-service payments or consumption as well as new capital goods imports) and tend to be cheaper than equity.

Before the 1970s, countries gained access to the financial markets rather

gradually. They needed a reputation for sustained, sound economic performance and a proven capability to service credits from suppliers before
they became attractive lending prospects for bankers. The transition in
external financing patterns was accelerated for most developing countries
during the 1970s. A pivotal factor was the income transfer associated
with the oil shock, and for many economies financing needs were amplified
by the collapse of the commodities boom of 1974. External finance was
used to ease the pain of adjustment to income loss and to compensate for
the export earnings cycle, as well as to augment domestic savings and serve
the needs of trade.

Many developing countries which otherwise might not have expected to
finance adjustment from the markets enjoyed expanded access because of
the nature of the oil shock. Oil-exporting countries deposited the largest
part of their new-found earnings in the financial markets, and to the commercial banks fell the task of 'recycling' the oil surpluses. The volume of
funds available for lending and the institutional and prudential constraints
on banks' portfolios aided countries that had not previously graduated to
market-borrowing to satisfy substantial portions of their financing needs in
the financial markets.

With hindsight, and in the absence of a similar payments disequilibrium
later in the decade, many countries might have found their expanded access
to markets was once-for-all. However, the failure of the global economy to
return to the pre-1973 growth path and the renewed payments imbalances
of the late 1970s have maintained the financing requirements of developing
countries at elevated levels and ensured the continuing widespread involvement of banks in development finance.

A legitimate question is whether the current heavy bank involvement
constitutes too much, too soon. Although the continued growth of bank-
lending to developing countries is certain, nothing guarantees that this
growth will be smooth or even continuous. The difficulties of both borrowers and lenders in the depressed conditions that now afflict the global
economy tend to colour judgements on the appropriateness of the current
level of involvement of banks. Both views described earlier support the
position that bank involvement has developed too fast and has gone too
far because the stability of international financial intermediation is threatened or because developing countries are experiencing such difficulty in
servicing their debt that their policies for growth are excessively constrained.

Because of the certainty of continuing involvement of commercial banks
in development finance, those commentators that point to the dangers of
the current situation should feel obligated, on the first side, to describe a
process of international financial intermediation that can meet the test of

participation by the developing countries, and, from the other, to reassess the ultimate contribution of external capital to the development process. As this paper shows, loan finance is the predominant avenue for net resource inflow to developing economies.

The intentions of this paper are modest. It steps back from current difficulties in financial markets to analyse development finance during the 1970s, the role of banks in this process and some of the implications for managing the debt of developing countries. In doing so, it does not break new ground. Similar studies have been undertaken by others, and information on the status of developing countries' debt and commercial banks' lending is published regularly by the major reporting services of the International Monetary Fund (IMF), the Bank for International Settlements (BIS), the Organisation for Economic Co-operation and Development (OECD) and the World Bank.[5] Any novelty in the paper stems from the advantage of access to the unique source of data residing in the World Bank's Debtor Reporting System (DRS); and bank-lending is analysed from the viewpoint of the DRS rather than the more current data from the BIS that lie at the heart of many other studies. The DRS has a broader coverage of term-lending; and by excluding short-term loans (those with an *original* maturity of less than twelve months) that comprise much of the data reported to the BIS, there is a presumption that trends are more closely related to the role of banks in financing development, or at least adjustment, than they are to the financing of trade.

The other innovation offered here is a grouping of developing countries that differs from some of the more traditional divisions used in comparative analysis. The benefits from borrowing abroad, the types of loans that are available – especially from financial markets – and the problems raised in debt management are related to broad considerations of creditworthiness and past borrowing patterns as well as the policy-determined effectiveness with which external finance is used. Countries' abilities to use foreign capital on market terms efficiently and to manage it competently are a function of the stage of their progression from dependence on aid to integration in the financial markets.

The classification of developing countries into three groups comprises the rest of this introduction. The chapter then examines the role of debt capital in the balance-of-payments' experience of these groups. For each, the oil shock is shown to have raised net use of external resources by a percentage point of GDP or more, and foreign resource inflow is shown to depend mainly on loans. It next establishes the role that banks have played in this process as reflected by DRS data. Finally, it illustrates that resource inflows of the magnitude experienced in the 1970s could be sustainable in the 1980s, given similar developments in the global economy and the supplies of external finance. Some of the factors that, in practice, can enhance or inhibit the capacity of developing countries to manage their debt are considered.

Grouping Developing Countries

Table 5.1 lists the developing countries that report under the DRS and some indicators, based on data to the end of 1981, of their dependence on private lending. The countries are ranked according to the shares of private in total medium- and long-term debt over 1979–81. The groupings are based on these shares and the share of their debt that is on concessional terms.

Inevitably, breakdown into groups is fuzzy and consideration was given also to the shares of commitments and disbursements that are from private sources.[6] Thus, for seventeen countries in Group I – the 'market borrowers' – the selection criteria were that at least 70 per cent of total debt should be from private sources and no more than 15 per cent of outstanding debt should be on concessional terms.[7] The choice of the apparently arbitrary cut-off line of 70 per cent was supported by the shares of private loans in current commitments and disbursements. Except for Uruguay and Panama, no country in Group I obtained less than 75 per cent of new commitments from private sources in the period 1979–81, and (except for the Bahamas and Panama) disbursements from private sources were 83 per cent or more of total disbursements in this period. A comparison of these numbers with the countries at the top of Group II suggests that the cut-off is appropriate.

The countries in Group III – the 'aid recipients' – were less easy to identify clearly, and about a dozen lower-ranked countries in Group II might be added to the forty countries assigned to this group. The criteria for inclusion were a share for private debt of no more than 25 per cent of total debt with at least 50 per cent of total debt on concessional terms in the years 1979–81. However, as these criteria would exclude five countries (Benin, Central African Republic, Malawi, Niger and Sudan) that have comparatively high shares of private debt but poor current prospects for substantial new commitments from the private sector, the category was broadened to include all the least-developed countries for which data are available.

The remaining forty-one countries assigned to Group II – the 'mixed borrowers' – are indeed mixed. They include major financial market participants such as the Philippines, Portugal, Peru, Korea, Thailand, Morocco, Bolivia and Indonesia, and the aforementioned lower-ranked countries (some of which have re-scheduled their debt already) which share most of the characteristics of the aid-recipients. The dividing lines for the groups, therefore, are not clear-cut, but the characteristics of the average country within each group differ sufficiently for external financing patterns and prospective financing policies to be easily discernible.

In the DRS, debt from private sources includes mainly suppliers' credits, lending by financial institutions and bonds. A question that arises in analysing country groupings based on shares of private debt is how closely the conclusions will match those of analyses based on the banking statistics prepared by the BIS.[8] One hypothesis is that the countries that depend heavily on medium- and long-term private borrowing should be the most creditworthy for borrowing from the banking system. Even including short-term assets and liabilities, these countries would be expected to show a net liability position with BIS reporting banks. At the other extreme, countries that have little medium- and long-term debt from private sources are unlikely to be creditworthy for much short- or long-term borrowing from commercial banks that is not secured by deposits in the banking system. A ranking of countries by their net exposure to BIS banks might be expected then to correlate closely with the ranking based on DRS data for private debt.

To test this hypothesis, Table 5.1 provides a memorandum item that gives for each included country its net liability position as a percentage of its assets held in BIS banks.[9] As hypothesised, only one of the market participants (Group I) has net asset position with BIS banks, but 66 per cent of the aid-recipients (Group III) have net asset positions. Comfortingly, the mixed borrowers indeed have a mixture of net asset and net liability positions. On average, Group I countries have a net liability position of 186 per cent of their assets held in BIS banks; Group II countries have a corresponding net liability position of 118 per cent; and Group III countries (excluding Niger) have a net asset position of 9 per cent.

Clearly, groups that were formed by ranking on the net liability position *vis-à-vis* banks reporting to the BIS would not be identical to the ones used here. But there is a strong correlation between the two rankings. The Spearman rank correlation coefficient for all countries in Table 5.1 is 0.58. Without testing further, there is strong *a priori* evidence to indicate that the balance-of-payments experience of countries grouped by shares in private debt as measured by DRS data should correspond quite closely to groupings based on net borrowings as measured by BIS data.[10]

TABLE 5.1 Shares of loans from private sources in total medium- and long-term external debt, commitments, disbursements and debt service of developing countries: weighted averages 1979–81[a] (percentages)

	Debt from private sources	Commitments from private sources	Disbursements from private sources	Debt service to private sources	Debt on concessional terms[b]	Memo: Net liabilities to as a percentage of assets in banks reporting to BIS at end-1981[c]
Group I — Market Borrowers[d]						
Venezuela	97	100	99	97	0	20
Hong Kong	97	99	96	98	0	22
Mexico	90	88	93	94	1	358
Argentina	89	93	95	91	2	249
Brazil	88	88	92	93	3	932
Greece	88	88	89	88	3	69
Chile	84	97	97	86	7	168
Algeria	84	79	83	91	7	66
Bahamas	83	89	58	82	—	9
Nigeria	81	88	94	86	8	170
Ecuador	80	77	86	92	9	450
Yugoslavia	77	82	85	85	8	286
Ivory Coast	77	76	85	88	8	314
Uruguay	77	65	88	80	6	–39
Panama	75	67	79	87	12	71
Malaysia	74	76	83	82	9	5
Singapore	70	85	85	75	6	11
Group II — Mixed Borrowers[e]						
Zimbabwe[f]	84	72	70	86	6	137
Gabon	69	63	69	84	12	370
Portugal	68	74	79	71	7	313
Philippines	68	61	68	79	13	142

Trinidad and Tobago	67	72	58	83	2	-63
Korea, Republic of	62	70	75	80	16	438
Costa Rica	61	63	70	81	12	247
Thailand	60	60	72	84	16	114
Papua New Guinea	60	59	64	77	21	-27
Peru	59	62	67	76	18	177
Cyprus	58	67	71	76	11	-45
Kenya	51	43	58	62	30	-19
Colombia	50	70	74	78	21	36
Morocco	50	47	47	77	40	416
Dominican Republic	50	37	49	77	29	189
Indonesia	49	55	68	80	41	-25
Bolivia	49	48	42	73	31	258
Paraguay	48	47	61	70	30	6
Zaire	46	21	26	49	28	43
Mauritius	45	43	50	70	26	49
Cameroon	44	49	53	70	37	140
Togo	43	12	52	41	30	115
Congo, People's Republic of	42	73	69	63	42	339
Jamaica	42	34	37	75	29	152
Israel	41	45	43	68	44	-37
Nicaragua	41	1	0	30	28	462
Turkey	39	41	51	54	31	101
Honduras	39	38	54	69	29	345
Tunisia	39	29	44	64	43	17
Zambia	38	43	47	75	32	45

a   Data are drawn from 98 countries' reports under the DRS and from estimates by staff of the External Debt Division. Data are for loans of original maturities exceeding 12 months. Note that separate data for commitments of debt to private borrowers without public guarantee are not available; the assumption is that commitments are identical to disbursements in any year. This assumption will depress the share of private debt in commitments. As well, estimated or actual data for private non-guaranteed debt are available for only 42 countries, very few of which are in Group III. This introduces a (small) understatement of the role of debt from private sources in external financing. In averaging, weights are the shares of private lenders in total debt in each year.

b   The share of a country's debt that has a grant element of 25 per cent or more.

c   Calculated from BIS data (revised series) published April 1983. A negative sign indicates a net asset position *vis-à-vis* banks reporting to the BIS.

d   Countries for which private-source debt is at least 70 per cent of total debt and concessional debt is no more than 15 per cent of total debt.

TABLE 5.1 (continued)   Shares of loans from private sources in total medium- and long-term external debt, commitments, disbursements and debt service of developing countries weighted averages 1978–81[a] (percentages)

	Debt from private sources	Commitments from private sources	Disbursements from private sources	Debt service to private sources	Debt on concessional terms[b]	Memo: net liabilities to as a percentage of assets in banks reporting to BIS at end-1981[c]
Group II – Mixed Borrowers[e] (cont.)						
Guyana	37	27	25	68	41	145
Sierra Leone	35	40	58	89	50	−22
Lebanon	34	0	56	52	42	−80
Madagascar	33	39	42	49	44	300
Guatemala	32	31	28	65	25	−41
Senegal	32	10	27	75	42	149
Oman	28	80	47	62	27	−77
Barbados	28	47	39	58	36	−16
Liberia	28	11	26	73	47	168
Fiji	23	18	24	41	19	−44
Malta[g]	1	0	0	5	94	−97
Group III – Aid Recipients[h]						
Benin, People's Republic of	52	74	74	43	42	−58
Malawi	35	37	38	77	44	135
Niger	32	38	41	42	42	1,087
Central African Republic	32	5	5	15	47	0
Sudan	27	11	10	11	43	18
Ghana	24	2	8	34	60	−21
Jordan	22	16	22	60	66	−83
Lesotho	21	21	36	83	71	−85
Uganda	20	13	18	38	44	−36
Burma	19	13	23	57	80	105
Egypt, Arab Republic of	17	50	47	61	74	−21
Guinea	17	26	32	15	66	547

Mauritania	17	7	10	70	68	−44
Western Samoa	16	0	0	56	64	0
Swaziland	15	0	0	43	59	−78
Chad	13	28	17	44	84	21
Sri Lanka	11	18	34	28	84	−10
Gambia, The	10	16	16	49	84	4
Tanzania	9	19	18	44	71	37
Seychelles	7	33	19	0	71	−80
Haiti	6	22	21	32	90	−37
Ethiopia	6	15	19	28	81	−92
Pakistan	6	8	19	26	85	−20
Syrian Arab Rep.	5	3	6	13	67	−34
Burundi	4	8	3	67	90	−90
Upper Volta	4	13	8	24	86	−84
India	4	8	13	11	90	−59
Maldives	3	3	8	20	88	−50
Bangladesh	3	1	4	28	93	15
Mali	3	0	2	10	93	393
Botswana	2	3	3	7	55	−85
El Salvador	1	12	2	19	50	−22
Yemen, Arab Republic of	0	0	2	7	98	−83
Somalia	0	3	6	7	95	−72
Nepal	0	2	0	0	99	−99
Comoros	0	0	1	0	98	−50
Djibouti	0	0	0	16	86	−95
Rwanda	0	0	0	0	100	−94
Solomon Islands	0	0	0	0	100	i
Yemen, People's Democratic Republic	0	0	0	21	100	−97

e Countries not satisfying the requirements for inclusion in Group I or Group III, except Zimbabwe and Malta.

f Zimbabwe qualifies for Group I but this is because of its past political status and lack of access to external capital rather than substantial capacity for borrowing in financial markets. Therefore, it has been assigned to Group II.

g Malta qualifies for Group III but is excluded on income grounds.

h Countries for which private debt is less than 25 per cent of total debt and at least 50 per cent of debt is concessional, or countries that report to the DRS and are classified as 'least developed' by the UN.

i Not available.

II   THE ROLE OF FOREIGN BORROWING IN BALANCE-OF-PAYMENTS FINANCING: 1968–81

Conventionally, analyses of the contribution of external finance to development have emphasised its role in raising investment in developing countries. The other uses for foreign borrowing have received less attention, except that recently the implications of financing adjustment have been scrutinised closely.[11] Balance-of-payments data of the required consistency and completeness are available for many countries from 1968, so analysis of these data covers periods, of about the same length, during which the investment motive (1968–73) and the adjustment motive (1975–81) for external borrowing may have predominated.

Data used in the analysis are from IMF balance-of-payments information as maintained in World Bank files. Not all series are complete for all countries; in particular, data essentially complete for the full period are available for only twelve Group III countries.[12] In order to use as much information as possible, and given groupings large enough to eliminate systematic bias, balance-of-payments data for each country have been included in group totals for each available year. The data have been normalised so that balance-of-payments aggregates are expressed as percentages of the GDP of the countries for which data are included.

Four broad categories of *net uses* of external finance were identified as were three broad categories of *net sources*. The balancing item – assigned as a net source of foreign funds – ensured equality between net use and net availability. The four net uses of finance are: (i) the balance on goods and non-factor services – the resource balance; (ii) net investment income paid abroad; (iii) net labour income paid abroad (including private transfers and workers' remittances) and (iv) additions to reserves. A negative resource balance indicates a surplus on the balance of goods and non-factor services and, for all groups of countries, net labour income paid abroad was always negative. That is, labour earnings and private transfers have supported a consistent resource inflow to the groups of developing countries over the period examined.

External finance is provided by net official transfers (conventionally viewed in the World Bank as a financing item), net direct investment and net flows of medium- and long-term (MLT) loans (i.e. those with original maturities exceeding twelve months). The balancing item includes net movements of short-term debt, errors and omissions, and counterpart items (chiefly monetisation and demonetisation of gold, allocation of SDRs and valuation changes in reserves).

The results of the analysis for each group of developing countries are illustrated in Figure 5.1 and underlying data are found in Annex Table 1. As anticipated, patterns of development finance have differed markedly between the groups of developing countries.

Market Borrowers – Group I

Net annual use of foreign finance for market borrowers generally has been in the range 2.5–3.5 per cent of GDP. The peak was 4.9 per cent in 1978, and the trough 2.1 per cent in 1969. Perhaps surprisingly, the major use of external finance from 1968–81 was to service foreign capital. These payments have been remarkably stable, around 2 per cent of GDP a year, and in only four years – 1972, 1975, 1976 and 1978 – have net capital-service payments used less than half the finance available. The apparent stability is contradicted by the changes within net investment payments. In 1968, 75 per cent of these payments were in respect of direct investment; all other payments – mainly interest on medium- and long-term debt – accounted for the remaining 25 per cent.[13] By 1981, the shares had been reversed, an accurate reflection of the increasing importance of debt-financing relative to equity for countries creditworthy for borrowing in the financial markets.

Extremes of the resource balance for the group were achieved within a year of each other; there was a net resource outflow of 0.1 per cent of GDP in 1974 followed by a resource inflow of 3.0 per cent of GDP in 1975. The net resource inflow has averaged 1.3 per cent of GDP a year for the full period, but the average for 1975–81 has risen to 1.9 per cent, from 1.0 per cent in the period 1968–73.

Net labour income receipts have reduced external financing requirements by around 0.66 per cent of a GDP a year. Reserve accumulation has amounted to as much as 2.3 per cent of GDP (in 1974) and as little as 0.1 per cent (in 1975 and 1981) but the average annual use of external finance for reserves was about 0.9 per cent of GDP over the whole period.

On the sources side, net official transfers have been of negligible importance. Net direct investment has been consistently between 0.8 and the 1981 peak of 1.1 per cent of GDP a year over the whole period. The principal source of finance since 1969 has been net MLT lending; in the period 1973–81, it accounted for 80 per cent of the net availability of external finance. Figure 5.1 illustrates, however, that the predominance of debt financing is not just a recent phenomenon. There has been a rising trend to the inflow from foreign borrowing since 1968.

For the market borrowers then, balance-of-payments analysis for 1968–81 reflects their maturity in external financing and establishes that

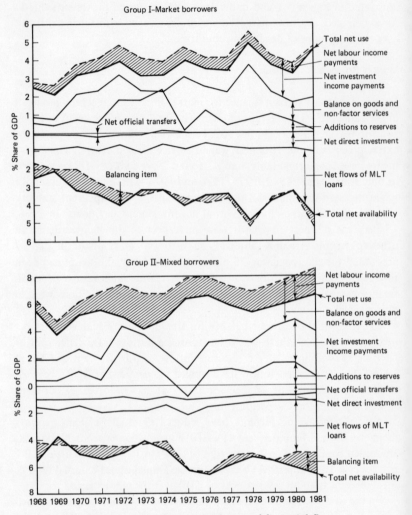

FIGURE 5.1   *Sources and uses of financial flows*

(i) MLT borrowing has consolidated its position as the dominant source of external finance; (ii) net service payments on foreign investment have been the most stable and largest users of external finance; (iii) the composition of capital—service payments has changed, with the share of direct investment falling from 75 to 25 per cent of the total; and (iv) the annual supplement to domestic resource availability provided by external finance

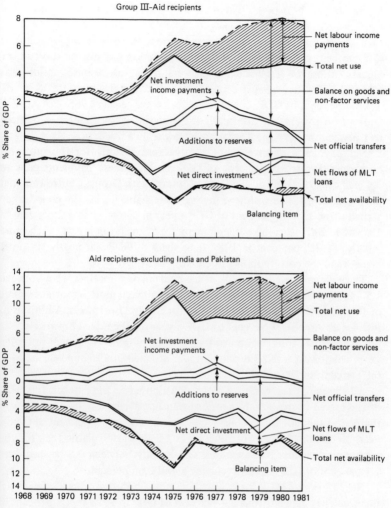

FIGURE 5.1 (continued) *Sources and uses of financial flows*

has been a modest 1.3 per cent, but it has increased by almost one percentage point of GDP a year during the adjustment period since 1974.

Mixed Borrowers – Group II

External finance has consistently supported a substantial resource inflow for the mixed borrowers. The very different circumstances of individual countries within the group mean that the uses and sources of finances for each differ very widely; but, for the group, the lowest resource inflow (2.8 per cent of GDP in 1969) during the period was not far short of the highest inflow to the market borrowers. The peak resource inflow was achieved in 1975 – 6.9 per cent of GDP; the annual average for 1975–81 was 4.4 per cent of GDP, compared with 3.6 per cent in 1968–73. As with Group I borrowers, the aftermath of the oil shock saw an increase of close to 1 per cent in the annual resource inflow from abroad.

Net payments of investment income rose steadily for this group of borrowers. From 1.5 per cent of GDP in 1968 these payments grew to 3.4 per cent of GDP in 1981. By contrast with Group I borrowers, net payments of direct investment income were stable during the period; they actually rose from 1 per cent of GDP a year in 1969–71 to 1.2 per cent in 1979–81. But other investment income payments increased much more rapidly; at 2.3 per cent in 1981 their share of GDP was nearly six times higher than the corresponding figure in 1968.

Through most of the 1970s, net labour income receipts were between 1.5 and 2 per cent of GDP a year; they were a much more important source of foreign exchange for Group II than for Group I borrowers. Additions to reserves absorbed 0.9 per cent of GDP a year for the mixed borrowers. Net use of external capital was consistently in the range 5–6 per cent of GDP a year. The lowest level, 3.8 per cent was attained in 1969 and the highest, 6.6 per cent, in 1976 and 1981.

All the major categories of flows contributed to the external financing of the mixed borrowers. Net official transfers declined in importance over the period falling from around 1 per cent to about 0.75 per cent of GDP a year. Net direct investment flows were a little more volatile than for the market participants but were still consistently between 0.5 per cent and 1.1 per cent of GDP a year, averaging about 0.66 per cent.

Net inflows of MLT loans were the most important source of external finance. They ranged from 2.4 per cent of GDP in 1973 to 4.8 per cent in 1976, and averaged around 3.5 per cent a year for the period. Since 1974, term loans have met over 60 per cent of the mixed borrowers' requirements of external finance. For this group, the balancing item is consistently positive, reflecting the importance of short-term debt as a source of funds. It provided more than 20 per cent of available external finance in two years, including 1981.

The lessons from balance-of-payments analysis for 1968–81 for the mixed borrowers are that: (i) MLT debt financing has been the predominant source of external finance over the whole period; (ii) net official transfers and direct investment have both been stable sources of external finance, jointly providing about 1.5 per cent of GDP a year; (iii) short-term debt has been a consistent source of external capital; (iv) service payments on foreign-owned capital have risen sharply as a share of GDP, with most of the rise attributable to interest payments; and (v) the annual resource inflow supported by external finance has been substantial — about 4 per cent of GDP a year.

Aid Recipients — Group III

Analysis of the balance-of-payments data for these borrowers is handicapped by the lack of complete time series for most countries. As well, the impact of India and Pakistan on the group is so large that their exclusion changes the picture considerably. Accordingly, Figure 5.1 illustrates the balance-of-payments experience of the whole group and the group without India and Pakistan.[14] In general, retaining India and Pakistan in the group tends to reduce the uses and sources of external finance as a share of GDP without changing the underlying trends of the component items.

On the uses side, net resource inflow jumped in the period 1975—81 to 6.3 per cent of GDP a year (11.7 per cent, excluding India and Pakistan), compared with 1.8 per cent a year (4.0 per cent, excluding India and Pakistan) in 1968—73. The deterioration of their economies after 1974 led the aid-recipients into a much greater dependence on foreign resource inflow, despite which the growth of most of them has been very disappointing during this period. In part, the increased absorption of foreign resources has been supported by the strong growth of net labour income receipts. For all the countries, these now amount to more than 3 per cent of GDP a year (1979—81), compared with 0.2 per cent a year (1969—71); excluding India and Pakistan, corresponding figures are 4.9 and 0.1 per cent.

By contrast with the other groups, net investment income payments by aid-recipients have declined steadily as a proportion of GDP over the observation period. This reflects both the net asset position of these borrowers with BIS banks and the low levels of direct investment in their economies. Additions to reserves have absorbed a low share of external finance, excepting 1976 for India and Pakistan, 1972 and 1973 for the sub-group, and 1977 for all countries.

The net use of external finance averaged 4.6 per cent of GDP a year in 1975—81, up from 2.4 per cent in 1968—73; excluding India and Pakistan, the corresponding figures are 8.6 and 4.8 per cent. The pattern is the same as for the market and mixed borrowers, but net use of external finance is substantially higher if India and Pakistan are excluded from the other aid-recipients. When these economies are included, use is intermediate between borrowers in Group I and Group II. The acceleration in foreign resource use predated the oil shock and coincided with an upturn in official grants and concessional lending in 1972.

Except for 1979, net direct investment flows have been a negligible source of external finance, though they have risen in importance since 1976. The preponderance of external financing has been divided — almost equally — between official grants and (mostly concessional) lending; grants have been more important if India and Pakistan are excluded. For the group excluding India and Pakistan, official grants provided 4.4 per cent of GDP a year in 1975–81, compared with 2.8 per cent in 1968–73, and foreign borrowing provided 3.5 per cent of GDP a year in the latter period, compared with 1.5 per cent in the earlier. With India and Pakistan included, the rise in debt-financing is not so marked between the two periods, reflecting the longer-term involvement of official lenders in these two economies.

For aid-recipients, the general conclusions of the analysis are that (i) grants and loans jointly have met the rising need for external finance; (ii) net labour income payments have been an increasingly important source of foreign exchange earnings; and (iii) service payments on foreign investment have been a declining share of the uses of foreign finance, notwithstanding the debt-management difficulties of some of the countries in the group.

Overall, this analysis establishes the rise in the external financing needs of all the groups of the developing economies in the adjustment period of the 1970s and the importance of external borrowing in supporting resource inflow. Loans are the principal source of development finance. Net direct investment flows are barely sufficient to cover service payments on prior investment. Grants are important for the mixed borrowers and for the aid recipients, but debt is of equal or greater importance for each of these groups. The conclusion is that if net inflows of foreign resources are important in promoting growth and development, then external borrowing is, and has been, the principal vehicle through which these benefits are conveyed to a developing economy.

III THE CHANGING FACE OF DEBT FINANCING AND THE CENTRAL ROLE OF THE BANKS: 1970–81

The primacy of debt capital in development finance and the stepped-up resource inflow to all groups of developing countries since 1974 raise questions about how long the process can continue. The algebra of foreign borrowing is well-established.[15] To maintain a positive net transfer of resources through foreign borrowing the growth of debt must exceed the interest rate. This was clearly the case for most borrowers throughout the 1970s but with the slowdown of borrowing and high interest rates – at least for market borrowing – in 1981–3, the necessary conditions for a net resource inflow may not now be met. This depends on the terms of borrowing, which in turn are largely determined by the source of the loans. Most lending from official sources is on much softer terms than lending from the financial markets. As well as its growth, the structure of debt therefore becomes important; differential terms imply different gross borrowing requirements for a given net transfer of resources.

Data from the DRS track developments in the MLT debt of the groups of developing countries discussed above. These developments should compare closely with the net flow data shown on the balance-of-payments accounts. But there will be differences; the main one results from the exclusion of the asset position of developing countries in the DRS. A consequence is that the capital inflow from MLT is overstated by DRS data.[16]

Data from the DRS reveal clearly the changing patterns of lending to developing countries between 1970, the first year for which comprehensive data are available, and 1981, the last such year. For market borrowers, MLT debt grew from $27 billion in 1970 to $238 billion in 1981, a trend rate (by least squares) of 23 per cent a year. Debt from private sources grew by 25 per cent a year; that from official sources grew by 13 per cent a year. For the mixed borrowers, debt was $23 billion in 1970 and grew to $154 billion in 1981 – or a trend rate of 20 per cent a year. Debt from both private and official sources grew by 20 per cent a year. The aid-recipients' debt was $16 billion in 1970 and $70 billion in 1981, a trend growth of only 15 per cent a year. The trend growth of debt from both private and official sources was 15 per cent a year.

Hence, the groups' shares in the total debt of developing countries have changed considerably over the decade. The market borrowers' debt increased from 41 per cent of the total in 1970 to over half of the debt in 1981. The mixed borrowers' share fell from 35 to 33 per cent, and there was a sharp fall in the aid-recipients' share – from 25 per cent of the debt in 1970 to less than 17 per cent in 1981. In the light of the balance-of-payments data analysed earlier, these movements appear somewhat paradoxical; the much more rapid growth in the debt of market borrowers was associated with a comparatively small expansion in the net flows to them when measured in GDP terms.

An obvious part of the explanation is the higher GDP of the market borrowers relative to the initial level of debt, but another important factor is the initial composition of debt, and the differential growth of borrowing from private sources, essentially on market terms, compared with borrowing from official sources, generally on subsidised terms. The importance of borrowing from private sources in the overall debt picture for the groups of countries is illustrated in Figures 5.2 and 5.3.

The continuous lines in Figure 5.2 refer to the left-hand axis and show the evolving shares of private-source in total debt of the groups of developing countries.[17] For the market borrowers, almost 70 per cent of debt in 1970 was from private sources and the share increased steadily to 87 per cent in 1981. Over the same period, disbursements of loans from private sources rose from 82 to 92 per cent. The higher share and generally harder terms of private-source debt have necessitated a comparatively rapid growth of debt to support a rise in resource inflow (as a share of GDP).

By contrast, the very low service-costs of official capital and the high proportion of debt from official sources have enabled the aid-recipients to enjoy a substantial increase in net inflows of loan capital during the

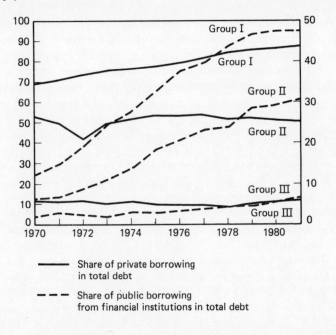

Source: DRS

FIGURE 5.2   *Share of private debt and of public debt to financial institutions in total debt, 1970–81 (percentages)*

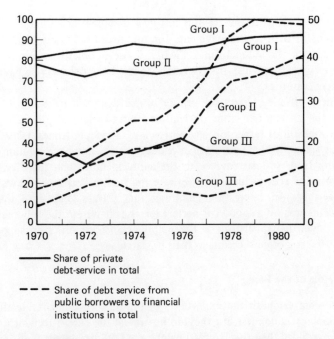

Share of private
debt-service in total

Share of debt service from
public borrowers to financial
institutions in total

Source: DRS

FIGURE 5.3 *Share of debt service payments to private sources and to financial institutions from public borrowers, 1970–81 (percentages)*

1970s with comparatively slow growth in debt. For aid-recipients, the share of debt from private sources peaked at 11.5 per cent in 1981 (see Figure 5.2) and it has been very stable, lying in a range of 9–11 per cent during the period.

Somewhat surprisingly, given the large number of countries in Group II that are major borrowers, the share of private source in total debt also has been stable for the mixed borrowers, but while the share has moved comparatively narrowly (a range of 42–54 per cent) the stability is suspect. A decline in the share of concessional lending from bilateral creditors (from 33 per cent in 1970 to 23 per cent in 1981) has been offset partially by a rising share for multilateral lending and for official (bilateral) capital on market terms. Although public borrowing from private sources has increased strongly over the period (as discussed later) estimates of private borrowing from private sources show a sharply declining share, thus slowing the overall rise in the share of private debt.

The solid lines and left-hand axis of Figure 5.3 show the importance of private-source debt in debt-service payments. The shares are again fairly stable for Groups II and III. But private-source debt accounts for 72–78 per cent of debt-service payments for the mixed borrowers, and 30–41 per cent for the aid-recipients. Clearly, a rise in borrowing from private sources would add disproportionately to the total debt-service payments of these countries.

These differing shares for private source debt and debt-service result from the differential terms on lending from official and private sources. The evolution of terms for new borrowing is shown in Annex Table 5A.3. Terms generally hardened during the decade – the notable exception is for lending from official sources to the aid-recipients – and the divergence between the cost of funds from private and from officials sources widened appreciably. An interesting feature is that private lending to the aid-recipients was on as good (or better) terms as it was to the other groups. The principal explanation is the preponderance of officially supported suppliers' and buyers' credits in their private loans.

The Role of the Banks

These data establish the importance of private source in total lending to developing economies, but they do not reveal the extent to which banks have expanded their role. Unfortunately, the DRS has detailed information only on the public and publicly guaranteed debt of the developing countries. A substantial proportion of the borrowing of many countries is by private borrowers without government guarantee; the principal sources are commercial banks, suppliers and parent companies.[18] Specifically, of the market borrowers' total debt, private non-guaranteed debt has accounted for between 25 and 40 per cent in 1970–81. A guess would be that around 80 per cent of it is owed to banks. The mixed borrowers' private non-guaranteed debt has been about half as important (a range of 11–26 per cent of total debt), and for aid-recipients it has been negligible – no more than 1 per cent of total debt. Estimates indicate a declining role for non-guaranteed debt, a reflection of the increasing creditworthiness of public borrowers for loans from private sources and, possibly, of a systematic tendency to underestimate non-guaranteed debt in recent years or to overestimate it in earlier years.

Recognising that the exclusion of private non-guaranteed debt understates the importance of bank lending while, at least for market participants, overstating its growth, the right-hand axes and the broken lines of Figures 5.2 and 5.3 illustrate the dominant role of bank lending to public borrowers in the overall growth of developing countries' debt. For market borrowers, public debt owed to banks increased from $3 billion to $113 billion between 1970 and 1981, a trend rate of almost 40 per cent a year. As a result, the share of this debt in the total rose from 12 to 47 per cent (Figure 5.2) and of debt-service payments in the total from 17 to 48 per cent (Figure 5.3). About eight percentage points of the gain in the banks' share of public debt stems from the decline in the share of suppliers' credit, so there has been a pronounced shift within private lending to the banks and away from suppliers and bond-holders, as well as a shift from official to private lenders.

For mixed borrowers, the stability of the share of private in total debt disguises the explosion of bank-lending to them. In 1970, their public debt owed to financial institutions was just over a billion dollars; by 1981, it was $47 billion – a trend growth of 40 per cent a year. Figure 5.2 shows public borrowing from financial institutions rising from 6 per cent of total debt in 1970 to 30 per cent in 1981. As with Group I countries, bank-lending gained relative to suppliers' credits and bonds. The debt-service payments made to banks by public borrowers have increased similarly – from 9 per cent of the total in 1970 to 41 per cent in 1981.

Only for the aid-recipients has the role of bank-lending remained a small part of the debt picture, and even for these countries lending from the banks has grown by 28 per cent a year.[19] From $283 million in 1970, public debt from the banks rose to $4.4 billion in 1981; that is an increase from 2 per cent to more than 6 per cent of the total debt. Debt-service payments to the banks rose from 5 to 14 per cent of the total during the same period.

The increasing importance of bank-lending has far-reaching implications for the debt-management strategies of developing countries. Bank loans cost more than most other forms of borrowing and the costs have been rising during the decade. Unfortunately, DRS data do not permit a disaggregation of bank lending into its two main components: buyers' credits, generally officially supported and for the purchase of specific goods; and financial credits, including both direct loans and syndications, which provide free foreign exchange. Variable interest rates are rising in frequency for all private loans but, while they are almost universal for financial credits, large volumes of buyers' credits are still extended at fixed rates.

For these reasons, the trend in the costs of borrowing from the banks are difficult to discern. The changing composition of loans obscures the underlying cost of borrowing each type of loan. Difficulties are caused also by the variety of currencies that are borrowed; interest rates are currency specific and exhibit wide differentials. This said, the terms of bank-lending to public borrowers in the groups of developing countries are shown in Table 5.2. Other than the tendency for interest rates to rise

TABLE 5.2 Average terms on bank lending to public borrowers: selected years: 1971–81[a] (per cent, years)

	1971	1973	1975	1977	1978	1979	1980	1981
Group I								
Interest Rate (%)	7.8	9.8	8.9	8.2	10.3	12.4	13.5	16.2
Maturity (years)	6.8	11.4	6.6	7.3	8.5	8.5	8.1	8.1
Grace Period (years)	2.7	4.7	2.6	3.0	3.9	4.1	3.7	3.4
Group II								
Interest Rate (%)	7.5	9.9	9.1	8.1	9.8	11.8	13.6	14.3
Maturity (years)	9.5	9.4	7.8	8.1	9.5	9.1	9.1	9.5
Grace Period (years)	2.2	3.1	2.7	2.8	3.3	3.4	3.2	3.5
Group III								
Interest Rate (%)	7.1	8.1	9.3	7.4	10.8	10.2	12.2	13.2
Maturity (years)	4.0	9.2	12.3	8.2	9.0	10.8	9.5	7.9
Grace Period (years)	1.6	2.1	2.0	2.6	2.8	2.6	2.9	2.3

[a] Terms on loan commitments in year indicated.

for all groups of countries, there are few regularities. An exception is that grace periods are longest for market participants, followed by mixed borrowers and then aid-recipients. Probably this stems from the larger share of syndicated loans in the borrowing of the more creditworthy countries. A notable feature of the data is that aid recipients do not pay higher interest rates nor do they face shorter maturities. This may indicate a higher proportion of buyers' credits in lending than for the other groups, but the currency composition of borrowing and favourable terms for isolated, large, market issues could be equally important explanatory factors.

To summarise, these data show how private lending, especially from the commercial banks, has been the driving force behind the increased resource inflow to developing countries during the economic adjustment phase of the middle and late 1970s. By 1981, around 75 per cent of new commitments to the market borrowers was from banks; for the mixed borrowers the figure was more than 40 per cent; and for the aid-recipients only 5 per cent. A benefit of this inflow was an enhanced ability to maintain comparatively high growth. Not all countries adjusted, however; some have maintained excessive consumption and inefficient investment programmes, with the result that debt-servicing problems of sufficient severity to compel countries to re-schedule their external debt have been frequent occurrences in the early 1980s. The cost of loans from banks is high compared with other forms of loan capital – and it has risen steadily, latterly even in real terms. The prospect that the elevated participation of banks in development finance will be sustained, and indeed increase, throughout the 1980s has important implications for debt-management to which we now turn.

IV MANAGING DEVELOPING COUNTRIES' DEBT

The policy implications of the rise in developing countries' external debt and their continuing need for an inflow of foreign resources are clear. To maintain the required flow of lending, market participants must establish creditworthiness as a central policy objective; the potential disruption to their economies resulting from even a partial exclusion from the financial markets would be great. Their expanding role in global trade and finance ensures that the external sector will exercise a strong constraining influence on their policy options during the 1980s.

The aid-recipients have much less autonomy in controlling the inflow of external resources; throughout the 1980s the supply will depend on official aid. All their external borrowing has the potential to create debt-management difficulties.

For the mixed borrowers, a crucial problem is to maintain an appropriate balance in financial inflows. As they continue to raise their borrowing from the banking sector, they must take steps to secure their credit-worthiness. At the same time, they need to maintain access to official flows on appropriate terms to support infrastructure investment and other long-lived development projects.

Simulations prepared for this paper show that an inflow of resources associated with MLT borrowing comparable to, or even greater than, the inflows of the 1970s could be sustained throughout the 1980s, without leading to evidently unmanageable levels of debt and debt service. The results of one of these simulations are described here.[20]

Key assumptions are provided in Table 5.3 and the results are shown in Table 5.4. The most important assumption is that access to finance is not disrupted. The simulation takes as inputs the DRS projected disbursements against committed but undisbursed loans and the projected debt-service payments against all outstanding debt; the average terms of borrowing from 1979–81 as the terms on new loans; and the levels of commitments in 1981 as the base for new borrowing. For the simulation, GDP growth was projected at the trend rate for 1971–81 and commitment growth was projected as shown in the table. The growth assumptions are arbitrary and, in particular, they take no account of the effects of falling inflation. They are felt to be reasonable, however, and, within sensible limits, the results were not sensitive to growth-rate changes. The obvious impact of adjusting GDP growth relative to growth in borrowing was a fall-off (or rise) in external capital inflows measured as a share of GDP.

Comparing Table 5.4 with Annex Table 5A.2 shows that, under the assumptions in Table 5,3, net flows and net transfers in the 1980s are comparable to those in the 1970s. They tend to be lower for the market borrowers and higher for the aid-recipients. For Group I and Group II borrowers net transfers recover from the depressed levels of 1981–82 to peak around the middle of the decade and then stabilise; for the aid-recipients (which include India and Pakistan) the high growth projected for official loans permits a rising net transfer throughout the decade.

The debt-service obligations associated with the scenario would be highest for the market borrowers — reflecting the high and rising share of their finance from private sources — but even for this group, it would fall from 5 per cent of GDP in 1982 to 4 per cent in the mid-1980s before rising again to just over 5 per cent in 1990 (see Annex Table 5A.4 for details). For the mixed borrowers, debt-service would fluctuate more narrowly between a 'high' of 4.8 per cent of GDP in 1982 and 1990 and a 'low' of 4.3 per cent in 1984. For aid-recipients, again reflecting the rapid

TABLE 5.3 *Key data and assumptions for projected borrowing: 1982–90*

	Trend growth 1971–81[a] (per cent per year)			Projected growth 1982–90 (per cent per year)			Projected terms 1982–90[b]		
	Commitments	Debt	GDP	Commitments	Debt	GDP	Interest (percent)	Maturity (years)	Grace (years)
Market Borrowers									
Official loans	12	13⎫	19	10	16⎫	19	8	15	4
Private loans	24	26⎭		20	22⎭		14	9	4
Mixed Borrowers									
Official loans	20	20⎫	17	15	17⎫	17	6	21	6
Private loans	19	20⎭		20	20⎭		12	10	3
Aid Recipients[c]									
Official loans	17	15⎫	13	20	15⎫	13	3	31	7
Private loans	21	15⎭		10	13⎭		10	11	2

a By least squares.

b Based on Average Terms for new loans: 1979–81.

c For acid recipients, the implausibly high trend rate for the growth of private debt in the 1980s reflects the high level of private-source commitments in 1981 (largely influenced by India's borrowing in the syndicated-loan market). If the growth rates of commitments are lowered – to 15 per cent a year for official loans and 5 per cent for private – the trend growth rates for official and private debt fall to 13 and 10 per cent respectively. Further results of this change are that, in 1990, debt falls to 18 per cent (from 21 per cent) of GDP and the net transfer falls to 1.8 per cent (from 2.7 per cent – see Table 5.4) of GDP.

TABLE 5.4 *Projected net flows and net transfers of medium- and long-term loans to groups of developing countries, 1982–90 (percentages of GDP)*

	1982	1983	1984	1985	1986	1987	1988	1989	1990
Group I									
Net Flows[a]									
Official	0.5	0.7	0.6	0.5	0.4	0.3	0.3	0.2	0.2
Private	2.1	2.8	3.8	4.3	3.9	3.6	3.6	3.5	3.4
Total	2.6	3.5	4.4	4.8	4.3	3.9	3.8	3.7	3.6
Net Transfers[b]									
Official	0.3	0.5	0.4	0.3	0.2	0.1	0.1	0.1	0.0
Private	−0.1	0.8	1.7	2.1	1.6	1.2	1.2	1.1	1.0
Total	0.3	1.3	2.1	2.4	1.8	1.4	1.2	1.1	1.0
Group II									
Net Flows									
Official	2.2	2.8	2.6	2.3	2.1	2.1	2.0	2.0	1.9
Private	1.8	2.1	2.6	2.7	2.6	2.6	2.7	2.7	2.8
Total	4.0	4.9	5.1	5.0	4.8	4.7	4.7	4.7	4.7
Net Transfers									
Official	1.6	2.1	1.8	1.6	1.4	1.4	1.3	1.2	1.2
Private	0.3	0.7	1.1	1.2	1.1	1.1	1.1	1.1	1.1
Total	1.9	2.8	3.0	2.8	2.5	2.4	2.3	2.3	2.3
Group III									
Net Flows									
Official	1.9	2.0	2.3	2.4	2.4	2.6	2.8	3.0	3.1
Private	0.1	0.3	0.3	0.3	0.3	0.3	0.2	0.2	0.2
Total	1.9	2.3	2.6	2.7	2.7	2.8	3.0	3.2	3.4
Net Transfers									
Official	1.4	1.6	1.8	1.9	2.0	2.1	2.3	2.5	2.7
Private	−0.1	0.1	0.2	0.1	0.1	0.1	0.0	0.0	0.0
Total	1.3	1.7	2.0	2.1	2.0	2.2	2.4	2.5	2.7

[a] Net flows are defined as (gross) disbursements less repayment of principal.
[b] Net transfers are net flows less interest payments.

growth of official lending, projected debt-service would decline from 1.8 per cent of GDP in 1982 to 1.5 per cent in 1990.

These debt-service obligations seem very manageable, barring a disruption of lending. Hence, the conclusion from this exercise is that foreign lending could continue to provide a substantial resource inflow to developing countries during the 1980s. Especially for market borrowers, however, the potential for difficulty in managing debt will increase as the decade progresses. And the current disturbed lending conditions could jeopardise development-financing in the longer term; they have interrupted the flow of development finance in 1980–1 and there is no guarantee that lending at the rates projected here will resume in 1982 or thereafter.

Securing the benefits from foreign resource inflow requires that severe economic disruption resulting from the servicing of foreign-owned assets is avoided. Allowing for the four reasons for accumulating external debt described at the beginning of this chapter in practice explicit optimising behaviour in foreign borrowing often is ruled out. Most analyses of external borrowing are concerned with the robustness of the developing economies' debt-servicing capacity. The major concern of many creditors and also of some analysts working with governments of developing countries is not whether a particular borrowing strategy is optimal in some sense but whether it is sustainable.

Most analyses based on a simple growth model are of this nature: for a certain growth rate a developing economy needs a certain level of resources from abroad. The question is, can the resources provided by foreign borrowing be used productively enough to service the debt? Aliber (1980) has analysed two aspects of the sustainability of servicing debt, which he terms the liquidity and the solvency problems. In the short-term, a viable borrowing strategy can be put at risk by a shortage of foreign exchange to service the debt. In the longer term, debt cannot be serviced if the external resources do not produce enough domestic resources to meet the service obligations. Unlike firms, countries can be insolvent without being bankrupt; the income foregone in servicing the debt simply exceeds what was made available by the act of borrowing.[21]

For governments, a more appropriate terminology for these two threats to sustainability might be the transfer risk and the budgetary risk respectively. An important distinction is that the government can experience a liquidity or transfer problem in debt-management because of the service obligations of other domestic borrowers as well as those on its own (and its guaranteed) debt; but the budgetary problem affects only the public debt.[22] In many countries, especially when a domestic economic boom runs into an export shortfall, private borrowers have been able to deposit the required local currency payments with the central bank, and the external liability has then become the government's when a shortage of foreign exchange has prohibited the payment to the foreign creditor.

Both problems for debt management apply to each of our three groups of countries. A liquidity or transfer crisis is arguably more acute for countries that must roll-over high proportions of their debt. The short maturities of bank-lending point to difficulties of this kind for the market participants; but the emergence of such a crisis is probably less likely for countries that are familiar to private creditors, unless there is a sudden decline in confidence in the sustainability of their economic policies.[23] In practice, many Group I countries can cope with high debt-service ratios quite easily; but Group III countries, which borrow mainly official money for designated purposes, have less flexibility in apportioning the funds they receive from abroad, and so can experience serious debt-management problems at comparatively low levels of debt-service payments relative to exports.

The remainder of this Chapter is concerned with some of the issues in the management of external debt. No attempt is made to survey the theoretical literature; rather, the concern is to outline the stages of debt-management, as perceived in a practical and institutional sense by the External Debt Division of the World Bank, and to highlight within each of the stages the relevant issues for each group of developing countries.

Stages in the Debt Management Process

There are three interconnected stages in managing external debt. They are: (i) knowing the debt; (ii) deciding how much to borrow; and (iii) selecting financing techniques. Except for simple data-gathering, no stage can proceed without the others. For example, the borrowing decision depends on current indebtedness and on the available sources of finance. Similarly, financing techniques will depend on how much is to be borrowed and the volume and distribution of outstanding liabilities. The critical action is the decision to borrow abroad, but the decision can be made rationally only if the knowledge provided by the other stages is in place.

Knowing the Debt

A major concern of the World Bank lies in ensuring that a country has detailed knowledge of its debt. There are three major benefits from this. The first, obviously, is that future borrowing decisions are informed by accurate knowledge of the external obligations associated with past borrowings. A second is that countries which meet their obligations as they fall due enhance their reputations for sound debt-management. Costs of borrowing are lowered by eliminating interest and other penalties for late payments, by reducing management fees and (sometimes) spreads, and by lowering prices for goods bought on credit from suppliers. By increasing creditor confidence, access to finance is raised and stabilised. The third, which until recently was so unthinkable that it carried little weight when exhorting a country to improve its debt-monitoring systems, is that countries are in a much stronger position to re-negotiate their debt if they do encounter debt-servicing difficulties. Countries in less serious straits are in a much stronger position to re-finance their debt on advantageous terms.

The DRS of the World Bank requires that all its borrowers report their public debt on a loan-by-loan basis, with commitments reported quarterly and an annual update of transactions on all outstanding loans. Countries are also encouraged strongly to report (usually in aggregated form) the status of the non-guaranteed debt of the private sector. The requirement covers all loans of original maturity exceeding twelve months. Unfortunately, many countries report their public debt inaccurately, incompletely and late, and only a few report non-guaranteed debt. The data that are collected are published annually (for the end of the previous year) in *World Debt Tables*.

Data deficiencies are common to all three groups of countries and affect the debt-management policies of all three groups adversely. A presumption for market participants is that their more diversified and larger economies could reduce the need for good information as external borrowing should adapt itself to the policies adopted for the domestic economy. The difficulties of some of the strongest economies in Group I should reduce the cogency of this argument. Some Group I members have poor debt-reporting and monitoring mechanisms that will need to be strengthened considerably if their increasing debt to private sources is to be managed successfully.

The presumption that many of the mixed borrowers and the aid-recipients have weak debt-monitoring and reporting systems is sound. There is a close correlation between countries that have re-scheduled and weak reporting systems (though bad policy – partly stemming from bad, or no, data – has been the critical element). Many countries with poor statistical systems have avoided debt-servicing crises, however; in some cases, the information available from official creditors has been sufficient to prevent borrowers from losing control of their foreign debt.

Choosing How Much to Borrow

Existing policy models provide developing countries with very little guidance on how to play a borrowing strategy. For those aid-recipients that depend almost entirely on official lending on highly concessional terms a sound rule of thumb is to borrow whatever is available; but this advice breaks down as soon as they borrow at market terms, or when the constraint on supply is removed.

The three policy areas that are related most closely to external borrowing are domestic monetary policy, fiscal policy – specifically, the public investment programme and associated policies for raising revenue – and exchange rate policy. Most existing models of foreign borrowing neglect the essential interconnectedness of these policy decisions and, indeed, they are not well designed to deal with them.

Some recent contributions attempt to rectify this omission. Aliber (1982) considers the problems of balance-of-payments managers in an economy that has the potential for significant private borrowing from abroad. This analysis, which should be of most relevance to the market participants of Group I, points to the constraints on domestic policy imposed by external borrowing needs. To change investors' willingness to acquire external debt, policy-makers can influence the differential between domestic and foreign interest rates or their expectations about future movements in the exchange rate. Either policy change (e.g. raising domestic interest rates or depreciating the exchange rate) will affect domestic expenditure and investment.

In a series of papers, Kharas (1981a, b, and c) has related the foreign borrowing decision to associated domestic policy requirements and structural changes in the economy. He emphasises the importance of foreign borrowing to the public investment programme and the associated need for an expansion of revenue through an increase in the tax base. Here, solvency — or avoiding the budgetary problem — must be ensured by the government's willingness to raise taxes. His analysis appeals as being particularly relevant to Group II and Group III countries that borrow heavily to support public investment projects. Here, the decision to borrow requires particular attention to raising additional revenues for debt-servicing obligations. This is the more necessary because the predominantly project-supporting finance provided by official lenders generally will not contribute directly to meeting current debt-servicing needs.

Other recent contributions have emphasised supply constraints on the borrowing decision. Eaton and Gersowitz (1981a and b) have emphasised the analogy between the expropriation of direct investment assets and the repudiation of debt. They argue that creditors will restrict lending to an amount that ensures that a country's losses from the denial of access to markets after debt-repudiation would exceed the benefits from eliminating debt-service obligations. Sachs (1982, pp. 21—2) in discussion their work, points to the possibility that strict conditions for re-negotiating debt can work to the benefit of both creditors and borrowers by raising the amount creditors will lend before the fear of repudiation becomes operative.

The Sachs point, in practice, may have worked to some developing countries' detriment. Provisions for re-scheduling debt, rather than default, appear to have encouraged official agencies in creditor countries to support inflows of suppliers' and buyers' credits beyond the capacity of countries, especially Group II and Group III, to meet the service obligations. The elimination of 'moral hazard' through insurance could cause suppliers and banks to neglect the economic returns on the projects for which, and the policies of the governments to which, they lend. In a period of heightened need for external finance and a slowdown in the growth of official support, many governments will borrow beyond prudent limits if export credits are offered. For the debt manager, the problem is to explain to governments the paradox that an export credit at 8 or 10 per cent below market interest rates may not be a bargain.

In the absence of explicit policy models, the advisor must fall back on more or less *ad hoc* admonitions to governments.[24] The IMF (1982) has found a close correlation between sudden increases in borrowing from the markets and subsequent debt-management difficulties. To avoid problems, a useful rule of thumb for all governments is to follow a year of sharply higher borrowing by a consolidation, if not a retrenchment. Beyond that, other qualitative advice can be offered.[25] Particularly for the market borrowers, economic policies should maintain the confidence of external investors. Official flows tend to be fairly stable; private flows can be very volatile and the overhang of short-term obligations can complicate the problem of rolling-over maturing loans and borrowing sufficient for current needs. For them, in the three key policy areas already identified, this means (i) avoid subsidising foreign borrowing and maintain realistic differentials between domestic and foreign interest rates; (ii) avoid discriminating between tradable and non-tradable goods and maintain an exchange rate that provides incentives to producing for export or import replacement; and (iii) avoid subsidies to domestic consumers and investors and adopt taxation policies which generate the revenues required to service the debt resulting from public investment.

Selecting Financing Techniques

How much to borrow depends very largely on what can be borrowed. If a country has access to a large volume of funds on highly concessional terms, then domestic absorptive capacity — meaning the supply of complementary, investible domestic resources — may constrain the borrowing decision, rather than the debt-servicing capacity.

This is not a major consideration for the market borrowers. All their finance will be borrowed at market terms and their financing techniques are concerned with such things as currency exposure, timing of issues, negotiation of spreads and the management of outstanding issues, including exercising re-financing and prepayment options and supporting the secondary market, where relevant. For some of these countries, the volume of borrowing requirements measured against total flows through markets is significant so they also must take account of supply conditions; if major banks already hold substantial amounts of their paper, their ability to expand borrowing may be constrained even if their economies are performing well. Borrowing problems can be complicated by large amounts of short-term debt and, as Mexico's recent problems indicate, weakness in the economy can create severe management difficulties when large amounts of maturing loans must be re-financed at the same time that new funds are needed.

Notwithstanding their current problems, many of the Group I countries are already very sophisticated in their market management. There is no lack of advice in the banking community to assist them, but most have an indigenous capability for exploiting advantageous market conditions. Among these countries, Brazil took advantage of favourable market conditions in 1978 to restructure its debt and so eliminate a concentration of repayments in 1982–3. Mexico acted similarly in 1979, obtaining fine terms on a large volume of re-financed loans. Venezuela has exploited the oil-price increases to consolidate huge amounts of short-term debt into longer maturities at very favourable terms.

For the mixed borrowers of Group II, similar considerations apply to their loans from banks. But an additional concern is to ensure that debt from private sources provides as much leverage as possible. Most projects are financed by a mix of equity and debt, the latter consisting of a combination of loans from official sources, and from private sources with and without official support. To gain the maximum resource inflow from their debt-servicing capability these countries must obtain as much 'cheap financing' as possible to accompany the minimum amount of borrowing (usually around 15 per cent of the value of the project) at private market rates. Many Group II countries have learned to exploit the ready availability of officially-supported export credits in combination with a minimum amount of market-term borrowing.

The aid-recipients of Group III find their flexibility constrained by their limited debt-servicing capacity. They must be very cautious in expanding their borrowing on market terms. The fact that much of the official finance they do obtain is tied to specific imports or projects is one reason why they experience debt-management difficulties at much lower debt-service ratios than is the case for Group I, or the more creditworthy Group II countries.

Advising Developing Countries

In all groups, there are countries which can benefit from external advice on their debt-management options. Indeed, the troubles of the past few years have led to a sharply increased demand for these services by the developing countries. An interesting development is the number of countries now employing merchant banks to advise on debt management, though, in most cases, the banks have been called in to help countries to prepare for a re-negotiation of their debt. A major portion of the advisors' input has been devoted to data gathering, a function in which the scope for duplication of the activities of the international agencies is high.

The longer-term roles of the agencies that advise countries remain to be determined. As noted earlier, the World Bank has been principally concerned to ensure that countries have good data on their outstanding medium- and long-term liabilities. The countries, however, increasingly request advice on debt-management policy and on the establishment of computerised systems for monitoring loan transactions and generating reports for policy-makers. The Bank's longer-term commitment to maintaining debt data in developing countries does not preclude the beneficial involvement of other agencies — especially during crises — but, as much of their work is done on a one-shot contractual basis, there is a need to ensure the continuation of benefits to the countries when the contract terminates.

The rise in demand for debt-management advice is not a transitory phenomenon related to the current economic difficulties of many developing countries. The involvement of banks in lending to the developing countries probably will necessitate specialised assistance in managing debt and in techniques of financing throughout this decade. The expectation is that the major responsibility for monitoring debt will devolve to the international organisations, and that for advising on financing techniques to representatives of the banking community. The problem of how much to borrow will remain a grey area pending much better policy analyses of the impacts of borrowing on domestic policy actions. Developing countries will continue to exercise this decision subject to the constraints imposed on Groups II and III by the availability of official funds, and on Group I by the need to convince lenders of the soundness of overall economic policy and borrowing strategy.

Re-scheduling and Re-negotiating External Debt

Finally, lenders must accept that re-negotiations of the external debt of developing countries will remain a cost of doing business. Liquidity crises will emerge periodically — one hopes with less frequency than in the early 1980s — and they will have to be handled in ways that minimise costs to borrowers as well as lenders.

A re-scheduling is a financing technique — somewhat similar to a re-financing, fairly far removed from a prepayment and very remote from a default. The real costs of these negotiations lie in the time taken to reach agreement. The ablest administrators in the finance ministries of affected countries can be tied up for years, the IMF spends much time negotiating standby agreements, and frequently creditors are denied access to their funds and the interest on them during the prolonged negotiating process. When re-scheduling is arranged expediently both parties probably benefit.

Creditors — whether private or official — are usually compensated by better terms on their outstanding loans. Debtors, despite higher future debt-servicing obligations, presumably also benefit from the breathing space afforded by the re-scheduling.[26] Arrangements fail to benefit the partici-pants when the re-negotiation process has been deferred too long, or when economic management in the borrowing countries has been so poor that the re-scheduling is in lieu of a default. A device to circumvent a liquidity difficulty is then misused to combat insolvency.

To conclude: this chapter has demonstrated two things that are well-known and one that, possibly, is not. The importance of foreign borrowing in development finance and the importance of lending by banks certainly are no secrets. The continued viability of foreign lending as a vehicle for resource transfers has been a subject of some dispute. But if continuing benefits from foreign borrowing are to be secured, the quality of developing countries' debt-management must improve further and costly disruptions in access to finance must be avoided. The last part of the chapter has offered some comments and suggestions that could aid this process.

APPENDIX: NOTE ON THE AVAILABILITY OF BALANCE-OF-PAYMENTS DATA

Balance-of-payments data for the country groups are presented for 1968–81. In some instances, however, data are either unavailable or incomplete. This note lists, by group, those countries and years for which data are not available. Table 5.1 provides a complete listing of the countries in each group.

Group I　　Complete data are available for seventeen countries with only minor exceptions in 1981 (Algeria, Yugoslavia). Data for Hong Kong and the Bahamas are not available.

Group II　　Data are essentially available for forty-one countries. Data are not available for Lebanon.

　　　　　　Countries for which partial data are available are:

	years not available
Cameroon	68, 69, 80, 81
Congo	68–70
Dominican Republic	81
Liberia	68–74
Madagascar	68, 80, 81
Nicaragua	80, 81
Oman	68–73
Papua New Guinea	68–75
Portugal	68–71

Senegal	79−81
Togo	80, 81
Zaire	78−81
Zimbabwe	68−76

Group III The data for this group are very incomplete. There are twelve countries for which virtually complete data exist; twenty-one countries for which partial data exist, although the years available vary from country to country; and seven countries where no data are available.

Countries with full data are:

Burma	Malawi
Egypt	Rwanda
Ethiopia	Somalia
Ghana	Sri Lanka
Haiti	Sudan
India	Syria

Countries with partial data are:

	years not available
Bangladesh	68−72
Benin	79−81
Botswana	68−74
Central African Republic	81
Chad	78−81
El Salvador	81
Gambia	68−69
Jordan	68−70
Lesotho	68−74
Mali	69
Mauritania	71, 72
Nepal	68−75
Niger	77−81
Pakistan	68−71
Swaziland	68−73
Tanzania	81
Uganda	81
Upper Volta	80, 81
Western Samoa	75−81
Yemen, A. R.	68−73
Yemen, P. D. R.	68−72, 81

Countries for which data are not available:

Burundi	Maldives
Comoros	Seychelles
Djibouti	Solomon Islands
Guinea	

The methods for incorporating incomplete data into group aggregates are described in the chapter.

ANNEX

TABLE 5A.1 Uses and sources of external finance for groups of developing countries: 1968–80^a (percentages of GDP)

	1968^b	1969	1970	1971	1972	1973	1974	1975	1976	1977	1978	1979	1980	1981
Group I – Market borrowers														
Uses of external finance														
Balance on goods and non-factor services	0.3	0.3	1.4	1.8	1.4	0.5	-0.1	3.0	1.3	1.8	3.0	1.3	1.0	1.8
Net investment income payments^c	2.0	1.9	1.8	1.8	1.7	1.9	1.7	1.5	1.6	1.9	1.9	2.1	2.3	3.0
of which														
Direct investment	(1.5)	(1.4)	(1.3)	(1.2)	(1.0)	(1.3)	(1.1)	(0.8)	(0.7)	(0.9)	(0.8)	(0.7)	(0.6)	(0.7)
Other investment	(0.5)	(0.4)	(0.5)	(0.6)	(0.6)	(0.6)	(0.6)	(0.7)	(0.9)	(1.0)	(1.1)	(1.4)	(1.6)	(2.3)
Net labour income payments^d	-0.3	-0.5	-0.6	-0.7	-0.8	-0.9	-0.7	-0.6	-0.7	-0.7	-0.6	-0.5	-0.5	-0.1
Additions to reserves	0.5	0.4	0.7	0.5	1.8	1.8	2.3	0.1	1.2	0.4	0.7	1.0	0.6	0.1
Total Net Use – Net Availability	2.5	2.1	3.2	3.4	4.0	3.2	3.2	4.0	3.5	3.4	4.9	3.8	3.3	4.7
Sources of External Finance														
Not official transfers	0.1	0.1	0.1	0.2	0.1	0.1	-0.1	0.0	0.0	0.0	0.0	0.0	0.0	0.0
Net direct investment	0.8	0.8	0.7	0.8	0.6	1.0	0.8	0.9	0.6	0.8	0.9	0.7	0.9	1.1
Net flows of MLT loans	0.8	1.1	1.2	1.8	2.6	2.4	2.5	2.8	3.3	2.9	4.3	2.7	2.4	4.2
Balancing Item^e	0.7	0.0	1.2	0.7	0.7	-0.3	0.1	0.2	-0.4	-0.4	-0.3	0.3	-0.1	-0.6
Group II – Mixed borrowers														
Uses of External Finance														
Balance on goods and non-factor services	4.5	2.8	3.6	4.8	3.0	3.1	4.3	6.9	5.0	4.0	3.8	3.1	3.4	4.6
Net investment income payments^c	1.5	1.5	1.6	1.5	1.7	1.7	1.8	2.0	2.1	2.1	2.3	2.6	3.1	3.4
of which														
Direct investment	(1.1)	(1.1)	(1.0)	(0.9)	(1.0)	(1.0)	(1.4)	(1.2)	(1.1)	(1.0)	(1.1)	(1.1)	(1.3)	(1.1)
Other investment	(0.4)	(0.4)	(0.6)	(0.6)	(0.7)	(0.7)	(0.5)	(0.8)	(1.0)	(1.1)	(1.2)	(1.5)	(1.8)	(2.3)
Net labour income payments^d	-0.9	-0.9	-1.0	-1.3	-2.3	-2.6	-1.9	-1.6	-1.4	-1.3	-1.5	-1.8	-1.9	-1.9
Additions to reserves	0.4	0.4	1.0	0.4	2.6	2.0	0.6	-0.9	1.0	1.1	0.8	1.6	1.6	0.5
Total Net Use – Net Availability	5.5	3.8	5.1	5.5	5.0	4.1	4.8	6.3	6.6	5.9	5.3	5.6	6.1	6.6
Sources of external finance														
Net official transfers	1.0	1.0	1.0	1.0	0.9	1.1	0.9	1.1	1.0	0.9	0.8	0.8	0.8	0.7
Net direct investment	0.6	0.8	0.5	1.0	1.0	0.8	0.6	1.1	0.6	0.6	0.5	0.4	0.4	0.5
Net flows of MLT loans	2.6	2.6	3.0	2.5	2.7	2.4	2.6	4.1	4.8	3.7	3.8	4.4	3.8	3.9
Balancing Item^e	1.3	-0.5	0.7	0.9	0.3	-0.2	0.7	0.0	0.1	0.7	0.3	-0.1	1.1	1.4

Group III — Aid Recipients[f]

Uses of external finance

Balance on goods and non-factor services	1.9	1.3	1.6	2.3	1.6	2.2	4.8	5.9	4.3	4.2	6.2	7.0	8.0	8.5
Net investment income payments[c]	0.6	0.7	0.7	0.6	0.6	0.5	0.4	0.4	0.5	0.4	0.4	0.2	0.1	0.3
of which														
Direct investment	(0.1)	(0.1)	(0.1)	(0.1)	(0.1)	(0.1)	(0.1)	(0.1)	(0.1)	(0.1)	(0.1)	(0.1)	(0.1)	(0.3)
Other investment	(0.5)	(0.6)	(0.5)	(0.5)	(0.5)	(0.5)	(0.3)	(0.3)	(0.3)	(0.3)	(0.3)	(0.1)	(0.0)	(0.0)
Net labour income payments[d]	-0.2	-0.2	-0.2	-0.3	-0.5	-0.5	-0.8	-1.2	-2.0	-2.4	-3.2	-3.4	-3.4	-2.9
Addition to reserves	0.1	0.4	0.4	0.1	0.3	0.5	-0.1	0.3	1.5	1.9	1.0	0.7	0.2	-1.1
Total Net Use – Net Availability	2.5	2.2	2.5	2.7	2.0	2.7	4.3	5.4	4.2	4.0	4.4	4.5	4.8	4.7

Source of external finance

Net official transfers	0.6	0.9	0.9	0.9	1.1	1.8	3.3	2.4	1.9	2.1	1.7	2.5	2.0	2.0
Net direct investment	0.1	0.1	0.1	0.1	0.1	0.1	0.1	0.0	0.1	0.1	0.2	0.7	0.3	0.4
Net flows of MLT loans	1.7	1.3	1.0	1.4	1.2	1.2	0.7	3.1	2.3	2.3	2.2	1.5	2.0	2.0
Balancing Item[e]	0.1	0.0	0.4	0.4	-0.3	-0.4	0.2	-0.2	-0.1	-0.5	0.3	-0.2	0.5	0.3

Aid Recipients — excluding India and Pakistan

Uses of external finance

Balance on goods and non-factor services	3.3	3.2	3.7	5.0	3.9	4.9	9.7	11.9	10.1	9.7	12.1	12.4	11.5	14.2
Net investment income payments[c]	0.6	0.9	0.8	0.8	0.7	0.6	0.6	0.5	0.7	0.6	0.6	0.4	0.3	0.6
of which														
Direct investment	(0.3)	(0.3)	(0.3)	(0.3)	(0.3)	(0.3)	(0.3)	(0.3)	(0.3)	(0.2)	(0.2)	(0.1)	(0.2)	(0.1)
Other investment	(0.4)	(0.5)	(0.5)	(0.5)	(0.4)	(0.4)	(0.3)	(0.2)	(0.4)	(0.4)	(0.4)	(0.3)	(0.2)	(0.6)
Net labour income payments[d]	-0.0	-0.1	-0.2	-0.4	-0.7	-0.8	-1.4	-2.0	-3.6	-3.8	-5.1	-5.3	-4.6	-4.7
Additions to reserves	0.0	0.1	0.1	-0.2	1.1	1.4	0.0	0.5	0.5	1.7	0.4	0.7	0.3	-0.6
Total Net Use – Net Availability	3.9	3.8	4.4	5.3	5.0	6.1	9.0	11.0	7.7	8.2	8.0	8.2	7.6	9.5

Sources of external finance

Net official transfers	1.8	2.1	2.2	2.4	3.0	5.0	5.3	5.5	4.1	4.6	3.5	5.1	3.8	4.2
Net direct investment	0.3	0.3	0.4	0.2	0.2	0.1	0.2	0.1	0.2	0.3	0.5	1.5	0.6	0.9
Net flows of MLT loans	0.9	0.7	0.9	1.8	2.4	2.0	2.4	5.2	3.1	4.1	4.0	2.9	2.4	3.1
Balancing Item[e]	0.8	0.7	0.9	0.9	-0.6	-1.1	1.0	0.2	0.3	-0.8	-0.0	-1.3	0.8	1.2

a Groups of developing countries are as defined in text Table 5.1. Data are from the IMF as stored in World Bank files. Data for countries with incomplete time series are included for available years. Refer to the Appendix for further details. The aggregate GDP for each group is obtained for each year by summing the GDPs for countries for which complete balance-of-payments information is available for that year.

b This is the first year for which complete information is widely available.

c Investment income payments minus investment income receipts. 'Net other investment payments' includes interest earnings on revenues and interest payments on short-term debt.

d Comprises payments – receipts from nationals resident or working abroad and includes private transfers and workers' remittances.

e The balancing item includes net inflows of short-term debt, errors and omissions and counterpart items (including monetisation/demonetisation of gold, allocation of SDRs, and valuation adjustments to reserves).

f Data coverage for this group is very incomplete. Substantially complete time series are available for only 12 countries (Burma, Egypt, Ethiopia, Ghana, Haiti, India, Malawi, Rwanda, Somalia, Sri Lanka, Sudan, and Syria.

SOURCE: World Bank.

TABLE 5A2 Net flows and net transfers of medium- and long-term loans to groups of developing countries, 1970–81 (DRS data; percentages of GDP)

	1970	1971	1972	1973	1974	1975	1976	1977	1978	1979	1980	1981
Group I												
Net Flows[a]												
Official	0.4	0.3	0.4	0.5	0.6	0.5	0.3	0.3	0.3	0.2	0.3	0.3
Private	1.6	1.6	2.7	2.3	2.5	2.5	2.9	3.4	4.2	2.5	3.4	3.4
Total	2.0	1.9	3.1	2.8	3.1	3.0	3.3	3.6	4.4	2.7	3.6	3.6
Net Transfer[b]												
Official	0.2	0.2	0.3	0.3	0.4	0.3	0.1	0.1	0.1	0.1	0.1	0.1
Private	1.0	1.0	2.1	1.6	1.6	1.5	2.1	2.4	2.9	1.3	0.6	1.1
Total	1.2	1.2	2.3	1.9	2.0	1.8	2.2	2.5	3.0	1.4	0.7	1.1
Group II												
Net Flows												
Official	1.7	1.7	1.9	1.5	1.3	1.7	1.9	2.0	2.0	1.9	2.2	2.0
Private	1.1	1.2	1.6	2.1	2.3	2.5	2.3	2.2	1.7	2.6	1.9	1.8
Total	2.8	2.9	3.5	3.6	3.5	4.2	4.2	4.2	3.7	4.5	4.1	3.8
Net Transfers												
Official	1.4	1.4	1.5	1.1	1.0	1.3	1.5	1.6	1.5	1.4	1.6	1.4
Private	0.6	0.6	1.1	1.4	1.6	1.8	1.6	1.5	0.8	1.6	0.6	0.2
Total	2.0	2.0	2.5	2.5	2.6	3.2	3.1	3.1	2.3	2.9	2.2	1.6
Group III												
Net Flows												
Official	1.3	1.5	1.1	1.6	2.1	3.5	2.6	2.6	2.4	2.1	2.1	1.9
Private	0.1	0.1	0.2	−0.1	0.4	0.2	0.3	0.2	0.2	0.3	0.4	0.5
Total	1.4	1.6	1.3	1.5	2.5	3.7	2.9	2.8	2.6	2.4	2.6	2.4
Net Transfers												
Official	1.0	1.2	0.8	1.2	1.8	3.1	2.3	2.2	1.9	1.7	1.8	1.5
Private	0.0	0.0	0.1	−0.2	0.4	0.1	0.2	0.2	0.1	0.2	0.3	0.4
Total	1.0	1.2	0.8	1.1	2.1	3.3	2.4	2.3	2.0	1.9	2.1	1.9

a Net flows are defined as (gross) disbursements less repayments of principal

TABLE 5A.3 Average terms of commitments to public borrowers: total, official and private, 1970–81 (percentages, years)

	1970	1971	1972	1973	1974	1975	1976	1977	1978	1979	1980	1981
Group I – Market borrowers												
Total Commitments												
Interest Rate (%)	7.2	6.9	6.9	8.5	8.9	8.4	7.8	8.0	9.5	11.3	11.9	14.3
Maturity (years)	12.9	12.6	12.1	13.4	12.5	9.8	9.7	8.9	9.4	9.6	9.7	10.1
Grace Period (years)	3.4	3.6	3.4	4.7	3.8	3.2	3.2	3.5	4.0	4.1	3.7	3.7
Commitments from Official Source												
Interest Rate (%)	6.3	5.7	6.3	6.5	6.3	7.4	7.7	7.8	7.2	7.4	8.1	9.3
Maturity (years)	20.6	20.0	17.9	18.1	17.9	18.1	16.3	15.4	15.1	15.1	15.2	15.7
Grace Period (years)	5.1	5.1	4.9	5.5	4.9	5.1	4.5	4.0	4.0	4.4	3.8	4.0
Commitments from Private Sources												
Interest Rate (%)	7.7	7.5	7.3	9.4	10.0	8.6	7.8	8.1	9.8	11.9	13.1	15.5
Maturity (years)	9.1	8.1	8.8	11.4	10.1	7.5	7.9	7.5	8.6	8.7	8.1	8.7
Grace Period (years)	2.6	2.7	2.5	4.3	3.3	2.6	2.8	3.4	4.0	4.1	3.7	3.7
Group II – Mixed borrowers												
Total Commitments												
Interest Rate (%)	5.1	5.4	5.4	6.5	7.1	7.3	7.0	6.9	7.4	8.6	9.1	10.5
Maturity (years)	20.9	22.7	20.4	19.2	17.6	16.0	16.1	15.9	16.0	15.6	16.5	14.6
Grace Period (years)	5.3	6.7	6.1	6.0	5.3	4.7	4.9	4.9	4.8	4.8	4.9	4.3
Commitments from Official Source												
Interest Rate (%)	3.8	4.5	4.3	4.0	5.1	5.9	6.1	5.9	5.5	5.6	6.4	7.4
Maturity (years)	27.5	28.8	26.8	28.7	23.7	23.3	22.3	21.9	21.7	22.7	21.5	19.5
Grace Period (years)	7.0	7.9	7.4	8.0	7.0	6.6	6.8	6.7	6.1	6.2	6.1	5.5
Commitments from Private Sources												
Interest Rate (%)	7.3	7.1	7.3	8.7	9.0	8.7	7.9	8.1	9.4	11.2	12.8	13.5
Maturity (years)	9.9	11.6	9.5	10.7	11.7	8.7	9.8	8.7	9.6	9.5	9.5	9.8
Grace Period (years)	2.5	4.5	3.9	4.2	3.6	2.8	3.1	2.8	3.3	3.5	3.3	3.2

(Continued)

TABLE 5A.3 *Average terms of commitments to public borrowers: total, official and private: 1970–81 (percentages, years)*

	1970	1971	1972	1973	1974	1975	1976	1977	1978	1979	1980	1981
Group III — Aid recipients												
Total Commitments												
Interest Rate (%)	2.5	2.9	2.7	3.1	3.8	3.6	3.9	4.0	3.3	4.2	4.3	4.7
Maturity (years)	29.5	28.0	28.1	28.9	25.9	26.5	25.7	25.2	30.9	26.0	27.0	27.2
Grace Period (years)	8.7	6.8	6.7	7.4	7.6	7.8	6.8	6.4	7.4	6.0	6.3	6.2
Commitments from Official Sources												
Interest Rate (%)	2.0	2.3	1.9	2.3	2.8	3.1	3.2	3.4	2.3	3.0	2.5	3.3
Maturity (years)	32.4	30.7	31.7	32.3	28.6	27.9	28.0	27.2	34.0	28.5	31.1	32.3
Grace Period (years)	9.8	7.5	7.6	8.4	8.5	8.5	7.6	7.1	8.3	7.0	7.4	7.4
Commitments from Private Sources												
Interest Rate (%)	6.5	7.1	6.6	6.9	9.8	8.5	8.3	7.9	9.2	9.4	10.9	10.1
Maturity (years)	11.0	7.9	11.3	12.3	9.6	13.2	11.5	11.7	12.8	14.6	12.6	6.6
Grace Period (years)	2.1	1.6	2.2	2.5	2.1	1.8	2.4	2.1	2.0	1.6	2.1	1.1

SOURCE World Bank Debtor Reporting System.

TABLE 5A.4 *Projected debt service as a percentage of GDP: 1982–90*[a]

	1982	1983	1984	1985	1986	1987	1988	1989	1990
Market borrowers									
Official	0.4	0.4	0.4	0.4	0.4	0.4	0.4	0.4	0.3
Private	4.6	4.2	3.6	3.5	4.0	4.4	4.5	4.7	4.8
Total	5.0	4.6	4.0	3.9	4.4	4.8	4.9	5.0	5.2
Mixed borrowers									
Official	1.4	1.4	1.4	1.4	1.4	1.3	1.3	1.2	1.2
Private	3.4	3.1	2.8	3.0	3.2	3.3	3.4	3.5	3.6
Total	4.8	4.5	4.3	4.4	4.6	4.6	4.6	4.7	4.8
Aid recipients									
Official	1.3	1.3	1.2	1.1	1.1	1.0	0.9	1.0	1.0
Private	0.6	0.5	0.5	0.5	0.6	0.5	0.5	0.5	0.5
Total	1.8	1.8	1.7	1.7	1.7	1.6	1.5	1.5	1.5

[a] Projections are based on DRS data and the assumptions described on pages 118–20 of the text.

NOTES

1. See Hope (1981), especially pp. 53—4.
2. See OECD (1981) p. 4. Similar assessments were produced by the IMF (1981a) and, in an update of an earlier piece, by Solomon (1981).
3. Although this point is usually directed at lending through the private markets, much of this lending is guaranteed by the export credit agencies of creditor governments, so the financial strength of these agencies should be of at least equal concern.
4. See Eaton and Gersowitz (1981a) and (1981b).
5. For examples of earlier work see O'Brien (1981) and Dod (1981). A good discussion of recent developments in credit markets is in Morgan Guaranty's *World Financial Markets*, August 1982. See also IMF (1981a, 1981b, 1982), BIS (1981, 1983), OECD (1981) and World Bank (1981b).
6. Some exceptions have been made for countries that have had very disturbed access to markets (e.g. Zimbabwe) or that have not approached private markets for finance (e.g. Malta). In these cases, income per capita has over-ridden simple rankings in making the group assignments.
7. In revising the paper for publication, data have been updated to 1981. This caused some changes in ranking compared with the paper (based on 1980 data) presented to the conference but no substantive changes to the conclusion.
8. For example, in IMF (1982) market financing is analysed using a breakdown of countries according to the size of their debt owed to banks reporting to the BIS. See IMF (1982) page 12, Table 3, and the discussion on pp. 11—15.
9. The ratio is expressed as (liabilities — assets/assets) x 100.   A negative figure implies a net asset position with the BIS banks. Data are for positions at end—1981.
10. This liability measure based on BIS data is being used in similar work under way at the UN.
11. See, for example, *World Development Report 1981*.
12. See Appendix for details.
13. Because data on reinvested earnings are very incomplete, net payments of direct investment income will be understated by the same amount as net direct investment inflows. Hence, the importance of direct investment in financing patterns is biased downwards.
14. Complete data are available for Burma, Egypt, Ethiopia, Ghana, Haiti, India, Malawi, Rwanda, Somalia, Sri Lanka, Sudan, and Syria; aggregations over this subgroup of countries — with and without India — generate similar patterns to those shown in Figure 5.1 for the whole group.
15. See Goran Ohlin (1966), Benjamin King (1968), or Raymond Mikesell (1968).
16. The extent of the overstatement in equating DRS data to the net MLT loan position from IMF balance-of-payments information can be seen by comparing Annex Table 5A.2 (based on DRS data) with Annex

Table 5A.1. The preliminary nature of the balance-of-payments data in 1981 would account for the apparent contradiction in this year.

17. Recall that Group I countries are those with a share of private-source in total debt of 70 per cent or more in 1979—81 and Group III countries are those with a corresponding share of 25 per cent or less.

18. Lending by parent corporations to their direct investment affiliates is included in the non-guaranteed debt reported to the DRS. The IMF correctly records these flows in direct investment, so the role of private direct investment inferred from IMF balance-of-payments data would be comparatively more important than would be inferred from DRS data.

19. But growth has been very uneven. One or two large market placements in a given year (e.g. India in 1980) were enough to generate rapid growth.

20. The exercise was a pure simulation, in the sense that no analysis was undertaken to relate the projected GDP growth to a required growth in loan commitments. The projected GDP growth could be associated with a much higher, or lower, growth of borrowing.

21. Note that this is couched in terms of investing the resources but the same point would hold when borrowing was to defer the cost of adjusting to a permanent, current income loss.

22. This is not certain if a country is forced to re-schedule. Claims against non-guaranteed debt of private borrowers may be represented as part of the debt to be rescheduled and, in practice, some governments have had little option but to meet these claims because of their poor records of what they owe. See further comments on data deficiencies in borrowing countries below.

23. Since this was written, the problems of many market borrowers have lent support to the points made here.

24. Among the less *ad hoc* are the policy prescriptions obtaining from the work of Gershon Feder and his collaborators. See, for example, Feder and Just (1979).

25. For a recent collection see Yves Maroni (1982).

26. Some commentators (e.g. Hardy 1982) show that borrowers can face a higher present value of debt-service payments after the re-scheduling than before. At a fixed discount rate, this is necessary to compensate lenders for changing the terms. From the borrowers' viewpoint the appropriate discount rate cannot be the same. A re-scheduling takes place because current imports are valued more highly than meeting current debt-service obligations, a development that was not anticipated when the loans were contracted.

REFERENCES

Robert Z. Aliber (1980) *A Conceptual Approach to the Analysis of External Debt of the Developing Countries*, World Bank Staff Working Paper 421 (Washington, DC: World Bank).

Robert Z. Aliber (1982) *The Management of External Debt*, External Debt Division Working Paper 1982–2 (Washington, DC.: World Bank).

Bank for International Settlements (1981) *Fifty-First Annual Report, 1st April 1980–31st March 1981* (Basle:.BIS).

Bank for International Settlements (1982) 'International Banking Developments – fourth quarter 1982' (Basle: BIS).

David P. Dod (1981) 'Bank Lending to Developing Countries: Recent Developments in Historical Perspective', *Federal Reserve Bulletin*, vol. 67 (Washington, DC).

J. Eaton and M. Gersowitz (1981a) 'Debt with Potential Repudiation: Theoretical and Empirical Analysis', *Review of Economic Studies*, vol. 48.

J. Eaton and M. Gersowitz (1981b) *Poor Country Borrowing in Private Financial Markets and the Repudiation Issue*, Princeton Studies in International Finance 47 (Princeton University).

Gershon Feder (1978) *Economic Growth, Foreign Loans and Debt Servicing Capacity of Developing Countries*, World Bank Staff Working Paper 274 (Washington, DC: World Bank).

Gershon Feder and Richard E. Just (1979) 'Optimal International Borrowing, Capital Allocation and Credit-worthiness Control', *Kredit und Kapital*, vol. 12.

C. S. Hardy (1982) *Rescheduling Developing Country Debts, 1956–80: Lessons and Recommendations*, Overseas Development Council Working Paper 1, (Washington, DC: Overseas Development Council).

Nicholas C. Hope (1981) *Developments in and Prospects for the External Debt of the Developing Countries: 1970–1980 and Beyond*, World Bank Staff Working Paper 488 (Washington, DC: World Bank).

International Monetary Fund (1981a) *External Indebtedness of Developing Countries*, IMF Occasional Paper 3 (Washington, DC: IMF).

International Monetary Fund (1981b) *International Capital Markets: Recent Developments and Short-term Prospects*, IMF Occasional Paper 7 (Washington, DC: IMF).

International Monetary Fund (1982) *Developments in Capital Markets*, IMF Occasional Paper 14 (Washington, DC: IMF).

H. Kharas (1981a) *The Analysis of Long-run Creditworthiness: Theory and Practice*, Domestic Finance Study 73 (Washington, DC: World Bank).

H. Kharas (1981b) *On Structural Change and Debt Service Capacity*, Domestic Finance Study 74 (Washington, DC: World Bank).

H. Kharas (1981c) *Constrained Optimal Foreign Borrowing by Less Developed Countries*, Domestic Finance Study 75 (Washington, DC: World Bank).

Benjamin King (1968) *Notes on the Mechanics of Growth and Debt*, World Bank Staff Occasional Papers 6 (Baltimore: Johns Hopkins Press).

Yves Maroni (1982) 'How to Borrow Reasonably', unpublished International Finance Division Paper 203, Federal Reserve Board.

Raymond Mikesell (1968) *The Economics of Foreign Aid* (Chicago: Aldine).

Morgan Guaranty (1982) *World Financial Markets* (August).

Richard O'Brien (1981) *Private Bank Lending to Developing Countries*, World Bank Staff Working Paper 482 (Washington, DC: World Bank).

OECD (1980), *Geographical Distribution of Financial Flows to Developing Countries* (Paris: OECD).

OECD (1981), *External Debt of Developing Countries* (Paris: OECD).

Goran Ohlin (1966) *Aid and Indebtedness* (Paris: Development Centre of the OECD).

J. Sachs (1982) *LDC Debt in the 1980s: Risk and Reforms*, Working Paper 861, National Bureau of Economic Research (Cambridge, Mass.: NBER).

Robert Solomon (1981) *The Debt of Developing Countries: Another Look* (Washington, DC: Brookings Institution).

World Bank (1981a) *World Development Report 1981* (New York: Oxford University Press).

World Bank (1981b) *World Debt Tables*, Report EC–167/81 (Washington, DC: World Bank).

6 The Debt Burden Problem

BAHRAM NOWZAD

I INTRODUCTION

Reviewing some of the discussion on this question, one may be forgiven the impression that in some people's view there is no such thing as a 'debt burden problem', only a financing problem. This is somewhat akin to the proposition that there is no global population problem, there are just too many people in the world! Without wishing to launch into a semantic discourse, I should like to state at the start that, in my view, external debt does indeed pose a burden for many countries. It is the result of many factors, including, to some extent, the consequence of what happened in the 1970s, namely, that in response to severe structural shocks, insufficient attention was paid to adjustment. Resort to the considerable financing that became available was not accompanied by adequate efforts to effect basic policy changes. For this and many other reasons external debt problems have had, and are having, serious consequences for many countries: they pose a direct threat to growth prospects and create pressures on the international financial system.

External debt has become the focus of attention and debate for very good reasons: the rapid increase in the debt obligations of developing countries in the past decade, the changing nature of debt, the emergence of debt-servicing difficulties for many countries and periodic prophecies of disaster, to say nothing of recent events. Economists have not lagged behind the action, and these developments have been accompanied by an impressive growth in debt literature, devoted mostly to the problems of external debt. It has to be remembered, however, that this only looks at one side of the question, at the possible negative side of external debt. It is important to bear in mind that international lending and international borrowing have also a positive aspect and that, as economic history shows,

140

in many cases external finance is a crucial ingredient in development. Therefore, although this chapter deals with the debt burden problem, 'debt' and 'problem' should not be considered synonymous; other chapters deal with the positive side.

The debt burden problem is a very broad subject; I will deal with certain selected aspects. I make no attempt to present a thesis or a particular line of argument, but address three aspects of the question: first, recapitulation of certain basic facts and figures in order to provide an anchor for the discussion; second, a discussion of the debt burden problem in a conceptual framework; finally, a brief examination of the debt burden question in an empirical context.

II SELECTED FACTS AND FIGURES

One problem with aggregate debt statistics, as with other forms of aggregative data, is that they obscure wide variations among individual countries. With that caveat in mind, a broad overview of the magnitude of the debt question for developing countries is nevertheless useful.

The total debt of developing countries at the end of 1983 (including all types of obligations that may reasonably be considered as debt) was estimated to amount to around $600 billion. The medium- and long-term debt of non-oil developing countries accounted for about $510 billion of this total. This category had been growing at an annual rate of about 21 per cent in 1974–9 and at the lower rate of 15 per cent a year since 1980. The debt-service payments on these debts were growing at an annual rate of 26 per cent in 1974–9 and again at 15 per cent in 1980–1. The debt-service ratio increased from 14 per cent in 1973 to 24 per cent in 1982.

Perhaps more significant than the growth rates of the debt magnitudes mentioned above has been the change in the *terms* of debt. These have, in general, deteriorated – from the borrowers' point of view – over the past decade as an increasing amount of debt was contracted at commercial rates with higher interest rates and shorter maturities, compared with official loans.[1] For instance the average interest rate on developing country debt to private creditors rose from 9.0 per cent in 1973 to 13.1 per cent in 1980 (4.3 per cent and 5.3 per cent, respectively, for official creditors) while average maturity on the same debt fell from 10.9 years in 1973 to 9.1 years in 1980 (25.6 years and 24.4 years, respectively, for official creditors). These developments are starkly reflected in data on net financial transfer, a concept that measures disbursements of debt, minus amortisation payments, minus interest payments: it is thus a measure of the actual net resources that the borrowing country receives. This magnitude, for non-oil developing countries, rose from \$7.4 billion in 1973 to \$28.2 billion in 1978 but has fallen sharply since then, to \$19.8 billion in 1980.

Turning to the most recent period, 1980–2, a number of significant developments may be noted. First, we had the problem of Eastern European debt and what may be termed a 'shattering of illusions'. Until the early 1980s it was widely believed that commercial bank lending to Eastern European countries was safe, not only because these countries had had a good record in debt repayment but also because, if they encountered difficulties, they could count on ready assistance from their allies. This proposition is clearly no longer valid. A second important development has been the very large number of developing countries, mostly small and many of them African, that have encountered debt problems in these two years and have had to seek a renegotiation of their official debt in the Paris Club, and in some cases of their commercial banking debt as well. There were eight such cases in 1981 and the queue is already lengthening for 1982. And of course a third and highly significant development is the debt problem of major borrowers, such as Mexico, Argentina and Brazil, about which there already exists an avalanche of literature.

So much for the recent past. What about the immediate future? For this one may turn to the IMF's most recent *World Economic Outlook*, published in April 1982. First, the magnitude of interest payments on already-contracted debt during 1982–3 was expected to have a limiting effect on the reduction of current account deficits of developing countries. Second, any moderation in interest rates on new debt was likely to be more than offset by the increasing proportion of debt to which high interest rates apply as old obligations were repaid. Third, there was likely to be an increase in long-term debt to replace short-term debt contracted for the financing of the 1980–1 balance of payments deficits. Fourth, the increase in debt was likely to outpace the increase in export earnings, which would, of course, imply a worsening of the debt-servicing ratio.

The main theme that emerges from the foregoing, and the one which is perhaps of greatest concern, is that the debt burden of developing countries has serious implications and that unless this problem can be met, international capital flows may be severely disrupted with detrimental effects on economic growth. It also seems clear that developing countries must avoid short-term debt that would affect their medium-term prospects while maintaining the flows of capital and credit necessary for economic activity.

III DEBT BURDEN: THE CONCEPTUAL FRAMEWORK

Debt burden must be defined in the context of debt capacity: in short, how much should a country borrow? What is the optimal level of debt for a particular country? To the economist, optimality is, as always, very attractive. In practice, however, the concept of optimality is very difficult to apply and for this reason much of the applied literature is based on the more practical measure of sustainability.

In the development literature attention has frequently focused on two constraints to development – insufficiency of both savings and foreign exchange. External borrowing is seen as a means of easing these constraints. The framework for debt analysis has largely been based on growth-cum-debt models in which emphasis is placed primarily on external finance in its role of augmenting domestic savings and thereby permitting a larger volume of investment than would otherwise be possible. These models are, broadly speaking, of two varieties. One group analyses the path of debt under different assumed or target growth rates, given assumptions about consumption behaviour and the economy's technology. The Harrod-Domar model has frequently been used for this type of analysis. In this model output is determined according to fixed coefficients of technology; the investment ratio is determined by the target growth rate in conjunction with the fixed capital-output ratio; the consumption (savings) function determines available domestic savings; and external borrowing is residually determined to fill the gap between required investment and available savings. The emphasis in Harrod-Domar type models is on analysing the sustainability of the projected path of debt. In the second group of models, on the other hand, investment, savings, and debt are determined as a result of optimising behaviour; and the optimising condition is the equalisation of the marginal costs and marginal benefits of using external finance.

There are a number of problems with the above approaches. The former are rigid in structure and say little about how much a country should borrow – they are concerned with how debt will evolve under specific scenarios. Both approaches suffer from a narrow view of the role that can be played by external borrowing. The uses of external finance go well beyond the investment role which, as mentioned above, is the principal purpose in the growth-cum-debt models. External finance can be used for balance-of-payments purposes as a means of sheltering consumption from fluctuations in income, that is, for instance, to compensate for fluctuations in export receipts. It can also be employed, again for balance of payments purposes, to reduce the costs to adjustment to a permanent shift in an economy's income stream, that is, a permanent shift in the terms of trade. Moreover, external borrowing is affected by a host of institutional factors such as the structure of international financial markets, sovereign risk, public guarantees (by debtor or creditor institutions) and so on. As a result any simple, mathematical formula of optimality is unlikely to be found, to say nothing of the tremendous informational obstacles that would have to be faced in attempting to put it to practical use.

IV   DEBT BURDEN: AN EMPIRICAL APPROACH

The literature on the debt burden makes a distinction between two broad categories of debt problems, those classified as being of a financial or liquidity nature and those that are classified as economic or solvency problems. The first group covers, for instance, cases where difficulties are brought about by a sudden surge in debt-service payments (due to a bunching of maturities) or a sudden shortfall in exchange earnings (due to fluctuating exports). The second group refers to cases of more fundamental imbalance where the country simply cannot generate sufficient earnings to meet its debt obligations and other basic foreign exchange needs; in other words cases where a country is living continuously beyond its means. In practice the distinction is not always clear-cut and frequently elements of both types of difficulties are present in actual debt-problem cases. Of greater interest than the classification of difficulties are the characteristics of the economies that have encountered debt-servicing difficulties.

The External Finance Division of the Fund recently undertook two simple and limited surveys of debt-problem countries. These were not based on sophisticated or complex models but rather involved an empirical analysis of the economies of a group of countries facing debt problems with the main purpose of seeing what, if any, broad conclusions can be drawn. In both these exercises the results basically confirmed results that would intuitively suggest themselves. Nevertheless, the exercises were useful.

In the first exercise we looked at the countries that encountered debt difficulties in 1975–80. (Debt difficulties were classified as those that required countries to seek or actually undergo a debt re-negotiation. It must, however, be recognised that this cannot be the sole criterion of a debt problem in that, for example, a country facing debt-burden difficulties may try to cope with them by cutting back on imports or by imposing restrictions).

One conclusion was that the debt problem could not be explained solely by developments in the years immediately preceding the debt crisis but, rather, reflected the cumulative effect of external and internal imbalance attributable to a number of factors. To some extent this conclusion runs counter to the popular view that debt difficulties occur because of sudden, recent, developments. A second conclusion was the apparent paradox that in some cases there was an *improvement* in the balance of payments just before the debt crisis. This occurred where depleted reserves, the lost potential for new borrowing, and an accumulation of arrears dictated adjustment (which often meant a sharp decline in imports).

There were specific factors at work in a number of cases, and these included natural disasters (which led to sharp increases in imports) or political developments (which led to sharp falls in capital flows, that is, reduced inflows and/or increased outflows). The pursuit of expansionary monetary and fiscal policies was characteristic of most of the cases leading to a sharp increase in imports. This was generally due to both domestic factors and external developments. The balance of payments was affected by a number of factors other than debt, including changes in energy prices, loss of export competitiveness, and sharp turnarounds in the services account (sometimes because of changes in remittances). The balance-of-payments difficulties frequently led to attempts to finance the current account with borrowing. Much of this was relatively short-term and high-interest-rate debt thus attempts to compensate for balance of payments deficits often led to sharply higher debt obligations. Also, problems were sometimes aggravated by a fall in long-term official capital flows and a reduction in private capital flows, or an increase in private capital outflows.

The second survey was a comparative one. It was based on a comparison of a group of twelve countries that encountered debt-burden problems during 1972–9 compared with all other non-oil developing countries. Again the results threw some light on the debt-problem issue and mainly confirmed one's intuitions; they demonstrated no causality and suggested no firm conclusions regarding the conditions necessary for the emergence of debt-burden problems.

The principal results of this empirical work can be summarised as follows:

1. the group of twelve countries in the study began the period with a

larger volume of debt compared with the size of their economies than the other countries (for the group, this was 17 per cent of GDP, compared with 14 per cent for the others);

2. the ratio of debt increased by twice as much for the group as for the others (1.1 per cent of GDP as against 0.6 per cent, respectively) and the group contracted debt under increasingly less favourable conditions;

3. the group had a weaker balance-of-payments situation, making them more susceptible to debt problems; the current account deficit for the group was about 4.3 per cent of GDP as compared with 4 per cent for the others, and therefore the group had to borrow more heavily to fill their savings gap;

4. the underlying structure of the balance of payments was weaker for the group, with export growth considerably slower than for the other countries; export growth for the group was 14 per cent on average as against 18 per cent for other countries, and therefore outstanding debt increased faster and the ratio of debt to exports deteriorated more rapidly for the group;

5. although the group had a larger amount of contracted debt compared with the size of their economies, this did not result in faster growth of GDP; indeed real GDP for the group increased on average at 3.6 per cent as against 5.2 per cent for the other countries; therefore not only was there a more rapid increase in the ratio of debt to GDP for the group, but the findings also suggest that less efficient use was made of the resources available;

6. the group had higher variability of exports as well as high concentration of exports and this was a very important factor in the triggering of debt crises; countries with higher export ratios would either have to maintain higher reserves or to contract lower absolute amounts of debt; in fact the opposite was the case.

V CONCLUDING REMARKS

There has been considerable analysis of debt-burden problems and much of it has helped to clarify the factors that should be focused upon and the questions that should be asked and studied. However, the search for a simple and easily applied rule of debt capacity – of how much a country should borrow – has been, and is likely to remain, elusive. The debt-service ratio, which is frequently used, has notorious shortcomings and the various evaluation procedures developed, which cover the entire spectrum from purely subjective evaluations to sophisticated models, suffer from a number of limitations.

It is perhaps unrealistic to expect a simple rule on debt capacity. This is because the concept of debt capacity is difficult to pin down. There is a wide range of motives for borrowing; there are numerous institutional and behavioural considerations; and whether or not debt becomes a problem depends upon different sets of variables that affect debt capacity. Whether or not a debt problem will arise is related primarily to consumption behaviour and the efficiency of investment. More specifically it is a function of exports, capital flows, import induced by domestic shocks, reserves, the availability of compensatory finance, the amount to which imports can be reduced, the level of interest and amortisation payments, and the level of imports considered essential. It is the interplay of these factors, and the difficulty of knowing how to combine them (to say nothing of the non-economic factors) and how much weight to attach to each of them that makes the formulation of a simple ground-rule difficult.

What lessons can one draw from this brief review? I think there are four. First, it is obvious that there are many countries for whom foreign debt constitutes a real burden and for whom such debt, in its most serious manifestation, is having a detrimental effect on their growth prospects. Second, this burden has been due to a number of factors including inadequate domestic policies, excessive borrowing by the country, unwise lending by banks and unfavourable external developments; in most instances it is probably a combination of all these factors that has brought about a debt-burden problem. Third, will there be a 'general crisis' bringing the international financial system to its knees? I think not. Given wise and timely policies, there is a sufficient awareness, and there are certainly enough resources, to prevent the situation from getting out of hand. Fourth, what can be done to alleviate the debt burdens of various countries? A great deal. There is a need for better debt-management and better debt-control. There is need for more cautious and a more studied attitude on the part of banks. More attention perhaps ought to be paid by all sides to the use that is made of borrowed resources, in other words whether funds borrowed today can be put to uses that will produce an income stream in the years to come and thus allow the debt to be serviced; and there ought to be, and there can be, improved arrangements for meeting and coping with debt problems.

NOTE

1. Data on public and publicly guaranteed debt indicate that in 1972–80 developing country debt to official creditors rose at an annual compound rate of 16.7 per cent and at a rate of 27.9 per cent to private creditors.

7 An Analytical and Taxonomic Framework for the Study of Exchange Controls

KATE PHYLAKTIS
AND GEOFFREY E. WOOD*

I INTRODUCTION

Controls on the international movement of capital have at one time or another been used by a majority of countries. These controls have sometimes been used under pegged exchange rates, and at other times under floating exchange rates. In this chapter we develop an analytical framework for classifying, and appraising the impact of, various forms of exchange control. This chapter therefore does not aim to study the workings of one set of exchange controls in detail, but rather to develop a tool-kit for such a study.

It begins by looking briefly at the various kinds of controls, and explaining how under competitive conditions we can calculate an appropriate price restriction (a negative or positive tax rate) that would have the same restrictive effect as any given quantitative restriction. In this way, we can express all restrictions in terms of a tax rate; this will facilitate the integration of the study of capital restrictions with that of trade restrictions. Next, it shows how exchange controls distort the traditional relationship

* The authors are indebted to John Black, David Llewellyn and Alan Winters for comments on this chapter.

149

between the rate of return on domestic assets and that on foreign assets. In particular, we look at three kinds of controls and examine how they affect the arbitrage relationship between domestic and foreign assets.

It then examines how exchange rate adjustment is affected by the imposition of capital controls. Effects occur because the interest rate parity relationship is a vital component in the asset market approach to balance of payments analysis. Thus, making various assumptions concerning the expectations formation mechanism, we are able to trace the effects of exchange controls on the exchange rate under floating exchange rates, and the effects on official international reserves under fixed exchange rates.

Finally, it summarises very briefly the results of the main previous studies which have tried to calculate the 'effectiveness' of capital controls. Our criterion here for judging the effectiveness is somewhat restricted. We do not look at capital controls as one instrument among a number of policy instruments intended to achieve a number of policy objectives. We simply consider whether the policy instrument affected the objective at which it was aimed. If the conclusion is affirmative then one can proceed to the next problem, of comparing the effectiveness and by-products of this instrument with those of others.

II CAPITAL CONTROLS

Capital controls have taken many forms, but almost all with the aim of reducing either capital inflows or capital outflows.[1] In the case of capital outflows, the purpose of the measures has almost always been to protect official reserves; in the case of capital inflows to preserve domestic monetary autonomy. The above arguments for controls apply under fixed exchange rates. Under flexible exchange rates, the main purpose of controls has been to prevent the exchange rate from fully adjusting.

It is important to stress at this point that the various capital controls generally affect more than one category of economic agents. Consider speculators and interest arbitrageurs, who might or might not belong to the banking sector and who might or might not be residents of the country imposing the controls. Although capital controls will impinge directly on one of the two categories, the other category might well also be affected. For example, assume speculators become more optimistic about the domestic currency (e.g. the Deutschmark). This increases the forward premium on the Deutschmark and modifies the behaviour of arbitrageurs, resulting in increases in capital inflows. The authorities impose a tax on non-resident bank deposits to stem this influx of capital. There will be a reduction in capital flows. However, if at the same time speculators revise their expectations because they believe that controls will be effective in preventing an appreciation, the reduction in capital flows will be greater as the forward rate will ease. If on the other hand they think it is a last ditch action with little hope of success they might well revise their expectations upwards, increasing capital inflows.

The main kinds of restrictions on capital flows are tabulated below.[2]

1. limits on the net foreign position or the net foreign position with foreigners;
2. swaps between the central bank and commercial banks;
3. a tax on non-resident bank deposits;
4. discriminatory reserve requirements on non-resident deposits;
5. dual exchange markets.

The first type of regulation limits the amounts of funds available to the banks for either arbitrage or speculation. Theoretically such a control should be more effective than other controls, which try to encourage or discourage capital flows through the use of economic incentives and disincentives, in that it sets an absolute limit irrespective of price incentives. This type of control has been used by several countries: Italy, the Netherlands, France, Japan and Sweden. The second type of regulation often aims to generate offsetting flows by making it profitable for the banks to place funds abroad. This type of control was extensively used by Germany during the 1960s. The last three types of regulation will be explained in detail in the next section. The imposition of a tax on non-resident bank deposits has been used extensively by Germany and Switzerland, while discriminatory reserve requirements have been used by Germany. The last system has been used by Belgium. Thus some restrictions are quantitative and others are price restrictions; of the five categories listed, only the first is quantitative.

Under competitive conditions the following proposition can be made; for each quantitative restriction there is an implicit tax rate which would produce the same restrictive effect.[3]

At this point, it is essential to stress that we are considering 'stock' rather than 'flow' exchange controls. By the former, we mean controls which affect the desired equilibrium composition of portfolios; by the latter, controls which affect the speed at which it is approached. An example of the former is a tax on foreign assets, and of the latter, deliberately sluggish administration – of permission to buy foreign currency

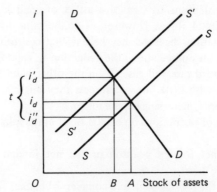

FIGURE 7.1   *The asset market in a capital importing country*

so as to invest overseas for example. Figure 7.1 shows a capital importing country. *SS* shows the desired amount of investments held in the country by foreigners at any interest rate. *DD* shows the net demand for capital at any rate after domestic purchases of assets; it is the difference between the desired stock of assets supplied and demand at each interest rate before foreign investors appear. It is downward sloping, reflecting the assumption that (*ceteribus paribus*) net indebtedness increased as interest rates fell. Equilibrium is initially at i_d, with foreigners holding OA of claims on the country. Suppose the authorities wish to reduce this. They can *either* restrict claims to OB (or less) or impose a tax (t) on interest receipts by foreigners equal to $i'_d i''_d$.[4] Either raises the domestic interest rate to i'_d, and reduces the foreign-held stock of capital to OB.

Where competitive conditions are no longer present, then, as Bhagwati shows in the trade case, the one-to-one correspondence between tariff and quota no longer holds; rather, for every quota there is a multiplicity of equivalent tariffs. The reason for this is straightforward; with a monopolistic supplier, the same price (*average* revenue) can correspond to an infinite number of *marginal* revenues.

III   CAPITAL CONTROLS AND INTEREST RATE PARITY

In this section it will be shown how capital controls affect international capital movements by examining how the relationship between the rates of return between assets in domestic and external markets is affected. The arbitrage activities of domestic banks, Euro-banks, and non-banking institutions ensure that:

1. the rates of return in the national and external markets are equalised
2. that the rates of return in different external markets are equalised through the availability of forward cover in the foreign exchange market
3. that the rates of return on assets in two different domestic markets will be the same.[5]

The introduction of restrictions on capital flows affects the above relationships in the same way as do the existence of transation costs in the securities and/or foreign exchange markets. Although the realised rates of return will be different from when such 'imperfections' did not exist, there will still be equilibrium in the markets, in the sense that there will be no unexploited profits to be made by making further transactions.[6]

Discriminatory Reserve Requirements on Non-resident Deposits

This kind of control has been extensively used by Germany — for most of the late 1950s, in the 1960s and early 1970s and again in 1978. The imposition of higher requirements on non-resident deposits discourages capital inflows because it increases the cost of funds borrowed abroad by domestic banks.

A domestic bank will borrow its own currency from the Euro-currency market if the effective cost of raising loanable funds from the Euro-currency market is less than the effective costs of raising loanable funds in the domestic market (the effective cost includes also the cost incurred by the reserve requirements on deposits). Thus by comparing the effective costs we find a relationship between the domestic and Euro-currency interest rates.

The effective cost per unit to a domestic bank of raising loanable funds in the Euro-currency market is:

$$i^e_{ec} = \frac{i_{ec}}{1 - m_e}$$

where i_{ec} is the Euro-currency deposit rate and m_e the domestic reserve requirement on non-resident deposits.

The effective cost per unit to a domestic bank of raising loanable funds in the domestic market is:

$$i_d^e = \frac{i_d}{1 - m_d}$$

where i_d is the domestic currency deposit rate and m_d the reserve requirement on residents' deposits.

Bank arbitrage will ensure that $i_{ec}^e = i_d^e$ and by substituting the definition above we have:

$$i_{ec} = i_d \left[\frac{1 - m_e}{1 - m_d}\right]$$

In the case of no capital controls $m_e = m_d$ and $i_{ec} = i_d$.

If we take the case of capital inflow controls, $m_e = m_d + T$:

$$i_{ec}^e = \frac{i_{ec}}{1 - (m_d + T)}$$

and

$$i_{ec} = i_d [1 - t] \text{ where } t = \frac{T}{1 - m_d}$$

The implication of having capital controls is that the domestic interest rate can be higher than the Euro-currency rate. At the same time the role of the domestic banks in the offshore *re-lending* of Euro-currencies is reduced because they are less able to take such *transactions on to* their balance sheets.[7] In addition, it implies that there will be a modification to the arbitrage relationship between i_d and a similar domestic rate in some other country.

Prohibition of Full Interest Payments on Non-resident Deposits

It can be shown how such a regulation affects the arbitrage relationship between domestic and foreign interest rates by examining the investment alternatives open to a non-resident.

In the case where there are no capital controls the return on a deposit held by a non-resident will be the interest rate payment (i_d) plus or minus any capital gain or loss which arises from fluctuation in the exchange rates.

$$r = \frac{S_t}{F_t}(1 + i_d)$$

where S_t is the spot exchange rate defined as domestic currency per unit of foreign currency, F_t is the forward exchange rate, regarded as an unbiased prediction of the future exchange rate expected to prevail at the time of the expiry of the deposit and i_d is the interest rate on the domestic deposit.

The return on a similar deposit held in the non-resident's home country is

$$r^* = (1 + i_f)$$

where i_f is the interest rate on the foreign currency deposit.

Arbitrage will ensure that the return on the domestic and foreign currency deposits is the same. In other words, the interest rate differential is equal to the forward discount on, for example, sterling, if the interest rate in the UK is greater than that of, for example, the US.[8]

$$i_d - i_f = \left[\frac{F_t - S_t}{S_t} \right]$$

If the domestic authorities prohibit the interest payment in full to the non-residents then the return on a domestic deposit held by a non-resident will be modified to:

$$r_E = \frac{S_t}{F_t} (1 + i_d^E) \text{ where } i_d^E = i_d(1 - t)$$

In this case the interest parity condition is modified to include another term:

$$i_d - i_f = i_d^t + \left[\frac{F_t - S_t}{S_t} \right]$$

A 'wedge' is interposed.

Dual Exchange Markets

The fundamental characteristic of a dual exchange market system is the channelling of current and capital transactions into separate exchange markets. The exchange rate for capital transactions is usually allowed to float freely (this exchange rate will be called the 'capital' rate) although some official intervention may take place. The exchange rate for current transactions is pegged, and official intervention takes place to prevent the rate from changing (this exchange rate will be called the 'current' rate).[9] By once more examining the investment alternatives open to a non-resident it can be shown how such an exchange rate system affects the arbitrage relationship between domestic and foreign interest rates.

The expected return to a non-resident investing in the home country is:

$$r = i_d \frac{ES_t^c}{S_t^f} + \frac{ES_t^f}{S_t^f}$$

where ES_t^c is the expected 'current' rate, S_t^f is the spot 'capital' rate, and ES_t^f is the expected spot 'capital' rate.[10] (The above expression for the rate of return implies that the interest payments will be transferred as a current item through the current account transactions. That is the usual practice.)

The expected return to a non-resident from investing in his own country is:

$$r^* = 1 + i_f$$

If the interest arbitrage operates costlessly, equilibrium in the financial market is achieved when:

$$1 + i_f = i_d \frac{ES_t^c}{S_t^f} + \frac{ES_t^f}{S_t^f}$$

The above condition is simplified to:[11]

$$i_f = i_d \left[\frac{1}{1 + p} \right] + f$$

where

$$p = \frac{S_t^f - S_t^c}{S_t^c}$$

$$f = \frac{ES_t^f - S_t^f}{S_t^f}$$

Two factors can make the i_d differ from i_f: a spread between the 'current' and 'capital' rates and expectations about the future 'capital' rate. These factors can either reinforce or offset each other. For example, an increase in the spot 'capital' rate will increase the premium and reduce the rate of return. At the same time if this increase is expected to reverse, there will be, in addition, an expected capital loss. If on the other hand it is believed that the exchange rate will keep on appreciating, there will be a capital gain which could offset the first effect.

Thus, assuming for the sake of example, that exchange rate expectations are regressive, if the authorities want to discourage capital inflows they will maintain the 'capital' rate at a premium over the 'current' rate. In the case of an attempt to discourage capital outflows, they will maintain the 'capital' rate at a discount below the 'current' rate.

IV CAPITAL CONTROLS AND THE ADJUSTMENT PROCESS UNDER FIXED AND FLEXIBLE EXCHANGE RATES

We shall now examine how capital controls affect exchange rate adjustment under fixed and flexible exchange rates. Our framework is based on the asset market approach to the balance of payments. It is shown that under fixed exchange rates, the imposition of capital controls enables a country to pursue an independent monetary policy in the short run (defined below); under flexible exchange rates, the imposition of capital controls prevents the exchange rate from adjusting to expected inflation rate differentials.

Adjustment Process under Fixed Exchange Rates

In our analysis we make use of the model developed by Dornbusch (1976). In such a model a balance of payments disequilibrium is reflected in a money-market disequilibrium. In the short-run the interest rate will have to change to restore equilibrium in the money market. However, this liquidity effect will be superseded by the change in foreign reserves, so that the domestic interest rate remains equal to the foreign interest rate.

The model can be set out in a simple four-quadrant diagram developed by Batchelor and Horne (1979).

Quadrant I shows how a desired money stock $M^d = M_0$ may be supplied by various combinations of domestic redit D^s and credit based on foreign currency reserves C^s. Quadrant II shows how the foreign assets C_0 would be multiplied to give a money stock contribution of C_0^s. Therefore the actual money stock M_0 consists of D_0^s credit based on domestic credit and C_0^s credit based on foreign sources. Quadrant IV shows the temporary effect on the interest rate i_d of a change in the money stock, with LL being the short-run liquidity preference schedule. Quadrant III reflects the fact that portfolios abroad will contain reduced stocks of domestic

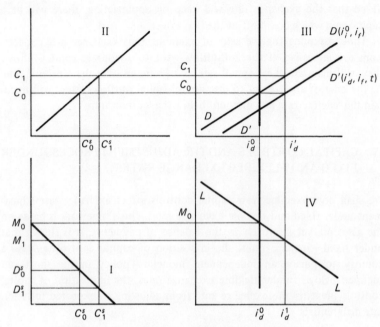

FIGURE 7.2   *Adjustment under fixed exchange rates*

bonds if their prices rise (i.e. interest rates fall) relative to the fixed price of foreign bonds. The stock of domestic bonds held by foreigners C_0 must be matched by domestic holdings of foreign money.

A fall in D will result in the short run in an increase in the interest rate in order to clear the money market. Thus, temporarily, the domestic interest rate will be higher than the foreign interest rate. This will increase the foreign demand for domestic assets, putting upward pressure on the exchange rate. This will necessitate intervention in the foreign exchange market by the monetary authorities, to purchase the excess foreign currency, resulting in an increase in foreign currency reserves. The total money stock will be unchanged but the division between the foreign and the domestic components will have changed; D will have fallen while foreign reserves will have increased. The domestic interest rate will fall to the original level since the money supply will be restored to the original level.

However, the adjustment is not yet complete because non-residents are not in equilibrium. They have more domestic bonds than they want to hold at the original level of the interest rate. As they try to get rid of them, the authorities will be obliged to buy them to prevent the exchange rate from changing. Thus in the end everybody has the same portfolio composition as before the monetary shock.

The implication is that independent monetary policy cannot be pursued. Monetary policy is dictated by the world economy. (We assume that the country is small and not in a position to affect the 'world' interest rate.)

Imposition of Capital Controls

As we have seen the imposition of capital controls will affect the rate of return on domestic assets held by non-residents. In the example given of a monetary contraction, the authorities will be able, by imposing capital inflow controls to maintain the domestic interest rate higher than the foreign interest (i_f) for as long as the capital control is in action. This can be shown again in Figure 7.2.

The *DD* curve in Quadrant IV shows the foreign demand of domestic bonds as a function of the interest rate differential between the domestic and foreign country. At the point of intersection with the vertical line the domestic and foreign interest rates are the same. If there are capital controls the foreign demand becomes in addition a function of the tax (*t*) which results from the imposition of controls. Thus in the case of capital inflow controls the *DD* schedule shifts to the right and a possible position is that such as $D'D'$. The domestic interest rate is higher than the foreign interest rate by the amount of the tax. The authorities have some degree of monetary independence. It is at this point that the short-run nature of this independence should be emphasised; for the *price level* consequences of using this independence will start to emerge, and will affect the exchange rate via the purchasing power parity relationship at some stage.

Adjustment under Flexible Exchange Rates

Under a floating exchange rate regime the exchange rate is determined in the long run by purchasing-power parity. But in the short run, because goods prices are sticky, interest-rate parity plays a key role. The model can be set out in a five-quadrant diagram (See Figure 7.3). Moving clockwise, quadrant I is the purchasing-power parity relationship. Quadrant II is the money (*M*)/price level (*P*) relationship; and hence quadrants I and II link money and the exchange rate. Quadrant III shows the temporary effect on interest rates of a change in the money stock with *LL* being the short run liquidity preference schedule. Quadrant IV shows the combination of the interest rate differential (*R*) and the domestic interest rate.

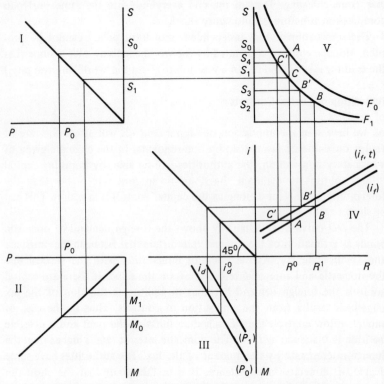

FIGURE 7.3 *Adjustment under flexible exchange rates*

Finally, quadrant *V* shows the combinations of *R* and the spot exchange rate (*S*) at which interest-rate parity holds, given the expected future spot-rate.

It is possible to generate various responses to a monetary shock, depending on how exchange rate expectations are formed: this is done in Batchelor and Horne (1979). For present purposes, it is sufficient to analyse rational expectations in the foreign exchange market. That shows the working of the model.

Suppose there is a fall in the quantity of money from M_0 to M_1. In the long run the price level (*P*) and the spot rate will fall by the same proportion. However in the short run the price level will not change, so the interest increases to i_d to clear the money market. Meanwhile the interest parity schedule in quadrant *V* has shifted downwards to combinations of *S* and *R* consistent with interest parity and the new expected spot rate. Hence in the short run *S* settles at a higher level (S_2) than the one consistent with long run equilibrium. Then as P starts to rise, so R goes back to R_0 and the exchange rate falls to S_1, the new equilibrium. Thus, the adjustment path of the exchange rate is ABC.

Imposition of Capital Controls

As already shown, the imposition of capital controls will affect the rate of return on domestic assets held by non-residents. Taking the example of the prohibition of full interest payments on non-resident deposits, the interest-rate parity condition was modified to include the tax rate which is implied by the controls.

$$i_d - i_f = i_d t + \left[\frac{E_t - S_t}{S_t} \right]$$

In this case R is expanded to include (t).[12] Therefore in quadrant IV there is an upward shift of the schedule. As a result in the short run (that is, with no price level changes) the exchange rate will appreciate less than when there were no controls, assuming that expectations about the exchange rate were not affected by the imposition of controls (i.e. it will move to S_3). Had market participants believed that capital controls would have been effective permanently the appreciation of the exchange rate would have been less (the FF schedule would have shifted between F_0 and F_1). However, as prices adjust to the fall in the money stock, the exchange rate will depreciate to S_4. In the diagram the adjustment path is now $A B' C'$.

V   THE EFFECTIVENESS OF CAPITAL CONTROLS

The imposition of capital controls can in principle have an impact on the interest-rate parity condition, the spot exchange rate and the forward exchange rate. As we have seen capital controls can be expressed in the form of a tax which modifies the interest-rate parity condition. *Rates of return* on domestic and foreign assets are still equalised, but the interest rates on these assets can differ by a different amount from when there were no controls. This effect depends on the prevailing exchange rate regime and on market participants' expectations. In a country under fixed exchange rates, the tax which results from controls is largely absorbed by the domestic interest rate. The reason for this is that the spot exchange rate is held fixed, while the forward rate will only move outside the bands around the par value when market participants expect a possible official change of parity. In a country under flexible exchange rates, the tax will be absorbed by the forward premium. How the burden of adjustment of the forward premium falls between the forward and spot exchange rates depends on investors' expectations. It was shown that even when they believe that controls are ineffective, there will still be an effect on the spot exchange rate, because the forward rate will change to reflect the effects of financial policies, as well as other real shocks, on the exchange rate.

Estimating the tax resulting from controls is much more straightforward than estimating the effect on exchange rates. It can be done by comparing the deviations from interest-rate parity when using national interest rates with those using external market rates. The former includes the impact of both transaction costs and capital controls, while the latter includes only the impact of transaction costs. Thus, their difference should capture the net effect of controls. Otani and Tiwazi (1981) in their study of the Japanese experience in 1978–81 show that capital controls whenever imposed caused distortions in the markets. They compared deviations from interest-rate parity when using a three-month Euro-yen, and a three-month Euro-dollar deposit, with deviations when using a three-month Gensaki bond and a three-month Euro-dollar deposit.[14] The deviations in the two interest parities were great throughout 1978 (especially in the first quarter) and again in 1980. During both periods capital controls were extensively used. The implementation of the new Foreign Exchange Control Law in December 1980, resulted in the deviations between the two interest parities disappearing.

A study of Germany has produced similar results.[15] Here, the author compares West German domestic and Euro-Deutschmark interest rates between 1973 and 1978.[16] Johnston found that for the period mid-1975 to end-1977, there was a very close relationship between the rates, but for the period 1973–4 and again in early 1978 when there were capital controls, there were substantial deviations.

What is characteristic of these experiences is the multiplicity of the controls. The Authorities had continually to resort to supplementary measures to counter methods of evasion. For a type of control to be effective, it should affect assets of all maturities. If the control only affects some assets, for example long-term but not medium- and short-term ones, then there will be 'segmentation' of the markets. The control will isolate the markets for assets affected by it, but capital will still flow via the markets which are not affected, namely, medium- and short-term ones.

Thus, for capital controls to be effective they have to affect all assets unless market participants have very strongly preferred habitats.[17]

Taking the example of Germany, between January 1973 and January 1974, there were discriminatory reserve requirements for non-resident bank deposits up to 95 per cent as compared with 13 per cent for resident deposits. However, capital inflows might not be affected, if non-residents by-pass the banks by placing funds with institutions outside the banking system which are not subject to minimum reserves. During this period therefore the German authorities imposed in addition a 100 per cent minimum reserve requirement against foreign loans contracted by West German companies, making it unprofitable for them to borrow externally (Barderpot Law). This regulation had to widen its coverage to include smaller sized transactions as time went on.

TABLE 7.1   *Three-month Euro-DM interest rate less West German three-month inter-bank rate.*

	Mean	Variance	No. of observations
1 Jan 1973 End Dec 1973	−6.42	5.89	46
1 Jan 1974 End July 1975	−0.23	0.27	87
1 Aug 1975 End Dec 1977	−0.15	0.03	120

SOURCE R. B. Johnston (1979).

If one looks carefully at the period after 1978, when the authorities imposed discriminatory reserve requirements once more on the level and growth of Deutschmark liabilities of domestic banks to non-residents, one notices that the Euro-Deutschmark rate dropped below the domestic interbank rate and subsequently returned to a normal level. The reason could be that that type of control was not enough to stem the capital inflow. Similar comments can be made about Japan, which has had the most comprehensive system of controls.

VI   SUMMARY

This chapter has concentrated on developing the techniques for a taxonomic analysis of exchange controls. It was first shown that, since the international capital markets are competitive, quantitative exchange controls can generally be regarded as having unique tax equivalents. The chapter has gone on to show the conditions under which exchange controls can affect domestic interest rates, the spot exchange rate, a forward exchange rate and the process of exchange rate adjustment.

NOTES

1. There are some exceptions e.g. the investment currency market in the UK, which aimed at ensuring a zero net outflow by UK residents, non-residents funds were left unregulated.
2. See Mills (1976).
3. See Bhagwati (1969) for the demonstration of this proposition in the context of international trade in goods and services. It should be noted also that strict equivalence holds only in the absence of uncertainty. This problem is set aside for the moment, as it is best dealt with when considering the individual cases where quantitative restrictions have been used; for the institutional setting this is important.
4. $i_d(1 - t) = i_d' = i_f$ where i_f is the 'world' interest rate.
5. Assume we have two currencies, the dollar and the Deutschmark; $i_\$$ and i_{DM} are the domestic interest rates on the dollar and the Deutschmark respectively; $i_{E\$}$ and i_{EDM} the Euro-currency interest rate on the dollar and the Deutschmark. Arbitrade ensures that if $i_\$ = i_{E\$}$, $i_{DM} = i_{EDM}$, $i_{DM} + f_p = i_{E\$}$. If i_{EDM} is higher than i_{DM} because, say, of capital controls, then f_p falls to maintain interest rate parity in Euro-currency interest rates. For an exposition of the simultaneous determination of the national interest rates, the Euro-currency rate and the forward premium (see Herring and Marston [1976]).
6. For elaboration of this concept of equilibrium see Levich and Frenkel (1975).
7. They may, however, act in the markets via off-balance-sheet transactions. This would be analogous to the use of banker's acceptances during the period of the IBELs restrictions in the UK. A description of this restriction and of how banks responded to it, can be found in Batchelor and Griffiths (1980).
8. The relationship given below between the domestic and foreign interest rates and the forward discount is a simplified version of

$$i_d - i_f = \left[\frac{F - S}{S}\right](1 + i_f).$$

For expository reasons we have made the traditional simplifying assumption that $(1 + i_f)$ is close to 1.
9. For a more detailed explanation of the operation of the dual exchange market see Fleming (1971 and 1974).

10. The foreign exchange rate is defined as foreign currency per unit of domestic currency. This definition facilitates the simplification of the arbitrage relationship.

11.

$$i_d \left[\frac{ES_t^c - S_t^c}{S_t^c} \right] \cong 0$$

since the 'current' rate is pegged.

12. $R = i_d(1 - t) - i_f$

13. The controls took the form of increasing reserve requirements on non-residents deposits, of prohibiting the purchase by non-residents of yen securities of various maturities, and of banning the purchase by non-residents of short-term treasury bills.

14. They assume that the interest on a three-month Euro-dollar deposit is equal to the interest on a three-month dollar deposit in the US; a reasonable assumption after the abolition of US capital controls in 1974.

15. R. B. Johnston (1979).

16. In this case, too, the author makes the reasonable assumption that the Euro-dollar rate is equal to the domestic dollar rate.

17. In fact the evidence from the term-structure literature is that the term structure appears to be best explained by a combined theory of expectations and risk aversion. See, for example, Van Horne (1970).

REFERENCES

R. A. Batchelor and B. Griffiths (1980) 'Monetary Restraint Under Credit Controls: The Lessons of the Current Practice in the UK', Discussion Paper No. 9, Centre for Banking and International Finance, The City University.

R. A. Batchelor and J. Horne (1979) 'Money, the Balance of Payments and the Rate of Exchange', *Annual Monetary Review* No. 1, Centre for Banking and International Finance, The City University, October.

V. Barattieri and G. Ragazzi (1971) 'An Analysis of a Two-Tier Foreign Exchange Market, *Banca Nationale de Lavoro, Quarterly Review*, No. 99, December.

J. Bhagwati (1969) 'On the Equivalence of Tariffs and Quotas', in J. Bhagwati (ed.), *Trade, Tariffs and Growth* (MIT Press).

R. E. Caves (1976) 'The Welfare Economics of Control on Capital Movements', in A. K. Swoboda (ed.) *Capital Movements and their Control* (Leiden: Sijthoff).

R. Dornbusch (1976) 'Expectations and Exchange Rate Dynamics', *Journal of Political Economy*, December.

G. Dufey and I. H. Giddy (1978) *The International Money Market* (New York: Prentice-Hall, Foundations of Finance Series).

J. M. Fleming (1971) 'Dual Exchange Rates for Current and Capital Trans-actions: A Theoretical Examination', in *Essays in International Economics* (Harvard University Press).

J. M. Fleming (1974) 'Dual Exchange Markets and Other Remedies for Disruptive Capital Flows', *International Monetary Fund Staff Papers*.

R. J. Herring and R. C. Marston (1976) 'The Forward Market and Interest Rates in the Eurocurrency and National Money Markets' in C. H. Stern, J. H. Makin, D. E. Logue (eds) *Eurocurrencies and the International Monetary System*, American Enterprise Institute for Public Policy Research.

R. B. Johnston (1979) 'Some aspects of the determination of Euro-currency Interest Rates', *Bank of England Quarterly Bulletin*, March.

A. Lanyi (1975) 'Separate Exchange Markets for Capital and Current Transactions', *International Monetary Fund Staff Papers*, vol. 22, November.

R. M. Levich and J. A. Frenkel (1975) 'Covered Interest Arbitrage: Un-exploited Profits?', *Journal of Political Economy*, April.

R. H. Mills (1976) 'The Regulation of Short-Term Capital Movements in Major Industrial Countries', in A. K. Swoboda (ed.) *Capital Movements and their Control* (Leiden: Sijthoff).

I. Otani and S. Tiwazi (1981) 'Capital Controls and Interest Rate Parity: The Japanese Experience, 1978–1981', *International Monetary Fund Staff Papers*, December.

UK (1980) House of Commons, Treasury and Civil Service Committee, Session 1979–80, *Monetary Policy*, November.

J. C. Van Horne (1970) *Function and Analysis of Capital Market Rates* (New York, Prentice-Hall).

8 Fiscal and Monetary Policies in a Flexible Exchange Rate Model with Full Employment and Static Expectations

EMMANUEL PIKOULAKIS

I INTRODUCTION

In an important paper Tobin and Buiter (1976) pursued the pioneering work of Blinder and Solow (1973) and (1974) further to confirm the Blinder and Solow key result that bond-financed fiscal expansions have permanent effects on aggregate demand. When Tobin and Buiter considered such a fiscal expansion in the context of a fully employed, closed economy, with flexible prices a very strong result was shown to emerge: the steady-state output increased through capital deepening. Unfortunately this result can be accepted only if price expectations adapt fairly quickly to price experience because only then is their model stable. Under static expectations their model is unstable. In this chapter we generalise the full-employment model with static expectations presented by Tobin and Buiter in two important respects. First we 'open up' the economy to trade in commodities and securities with the rest of the world in a regime of perfectly flexible exchange rates. Second, we discard the restrictive assumption that bonds and capital are perfect substitutes in portfolios by allowing for imperfect substitution. In turn, we use our model to reconsider the effects of a bond-financed fiscal expansion and we also use it to study the effects of an open-market operation.

The economy trades with the rest of the world in a home-produced good and in a foreign-produced good and it also trades in government interest-bearing debt. The economy is small in the sense that it has no influence on the foreign price of the foreign good and on the world interest rate. Claims on capital are not traded internationally. The exchange rate, the terms of trade and the market return on capital are all endogenously determined. The specification of the aggregate demand for the home-produced good resembles a specification suggested by Dornbusch and Fischer (1980). In 'opening-up' the Tobin-Buiter model we are able to study the effects of a bond-financed fiscal expansion and the effects of an open-market operations on variables such as the exchange rate, the terms of trade and the current account (or the capital account).

II THE MODEL: SHORT-RUN EQUILIBRIUM

Short-run equilibrium is defined by a set of asset-clearing equations and an equation which describes equilibrium in the goods market. Residents of the home country hold three kinds of assets: domestic money, bonds and claims on domestic capital. Domestic money is of the fiat kind issued exclusively by the monetary authorities. The nominal stock of such money is denoted by M. Private holdings of bonds consist of bonds issued by the home government and bonds issued abroad. These two types of bonds are considered to be perfect substitutes for each other and, therefore, they bear a common, net of tax, interest rate denoted by r. Foreign-issued bonds are assumed to be denominated in domestic currency. The nominal value of foreign issued bonds is denoted by B_f while the nominal value of bonds issued by the home government and held by private home residents is denoted by B_g. The sum of B_f and B_g is denoted by B. Bonds are assumed to be of very short maturity and are, thus, modelled like interest-bearing deposits. Claims on domestic capital are assumed to be equal in number to the units of capital domestically located. Capital and the domestically-produced goods are homogeneous. The stock of domestically located capital is denoted by K and the price of a claim to a unit of capital in terms of the domestically-produced good is set equal to one. Thus capital gains and losses on claims on capital are assumed away. The net of tax market yield on capital is denoted by ρ. The home country produces one type of good and it trades in two types of goods; the home good and a foreign good. The price of the foreign good expressed in domestic currency is denoted by eP^* where e is the exchange rate and P^* is the price of the foreign good expressed in foreign currency. The terms of trade is defined by $\lambda \equiv (eP^*/P)$ where P is the price of the home good expressed in domestic currency. Next we turn to the description of the behaviour that defines equilibrium in the market for assets and in the market for the home-produced good.

$$A \equiv \frac{\lambda(M+B)}{eP^*} + K \equiv m + b + K \tag{1}$$

$$\frac{\lambda M}{eP^*} \equiv m = L(r, \rho)A \tag{2}$$

$$L_r < 0, \quad L_\rho < 0$$

$$\frac{\lambda B}{eP^*} \equiv b = V(r, \rho)A \tag{3}$$

$$V_r > 0, \quad V_\rho < 0$$

$$F(K) - I\left[\frac{(1-t)F'(K)}{\rho}\right] = D(\lambda, A, y) + X(\lambda) + g, \tag{4}$$

$$y \equiv (1-t)F(K), \quad F'(K) > 0, \quad F''(K) < 0, \quad I'(\ ) > 0, \quad I(1) = 0$$

$$D_\lambda > 0, \quad D_A > 0, \quad D_y > 0, \quad X_\lambda > 0$$

Equation (1) defines the aggregate level of assets, A. Equation (2) describes momentary equilibrium in the money market while equation (3) describes momentary equilibrium in the bond market. By the asset constraint, equations (2) and (3) are sufficient to describe momentary (short-run) portfolio balance. These two equations follow a popular specification of portfolio balance according to which asset demands depend on all the expected real rates of return (net of tax) and on the level of assets. In our model money is non-interest bearing and expectations are static. Accordingly, there are only two asset returns to consider, r and ρ. By the small country assumption r is pre-determined in the rest of the world. Assets are assumed to be gross substitutes and the wealth elasticity of each asset demand is assumed to be unity (asset demands are proportional to wealth). Equation (4) describes equilibrium in the market for the home produced good. The left-hand side of this equation gives the supply of the home-produced good available for consumption, while the right-hand side gives the demand for the home-produced good for consumption purposes. In turn, this supply consists of the production of the home-produced good less the amount used for investment (capital formation). Production follows the standard neo-classical production function with constant returns to scale. Since there is no growth in the labour force there is no loss in generality in choosing units such that the labour force is set equal to one. Wages and prices are perfectly flexible and the supply of labour is assumed to be perfectly inelastic. Accordingly full employment prevails at all times. Investment follows a version of a specification made popular by Tobin according to which investment depends, positively, on the ratio of the marginal product of capital (net of tax) to the market yield on capital (net of tax). In steady-state equilibrium the market yield on capital equals the marginal product of capital and in the absence of growth, net investment is zero. In our model we ignore depreciation of the capital stock. Aggregate consumption demand for the home good consists of the sum of three components: home private demand given by $D( )$, foreign demand given by $X( )$ and government demand exogenously determined at a level equal to g. Home demand is taken to depend, positively, on the relative price of foreign goods, λ, the level of wealth and the net of tax domestic product. Foreign demand for the home good is taken to be an increasing function of the terms of trade, λ.

At any moment in time, M, B and K are predetermined. In a regime of perfectly flexible exchange rates M is policy-determined. Since B is the only internationally tradeable asset and M is policy determined, private residents cannot change B; only its composition. Finally K is short-run predetermined by past capital formation. In the long run both B and K, and possibly M as well, are endogenously determined. Substituting the definition of A, given by equation (1), into equations (2) to (4) we are left with three equations to determine e, ρ and λ (P is then determined via $P \equiv (eP^*/\lambda)$) in terms of M, B, K, r, P^*, g, and t.

Accordingly, the short-run solution of our model can be described by the following reduced form equations.

$$e = e(M, B, K; r, P^*, g, t) \tag{5}$$

$$e_M > 0, \quad e_B < 0, \quad e_K \gtrless 0, \quad e_g < 0$$

$$\rho = \rho(M, B, K; \ r, P^*, g, t) \tag{6}$$

$$\rho_M > 0, \quad \rho_B < 0, \quad \rho_K = 0, \quad \rho_g = 0$$

$$\lambda = \lambda(M, B, K; \ r, P^*, g, t) \tag{7}$$

$$\lambda_M > 0, \quad \lambda_B < 0, \quad \lambda_K \gtrless 0, \quad \lambda_g < 0$$

The signs of the partial derivatives reported above are derived in the Appendix. Since we shall not be concerned with variations in r, P^* and t, the partial derivatives of e, ρ and λ with respect to r, P^* and t have not been derived. At this point we should make it clear that the signs of e_M,

e_B, ρ_M, ρ_B, λ_M and λ_B reported above crucially depend on the assumption that $mV_\rho - bL_\rho < 0$. In words, the crucial assumption is that the elasticity of the demand for bonds with respect to the yield on capital is bigger, in absolute terms, than the elasticity of the demand for money with respect to the yield on capital. To put it differently, the crucial assumption is that bonds and capital are closer substitutes than money and capital. The reason we wish to make this assumption is that, as it turns out, it proves to be necessary and sufficient for the stability of our model.

III DYNAMICS AND THE STABILITY OF LONG-RUN EQUILIBRIUM

To help appreciate the dynamics of the model consider, first, the following identities:

$$B \equiv B_g + B_f \tag{8}$$

$$B^T \equiv B_g + B^F + B_M \tag{9}$$

where B^T is the total stock of government interest-bearing debt expressed in units of domestic currency and where B^F and B_M is the part of this stock held by the rest of the world and by the monetary authorities, respectively. From (8) and (9) we derive

$$B \equiv B^T + (B_f - B^F) - B_M \quad \text{and} \tag{10}$$

$$\dot{B} \equiv \dot{B}^T + (\dot{B}_f - \dot{B}^F) - \dot{B}_M \tag{10'}$$

In a perfectly flexible exchange rate regime $\dot{M} = \dot{B}_M$, that is, the issue of money derives exclusively from the part of interest-bearing government debt which is monetised by the monetary authorities. For the moment we shall assume that monetary policy is designed to monetise a constant proportion γ of budget deficits so that $\dot{M} = \dot{B}_M = \gamma \dot{B}^T$. Accordingly

$$\dot{B} = \dot{B}^T(1 - \gamma) + (\dot{B}_f - \dot{B}^F). \tag{10''}$$

The second term on the right-hand side above records the capital account balance expressed in terms of domestic currency. When this term is positive (negative) the capital account is in deficit (surplus). In a perfectly flexible exchange rate regime $\dot{B}_f - \dot{B}^F$ also records the current account surplus. An alternative expression for the current account surplus is the difference between saving and the sum of investment plus budget deficits. Regarding saving we shall assume that it reflects a stock adjustment process whereby wealth adjusts to its desired level. Desired wealth is taken to be a multiple $\hat{\mu}$ of domestic output. Accordingly, saving measured in units of the home good is specified by

$$s = \sigma(\hat{\mu}F(K) - A), \quad 0 < \sigma < 1 \tag{11}$$

where σ is the speed of adjustment taken to be constant. Budget deficits measured in units of the home good are defined by

$$\lambda \frac{\dot{B}^T}{eP^*} = g + \lambda g_F + \frac{r\lambda B^T}{eP^*} - tF(K) \tag{12}$$

In the above g_F measures the units of the foreign good consumed by the government and t is the proportional tax rate which is assumed to apply to all types of income that arise from the production of the home good. In what follows we shall find it convenient to treat $\lambda g_F + \lambda(rB^T/eP^*)$ as a policy variable to be denoted by $\tilde{g}$. The assumption is that the government adjusts g_F in a way such that it keeps $\tilde{g}$ constant thus offsetting variations that would otherwise arise from the endogeneity of λ, e and the accumulation or decumulation of B^T over time. Taking the above discussion into account and making use of equation (11), equation (12) (in its amended form discussed above) and the specification of investment given in equation (4) we can rewrite (10″) as follows:

$$\dot{B} = \dot{B}^T(1 - \gamma) + \frac{eP^*}{\lambda}\left[\sigma(\hat{\mu}F(K) - A) - I\left[\frac{(1-t)F'(K)}{\rho}\right]\right] - \dot{B}^T$$

$$= \frac{eP^*}{\lambda}\left[\sigma(\hat{\mu}F(K) - A) - I\left(\frac{(1-t)F'(K)}{\rho}\right) - \gamma(g + \tilde{g} - tF(K)) \right] \tag{13}$$

In what follows we shall consider only the case where $\gamma = 0$, i.e. the case where there is no flow monetisation of budget deficits. From the definition of assets given by $(\lambda(M + B)/eP^*) + K$ we obtain

$$\dot{B} = \frac{eP^*}{\lambda}\left[\sigma\left(\hat{\mu}F(K) - \frac{\lambda(M+B)}{eP^*} - K\right) - I\left[\frac{(1-t)F'(K)}{\rho}\right]\right] \tag{13′}$$

where e, ρ and λ are defined by (5) to (7). Accordingly $\dot{B}$ depends on $(M, B, K; \ r, P^*, g, t)$. The other dynamic equation to consider defines the evolution of capital which has been already described by

$$\dot{K} = I\left[\frac{(1-t)F'(K)}{\rho}\right] \tag{14}$$

The linearisation of (13′) and (14) around equilibrium yields the following system of differential equations:

$$\begin{bmatrix} \dot{B} \\ \dot{K} \end{bmatrix} = \begin{bmatrix} a_{11} & a_{12} \\ a_{21} & a_{22} \end{bmatrix} \begin{bmatrix} B - \bar{B} \\ K - \bar{K} \end{bmatrix} \tag{15}$$

where $\bar{B}$ and $\bar{K}$ denote the steady-state values of B and K, respectively. Stability requires that $a_{11} + a_{22} < 0$ and that $a_{11}a_{22} > a_{12}a_{21}$. As was mentioned above the assumption that bonds and capital are closer substitutes in portfolios than money and capital, reflected in the condition $mV_\rho - bL_\rho < 0$, is necessary and sufficient to ensure stability. Accordingly we shall make that assumption. In the Appendix we derive the expressions for $a_{11}, a_{12}, a_{21}, a_{22}$ and we use these expressions to state the stability conditions explicitly. Here it will suffice to report that $a_{11} < 0, a_{12} \gtrless 0$, $a_{21} > 0, a_{22} < 0$.

In Figure 8.1 we depict the $\dot{B} = 0$ locus and the $\dot{K} = 0$ locus. We shall make use of this diagram in our analysis that follows. Along the $\dot{K} = 0$ locus net investment is zero and the stock of capital is constant. Along the $\dot{B} = 0$ locus the accumulation of bonds by private residents is zero and the stock of these bonds is constant. Alternatively, when the flow of budget deficits is not monetised, that is, when $\gamma = 0, \dot{B} = 0$ implies $\dot{B}_f - \dot{B}^F = -\dot{B}^T$. In other words, when $\gamma = 0$ the combinations of B and K along the $\dot{B} = 0$ locus are those combinations which make the current account surplus (deficit) identically equal to the budget surplus (deficit). The slope of $\dot{K} = 0$ locus is given by $-(a_{22}/a_{21}) > 0$. A rise in K reduces the rate of capital accumulation since it reduces the net of tax marginal product of capital (since $F''(K) < 0$) while it leaves the net of tax market yield on capital unchanged (since $\rho_K = 0$). At the same time a rise in B reduces ρ ($\rho_B < 0$) relative to $(1 - t)F'(K)$ and it helps stimulate investment. This

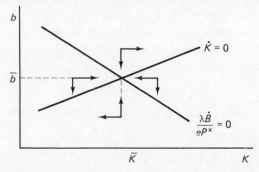

FIGURE 8.1   *The dynamics of capital and bond accumulation*

explains why a rise in K must be accompanied by a rise in B to maintain $\dot{K} = 0$. The slope of the $\dot{B} = 0$ locus is given by $-(a_{12}/a_{11}) \gtreqless 0$. By the stability condition that $a_{11}a_{22} > a_{12}a_{21}$ we obtain $-(a_{22}/a_{21}) > -(a_{12}/a_{11})$. Thus stability requires that the slope of the $\dot{K} = 0$ locus is numerically larger than the slope of the $\dot{B} = 0$ locus. Thus if the $\dot{B} = 0$ locus is to have a positive slope this slope must be less steep than the slope of the $\dot{K} = 0$ locus. In other words the $\dot{B} = 0$ locus must cut the $\dot{K} = 0$ locus from above. In our diagram we assumed, for simplicity, that $-(a_{12}/a_{11}) < 0$. For convenience of illustration we shall retain this assumption. Accordingly, a rise in K is assumed to require a fall in B to maintain $\dot{B} = 0$. To explain this we first note that around equilibrium a reduction in B reduces the real value of $(\lambda(M + B)/eP^*)$ and it also raises the market yield on capital since $\rho_B < 0$. Accordingly, around equilibrium a reduction in B stimulates saving and depresses investment and, given that $\dot{B}^T = 0$ around equilibrium, the current account turns into surplus which implies $\dot{B} > 0$. Here we should note that a reduction in B depreciates the exchange rate since $e_B < 0$ and it also worsens the terms of trade since $\lambda_B < 0$. As can be shown, the elasticity of e with respect to B is larger, in absolute value, than the elasticity of λ with respect to B. With a given P^* this calls for a reduction in λ/e when B is reduced and this is sufficient to explain the reduction in $(\lambda(M + B)/eP^*)$ that follows a reduction in B. A rise in K has opposing effects on the rate of accumulation of bonds. On the one hand such a rise raises output and thereby desired wealth and it also reduces the rate of capital formation. On the other hand a rise in K raises wealth directly and thus depresses saving. Here we assume, for convenience of illustration and without any substantial consequence, that on balance a rise in K depresses saving by more than it reduces capital formation, that is, we assume $a_{12} < 0$. Accordingly, around equilibrium a rise in K stimulates a decumulation of bonds and this requires a fall in B to maintain $\dot{B} = 0$. Above the $\dot{K} = 0$ locus, $\dot{K} > 0$ while below this locus $\dot{K} < 0$. Similarly above the $\dot{B} = 0$ locus $\dot{B} < 0$ while below this locus $\dot{B} > 0$. The intersection of the $\dot{K} = 0$ locus with the $\dot{B} = 0$ locus divides the plane in four areas and the arrows indicate the paths that B and K take when these variables happen to be in any of these areas.

IV   THE CONDITIONS FOR STEADY-STATE EQUILIBRIUM

At the steady state, $\dot{K} = 0$, $s = 0$, $\dot{B}^T = 0$, $\dot{B} = 0$ and also $\dot{M} = 0$. Without any flow monetisation of the budget deficit M is exogenous both in the short and in the long run. The conditions for steady-state equilibrium yield the following equations:

$$(1 - t)F'(K) = \rho \tag{16}$$

$$(I(1) = 0)$$

$$\hat{\mu}F(K) = m + b + K \tag{17}$$

$$(s(o) = 0)$$

$$g + \tilde{g} = tF(K) \tag{18}$$

$$(\dot{B}^T = 0)$$

$$\frac{\lambda \bar{M}}{eP^*} = L(r, (1 - t)F'(K))(\hat{\mu}F(K)) \tag{19}$$

$$\frac{\lambda B}{eP^*} = V(r, (1 - t)F'(K))(\hat{\mu}F(K)) \tag{20}$$

$$F(K) = D(\lambda, \hat{\mu}F(K), (1 - t)F(K)) + X(\lambda) + g \tag{21}$$

Equation (16) reflects the assumption that capital accumulation is zero when the marginal product of capital equals the market yield on capital. Equation (17) reflects the assumption that asset accumulation is zero when desired wealth equals actual wealth. Equation (18) is the balanced budget condition and, as in Tobin and Buiter is a key equation since it determines the steady state K in terms of $g, \tilde{g}$ and t. Equations (19) to (20) describe steady-state equilibrium in the money market and in the bond market, respectively. These equations incorporate the conditions described in (16) and (17). Given that K is determined by (18) and that M, r and P^* are exogenous, equation (19) determines λ/e or $P = (eP^*/\lambda)$. So here we have the familiar proposition that in the long run the domestic price level is determined in the money market. In turn equation (20) determines B while equation (21), which describes steady-state equilibrium in the market for the home good, determines the terms of trade λ. Finally, given λ/e determined in the money market and given that λ is determined in the home-commodity market the exchange rate becomes determinate. It is important here to note that the exchange rate at the steady state reflects both the equilibrium in the money market and the equilibrium in the home-good market.

V   AN INCREASE IN g FINANCED BY BORROWING

Let us, first, consider the impact effects of an increase in government expenditure on the home-produced good. As equations (5) to (7) suggest $e_g < 0$, $\rho_g = 0$, $\lambda_g < 0$. Accordingly an increase in g causes an impact appreciation in the exchange rate and an impact improvement in the terms of trade while leaving the market yield on capital unaffected. Moreover, the expressions for e_g and λ_g, derived in the Appendix, make it clear that e and λ fall by the same proportion leaving $P \equiv (eP^*/\lambda)$ unaffected. A glance at equations (1) to (3) verifies this last result immediately. Substituting equation (1) into (2) and (3) we are left with a system of two equations which can determine $P \equiv (eP^*/\lambda)$ and ρ in terms of M, B, K and r alone. Accordingly, the rise in g creates no impact effect on portfolio balance. In the home-good market, described by equation (4) the increase in g fully 'crowds out' $D(\ ) + X(\ )$ via the impact fall in λ. There is no impact 'crowding-out' of investment. This result is in sharp contrast to the standard short-run result that follows an expansionary fiscal policy. To quote from Tobin and Buiter, 'Expansionary fiscal policy, with constant nominal money stock, always raises the interest rate. Unless the demand for money is interest-inelastic and the *LM* curve vertical, it also raises the velocity of money and the prive level. Increased real government expenditure "crowds out" private investment and possibly also private consumption, to the extent necessary to equate total real demand to fixed real supply. But the short-run analysis does not trace the further effects of these changes in the rates of growth of capital and government debt.' Following our discussion immediately prior to the above quotation we can further observe that in the absence of any impact effects on P or ρ, keeping M and B constant, there can be no further effects in the rates of growth of capital and government debt. To put it differently there is nothing in the short-run equilibrium conditions nor in our dynamic equations that would suggest a shift in the $\dot{B} = 0$ and the $\dot{K} = 0$ loci. And yet equation (18) suggests that the steady-state K is increased. This inconsistency is resolved once one realises that the moment g is increased the government must issue either money or bonds to effect this increase. To put it differently either $dg = (dM/P)$ or $dg = (dB/P)$. In even more familiar terms the shift in the IS curve brought about by dg must be accompanied, simultaneously, by a shift in the *LM* curve. Once this is taken into account all is well. In what follows we shall assume that the increase in g is financed on *impact* by the issue of money so that $dg = \lambda(dM/eP^*) = (dM/P)$ and we shall also assume that the *continuing flow of budget deficits* is entirely financed by borrowing so that $\dot{M} = 0$. Thus, there is a once and for all increase in M by a discrete amount and a continuing issue (or retirement, as the case may be) of government interest-bearing debt. To incorporate this in our model we shall have to rewrite equations (5) to (7) as follows:

$$e = \widetilde{e}(M(g), B, K; \quad g, t, r, P^*) \tag{5'}$$

$$\widetilde{e}_g = e_M \frac{eP^*}{\lambda} + e_g$$

$$\rho = \widetilde{\rho}(M(g), B, K; \quad g, t, r, P^*) \tag{6'}$$

$$\widetilde{\rho}_g = \rho_M \frac{eP^*}{\lambda} + \rho_g = \rho_M \frac{eP^*}{\lambda}$$

$$\lambda = \widetilde{\lambda}(M(g), B, K; \quad g, t, r, P^*) \tag{7'}$$

$$\widetilde{\lambda}_g = \lambda_M \frac{eP^*}{\lambda} + \lambda_g$$

Returning to our dynamic equations (13') and (14), incorporating the results in (5') to (7') and making use of the expressions for e_M, ρ_M, λ_M, e_g, λg derived in the Appendix and of the definition of A we obtain that, around equilibrium,

$$\frac{\lambda}{e} \left(\frac{\partial \dot{B}}{\partial g} \right) = \frac{-\sigma(X_\lambda + D_\lambda)Ab(\widetilde{V}_\rho + \widetilde{L}_\rho)}{e\Delta}$$

$$+ \frac{I'(1)(X_\lambda + D_\lambda)\widetilde{V}(\ )K(1-t)F'(K)}{\rho^2 e\Delta} > 0 \tag{22}$$

and that

$$\frac{\partial \dot{K}}{\partial g} = \frac{-I'(1)(X_\lambda + D_\lambda)\widetilde{V}(\ )K(1-t)F'(K)}{\rho^2 e\Delta} < 0 \tag{23}$$

Accordingly both the $\dot{B} = 0$ locus and the $\dot{K} = 0$ locus shift upwards. As the above expressions indicate the shift in the $\dot{B} = 0$ locus is the larger resulting in a new intersection above and to the right of the old intersection. This is shown in Figure 8.2. The new equilibrium results in a higher K, $(\bar{\bar{K}} > \bar{K})$ and a higher b, $(\bar{\bar{b}} > \bar{b})$. The path to the new equilibrium is depicted by arrows. Along this path K declines initially but in time this decline is reversed and is followed by a rise in K. On the other hand B rises continually to its steady-state level.

Equation (18) confirms that K is higher at the new steady-state. From equation (17) we learn that wealth is also higher at the new steady-state. Equation (16) suggests that the rate of return on capital is reduced. Since steady-state ρ is reduced and steady wealth is increased both m and b are

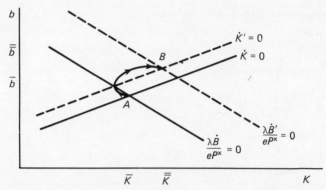

FIGURE 8.2   *The dynamics of capital and bond accumulation with an increase in government expenditure financed by borrowing*

higher at the new steady-state. Unfortunately one cannot unambiguously determine the steady-state effects on λ and e. The steady-state effects of a change in g on λ, e and λ/e remain an empirical question.

Finally consider the path of the current account balance. The locus along which this account balances is given by $\dot{B} - \dot{B}^T = 0$. Around equilibrium the slope of this locus is given by $(-[a_{12} + (e/\lambda)tF'(K)]/a_{11})$ which is numerically larger than the slope of the $\dot{B} = 0$ locus since $(-(e/\lambda)tF'(K)/a_{11}) > 0$. Whether the $\dot{B} - \dot{B}^T = 0$ locus can be steeper than the $\dot{K} = 0$ locus is an empirical question which opens up the possibility of two different types of path for the current account balance. Figure 8.3 illustrates this. One can easily verify that on an adjustment path above the $(\lambda(\dot{B} - \dot{B}^T)'/eP^*)$ $= 0$ locus the current account is in deficit whereas on an adjustment path below the $(\lambda(\dot{B} - \dot{B}^T)'/eP^*) = 0$ locus the current account is in surplus. Accordingly when the $(\lambda(\dot{B} - \dot{B}^T)/eP^*) = 0$ locus is steeper than the $\dot{K} = 0$ locus, as in Figure 8.3(ii), the current account is in deficit during the entire adjustment whereas when the $(\lambda(\dot{B} - \dot{B}^T)/eP^*) = 0$ locus has a slope which is smaller numerically than the slope of the $\dot{K} = 0$ locus, as in Figure 8.3(i), current account surpluses are followed by deficits. In Figure 8.3(i) from A to C there are surpluses whereas from C to B there are deficits.

VI   AN OPEN MARKET OPERATION

In what follows we examine the adjustments that arise from an open market operation. In particular we focus on the effects of a sale of bonds by the monetary authorities in exchange for money (that is, $dB = -dM$).

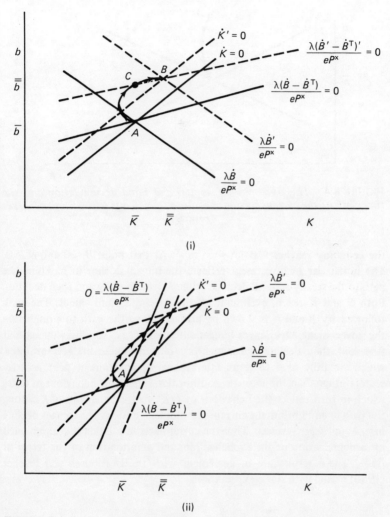

FIGURE 8.3 *Alternative time-paths of the current account balance-of-payments with an increase in government expenditure financed by borrowing*

In the stable case, that is, when $m\widetilde{V}_\rho - b\widetilde{L}_\rho < 0$, an open market operation consisting of a contraction of money and an expansion of bonds of equal amounts can be shown to result in an impact decline in e, λ and ρ. There are no steady-state effects. The adjustments in B and K are shown in Figure 8.4 At the instant of the open market operation described above

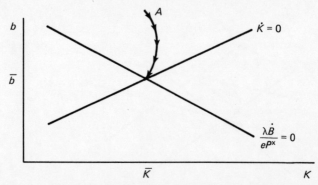

FIGURE 8.4   *The dynamics of capital and bond accumulation and the time-path of the current account balance-of-payments with an open market operation*

the economy reaches a point such as A. At that point $\dot{B} < 0$ and $\dot{K} > 0$. The initial rise in investment reflects the impact decline in ρ. Along the path to the steady-state, B declines while K rises initially and then declines. Both B and K reach, eventually, their old equilibrium values. The path followed by B and K is shown by arrows. Along the path to equilibrium the government experiences budget surpluses. These surpluses increase at first and they decline, subsequently, to zero. These budget surpluses, which are fully used to retire interest-bearing government debt held by sectors other than the monetary authorities, reflect the behaviour of taxes which in turn reflect the behaviour of $F(K)$ via the behaviour of K. Along the path to equilibrium the current account is in deficit. The impact decline in e, λ and ρ are reversed. Thus the current account deficit is accompanied by a depreciation of the exchange rate and deterioration of the terms of trade. These results are in agreement with the Dornbusch and Fischer (1980) model with static expectations.

VII   SUMMARY AND CONCLUSIONS

In this chapter we have constructed a version of the Tobin-Buiter (1976) full-employment model with static expectations and we have reconsidered the effects of a bond-financed fiscal expansion. In our version the economy is open to trade in commodities and securities with the rest of the world under a regime of perfectly flexible exchange rates. Also, in our version bonds and capital are allowed to be imperfect substitutes in portfolios. This imperfect substitutability proves extremely useful when the stability of the model is considered. In particular when bonds and capital are closer substitutes than money and capital the model is unambiguously stable. This suggests that the instability in the Tobin-Buiter model may stem from their restrictive assumption that bonds and capital are perfect substitutes in portfolios. In the course of our study we stumbled into a very important aspect of macro-economic modelling, namely, a fiscal expansion that unbalances the budget has immediate financing implications. The impact increase in government expenditures must be accompanied by an impact, discrete, increase in financing so that the *LM* curve must shift at the same time as the *IS* shifts. To repeat, this impact shift in *LM* is separate from and in addition to shifts in *LM* through time. In this Chapter we confirm the Tobin-Buiter results. Our open market experiment highlights the relationship between adjustments in the current account, the exchange rate and the terms of trade. In our model the exchange rate reflects both 'real' and monetary forces.

MATHEMATICAL APPENDIX

The Short-run (Impact) Effects of Variations in M, B, K and g on e, ρ and λ

Substituting equation (1) into equations (2) to (4) setting $p^* = 1$ and suppressing r we obtain

$$\frac{\lambda}{e} M \equiv m = \widetilde{L}(\rho)\left(\frac{\lambda}{e}(M+B)+K\right), \quad \widetilde{L}_\rho < 0 \qquad (2')$$

$$\frac{\lambda}{e} B \equiv b = \widetilde{V}(\rho)\left(\frac{\lambda}{e}(M+B)+K\right), \quad \widetilde{V}_\rho < 0 \qquad (3')$$

$$F(K) - I\left[\frac{(1-t)F'(K)}{\rho}\right] = D\left(\lambda, \frac{\lambda}{e}(M+B)+K, \right.$$
$$\left. (1-t)F(K)\right) + X(\lambda) + g \qquad (4')$$

Taking the total differential of $(2')$ to $(4')$ we obtain the following system of simultaneous equations

$$\begin{bmatrix} \alpha & \beta & \gamma \\ \hat{\alpha} & \hat{\beta} & \hat{\gamma} \\ \widetilde{\alpha} & \widetilde{\beta} & \widetilde{\gamma} \end{bmatrix} \begin{bmatrix} de \\ d\lambda \\ d\rho \end{bmatrix} = \begin{bmatrix} \phi dM + \psi dK + \theta dB \\ \hat{\phi} dM + \hat{\psi} dK + \hat{\theta} dB \\ \widetilde{\phi} dM + \widetilde{\psi} dK + \widetilde{\theta} dB - dg \end{bmatrix} \begin{array}{l} \text{(Money Market)} \\ \text{(Bond Market)} \\ \text{(Goods Market)} \end{array}$$
$$(5^*)$$

In (5*) the parameters of the three equations are as follows:

$$\alpha = \frac{1}{e}\,[\widetilde{L}(\ )(m+b) - m] = \frac{1}{e}\,[\widetilde{L}(\ )(A - K) - m] = -\frac{\widetilde{L}(\ )K}{e}$$

$$\beta = \frac{1}{\lambda}\,[m - \widetilde{L}(\ )(m + K)] = \frac{1}{\lambda}\,[m - \widetilde{L}(\ )(A - K)] = \frac{\widetilde{L}(\ )K}{\lambda}$$

$$\gamma = -\widetilde{L}_\rho(m + b + K) = -\widetilde{L}_\rho A$$

$$\hat{\alpha} = \frac{1}{e}\,[-b + \widetilde{V}(\ )(b + m)] = \frac{1}{e}\,[-b + \widetilde{V}(\ )(A - K)] = \frac{-\widetilde{V}(\ )K}{e}$$

$$\hat{\beta} = \frac{1}{\lambda}\,[b - \widetilde{V}(\ )(m + b)] = \frac{1}{\lambda}\,[b - \widetilde{V}(\ )(A - K)]\,\frac{\widetilde{V}(\ )K}{\lambda}$$

$$\hat{\gamma} = -\widetilde{V}_\rho A$$

$$\widetilde{\alpha} = \frac{-D_A(m + b)}{e}$$

$$\widetilde{\beta} = X_\lambda + D_\lambda + D_A\,\frac{(m + b)}{\lambda}$$

$$\widetilde{\gamma} = -I'(\ )\left(\frac{(1 - t)F'(K)}{\rho^2}\right)$$

$$\phi = \frac{\lambda}{e}\,(\widetilde{L}(\ ) - 1)$$

$$\psi = \widetilde{L}(\ )$$

$$\theta = \frac{\lambda}{e}\,\widetilde{L}(\ )$$

$$\hat{\phi} = \frac{\lambda}{e}\,\widetilde{V}(\ )$$

$$\hat{\psi} = \widetilde{V}(\ )$$

$$\hat{\theta} = \frac{\lambda}{e}\,(\widetilde{V}(\ ) - 1)$$

$$\widetilde{\phi} = -D_A\,\frac{\lambda}{e}$$

$$\widetilde{\psi} = F'(K)(1 - D_y(1 - t)) - D_A - I'(\ )\,\frac{(1 - t)F''(K)}{\rho}$$

$$\widetilde{\theta} = -D_A\,\frac{\lambda}{e}$$

Defining $\quad \Delta = \begin{vmatrix} \alpha & \beta & \gamma \\ \hat{\alpha} & \hat{\beta} & \hat{\gamma} \\ \tilde{\alpha} & \tilde{\beta} & \tilde{\gamma} \end{vmatrix} \qquad$ we obtain

$$\Delta = -\frac{K}{e}(X_\lambda + D_\lambda)(m\tilde{V}_\rho - b\tilde{L}_\rho) > 0$$

on the assumption that $m\tilde{V}_\rho - b\tilde{L}_\rho < 0$. To show that $m\tilde{V}_\rho - b\tilde{L}_\rho < 0$ implies that bonds and capital are closer substitutes than money and capital we define

$$(\epsilon m)_\rho \equiv \frac{-A\tilde{L}\rho}{m}, \quad (\epsilon b)_\rho \equiv \frac{-A\tilde{V}_\rho\rho}{b}$$

where $(\epsilon m)_\rho$ and $(\epsilon b)_\rho$ denote the elasticities in absolute terms, of the demand for money with respect to the market return on capital and of the demand for bonds with respect to the market return on capital, respectively. Accordingly,

$m\tilde{V}_\rho - b\tilde{L}_\rho < 0$ implies that

$$\frac{-(\epsilon b)_\rho bm}{A\rho} + \frac{(\epsilon m)_\rho bm}{A\rho} < 0,$$

which in turn implies that $(\epsilon b)_\rho > (\epsilon m)_\rho$.

The solution of (5*) yields the following results:

$$e_M = \frac{\dfrac{\lambda}{e}(X_\lambda + D_\lambda)[-\tilde{V}_\rho(b+K) - b\tilde{L}_\rho] + \dfrac{D_A A}{e}[-b(\tilde{L}_\rho + \tilde{V}_\rho)]}{\Delta}$$
$$+ \frac{\dfrac{\tilde{V}(\ )K}{e}I'(\ )\left(\dfrac{(1-t)F'(K)}{\rho^2}\right)}{\Delta} > 0$$

$$e_K = \frac{(m\tilde{V}_\rho - b\tilde{L}_\rho)\left[\dfrac{\lambda(X_\lambda + D_\lambda) + D_A(m+b) - \tilde{\psi}K}{\lambda}\right]}{\Delta} \gtreqless 0$$

$$e_B = \frac{\dfrac{\lambda}{e}(X_\lambda + D_\lambda)[m\tilde{V}_\rho + \tilde{L}_\rho(m+K)] + \dfrac{D_A A}{e}(m\tilde{V}_\rho + m\tilde{L}_\rho)}{\Delta}$$
$$\frac{- \dfrac{\tilde{L}(\ )K}{e}I'(\ )\left(\dfrac{(1-t)F'(K)}{\rho^2}\right)}{\Delta} > 0$$

$$e_g = \frac{\dfrac{K}{\lambda}(m\widetilde{V}_\rho - b\widetilde{L}_\rho)}{\Delta} < 0$$

$$\lambda_M = \frac{\dfrac{\lambda}{e}\dfrac{\widetilde{V}(\ )K}{e}I'(\ )\left(\dfrac{(1-t)F'(K)}{\rho^2}\right) - \dfrac{\lambda}{e}\left(\dfrac{bD_AA}{e}\right)(\widetilde{V}_\rho + \widetilde{L}_\rho)}{\Delta} > 0$$

$$\lambda_K = \frac{(m\widetilde{V}_\rho - b\widetilde{L}_\rho)\ \dfrac{D_A(m+b) - \widetilde{\psi}K}{e}}{\Delta} \gtreqless 0$$

$$\lambda_B = \frac{\dfrac{\lambda}{e}\dfrac{D_AA}{e}[m(\widetilde{V}_\rho + \widetilde{L}_\rho)] - \dfrac{\lambda}{e}\dfrac{\widetilde{L}(\ )K}{e}I'(\ )\ \dfrac{(1-t)F'(K)}{\rho^2}}{\Delta} < 0$$

$$\lambda_g = \frac{\dfrac{K}{e}(m\widetilde{V}_\rho - b\widetilde{L}_\rho)}{\Delta} < 0$$

$$\rho_M = \frac{(X_\lambda + D_\lambda)\dfrac{\lambda}{e}\dfrac{\widetilde{V}(\ )K}{e}}{\Delta} > 0$$

$$\rho_K = 0$$

$$\rho_B = \frac{-\dfrac{\lambda}{e}\dfrac{\widetilde{L}(\ )K}{e}(X_\lambda + D_\lambda)}{\Delta} < 0$$

$$\rho_g = 0$$

The Stability of the Long-run Equilibrium

The system of differential equations which describe the dynamics of the model is presented in the text and is reproduced immediately below.

$$\begin{bmatrix} \dot{B} \\ \dot{K} \end{bmatrix} = \begin{bmatrix} a_{11} & a_{12} \\ a_{21} & a_{22} \end{bmatrix} \begin{bmatrix} B - \bar{B} \\ K - \bar{K} \end{bmatrix}$$

Local stability requires that $a_{11} + a_{12} < 0$ and that $a_{11}a_{22} > a_{21}a_{12}$. Consider first the expressions for the a_{ij} ($i = 1, 2, j = 1, 2$) given below.

$$a_{11} = \frac{e}{\lambda} \left[\sigma \left(\frac{\frac{\lambda}{e^2}(X_\lambda + D_\lambda)(m\widetilde{V}_\rho + \widetilde{L}_\rho(m + K))(m + b)}{\Delta} - \frac{\lambda}{e} \right) \right.$$

$$\left. \times \frac{-I'(1)\frac{\lambda}{e}\frac{\widetilde{L}(\ )K}{e}(X_\lambda + D_\lambda)}{\Delta(1 - t)F'(K)} \right]$$

$$= \sigma \left[\frac{(X_\lambda + D_\lambda)(m\widetilde{V}_\rho + \widetilde{L}_\rho(m + K)(m + b)}{e\Delta} - 1 \right]$$

$$\times \frac{-I'(1)\widetilde{L}(\ )K(X_\lambda + D_\lambda)}{e\Delta(1 - t)F'(K)} < 0$$

$$a_{12} = \frac{e}{\lambda} \left[\sigma \left(\hat{\mu}F'(K) - \frac{(m + b)}{K} - 1 \right) - \frac{I'(I)F''(K)}{F'(K)} \right]$$

$$= \frac{e}{\lambda} \left[\sigma \left(\frac{\hat{\mu}F'(K)K - \hat{\mu}F(K)}{K} \right) - \frac{I'(1)F''(K)}{F'(K)} \right] \gtrless 0$$

$$a_{21} = \frac{-I'(1)(1 - t)F'(K)\rho_B}{\rho^2} = \frac{I'(1)\frac{\lambda}{e}\frac{\widetilde{L}(\ )K}{e}(X_\lambda + D_\lambda)}{\Delta(1 - t)F'(K)} > 0$$

$$a_{22} = \frac{I'(1)F''(K)}{F'(K)} < 0$$

Since $a_{11} < 0$ and $a_{22} < 0$, $a_{11} + a_{22} < 0$ and one of the two stability conditions is obviously satisfied. To establish the second stability condition we note, first, that $a_{11}a_{22} > a_{21}a_{12}$ implies that

$$\sigma \left[\frac{(X_\lambda + D_\lambda)(m\widetilde{V}_\rho + \widetilde{L}_\rho(m + K))(m + b) - e\Delta}{e\Delta} \right] \left[\frac{I'(1)(1 - t)F''(K)K}{(1 - t)F'(K)K} \right]$$

$$> \sigma\hat{\mu} \left[\frac{F'(K)K - F(K)}{K} \right] \left[\frac{I'(1)\widetilde{L}(\ )K(X_\lambda + D_\lambda)}{e\Delta(1 - t)F'(K)} \right]$$

Using the definition of Δ and the fact that $m + b \equiv A - K$ and that $m + K =$

$A - b$ we can show that $a_{11}a_{22} > a_{21}a_{12}$ implies that

$$\left[\frac{A(X_\lambda + D_\lambda)(m(\widetilde{V}_\rho + \widetilde{L}_\rho))}{e\Delta} \right]\left[\frac{I'(1)(1 - t)F''(K)K}{(1 - t)F'(K)K} \right]$$

$$> \hat{\mu}\left[\frac{F'(K)K - F(K)}{K} \right]\left[\frac{I'(1)\widetilde{L}(\ )K(X_\lambda + D_\lambda)}{e\Delta(1 - t)F'(K)} \right]$$

which is satisfied if and only if $\Delta > 0$, that is, if and only if $m\widetilde{V}_\rho - b\widetilde{L}_\rho < 0$.

REFERENCES

A. S. Blinder and R. M. Solow (1973) 'Does Fiscal Policy Matter?', *Journal of Public Economics*.

A. S. Blinder and R. M. Solow (1974) *The Economics of Public Finance* (Washington, DC: Brookings Institution).

R. Dornbusch and S. Fischer (1980) 'Exchange Rates and the Current Account', *American Economic Review*, Dec.

J. Tobin and W. Buiter (1976) 'Long-run Effects of Fiscal and Monetary Policy on Aggregate Demand', in J. Stein (ed.) *Monetarism* (Amsterdam: North-Holland).

Index